Section: 2

Profile Presentation

Of

James Wilson

"It is not about doing time; it is about doing something with the time."

My name is James Wilson, CDCR # AU5200. I am 45 years old. I am convicted for manslaughter, carjacking. And possession of a fire arm. I have been incarcerated 15 years. Since being in prison, I have completed the below-listed academic, rehabilitation, and pro-social activities, seeking to amend for my crimes, improve my life and community.

They are as follows:

1. Truly Redefine Yourself (T.R.Y.), a group I co-founded.

"Read a book, change your life. Write a book and change the world."

Introduction

There are three things that usually come together for an event, or movement to occur. They are: (1) <u>people</u>, (2) <u>ideas</u>, and (3) <u>timing</u>. I will start by acknowledging the people who have made our work, and this book, possible.

Progressive governors, legislators, wardens, and criminal justice advocates (like Initiate Justice and Ella Baker Center) to name a few, have carved out the rehabilitation space for us to exist, create, and evolve within. Your voices, and actions, have given us hope.

Next, I'd like to thank the citizens of California, and other states, that have supported, encouraged, and voted for progressive legislation that focuses more on rehabilitation than bare-knuckle punishment. Our work, and this book, is a small return on your trust, and investment, in us and the programs that reshape the lives of incarcerated individuals. This investment is preparing them for a future of success, better citizenship, and service.

Community Resource Managers (C.R.M.) and their assistants in every prison are the unsung heroes who work behind the scenes to locate, approve, and implement the rehabilitation programs that are now a permanent feature of almost every Department of Corrections across the United States. The "show" doesn't go on without the people who work behind the curtain to make it happen.

With this same gratitude, we could never forget the hundreds of Correctional Officers who are, and have been, instrumental in ensuring that self-help groups can operate within this prison environment.

To our family and friends on the outside: so many of you have been key players in our success; past present and future. Here are just some of these special men and women: Rabbi Brian Zachary Mayer (Religion Outside the Box), Jane Mayer, Alex Taylor, Robin Shanker, Leatta Poston, Tajai Massey, Lee Gibson (Initiate Justice), Karen McDaniel (Place 4 Grace), Nate Williams (Choices for Freedom), Marty Lemaster, Chaplain Harry Mukdani; and so many more that this book would be five times as thick if we were to name them all.

To the vast amount of those incarcerated who have taken the challenge to participate in rehabilitation programs, and the exceptional ones who create self-help groups for the larger incarcerated population: the fruits of your labors have been great indeed, and your efforts have created an infinite amount of possibilities for both yourselves, and countless others.

      You will read some profiles and accomplishments of incarcerated men in this book. Special thanks to our generous, and dedicated, editor and typist, Evan Gainer. He is the reason that these true stories, and ideas, are on paper, and (hopefully) contextually consistent and clear.

      Now, to ideas. There is an old saying that states: "Standing armies can not prevent an idea whose time has come." For decades (if not hundreds of years) there has been social, political, and institutional resistance to sensible rehabilitation efforts within our penal "justice" system, as well as freedom. The result has been the creation of the Prison Industrial Complex, mass incarceration, and billions of tax payer dollars being spent on incarcerating people for extended periods of time without effectively reducing crime, or making communities safer. The "Tough on Crime" approach to criminal "justice", according to some of it's former proponents, simply has not worked.

      Hopefully, by now you will have noticed the word 'justice' placed in quotations. This is because it has become abundantly clear that the way we define this term in American society is in dire need of revision, and reform. There is a need for new, and better ideas based on science, social factors, history, compassion, and the redemptive spirit of every human being. The facts have long since triumphed over the fiction that said, "once a criminal, always a criminal", and even moreso led to a belief that some people were born with a "crime gene" and were therefore "super predators" and "career criminals".

      Fortunately, these old tropes have been debunked, and more truthful (and worthwhile) ideas have taken their place within a majority of American citizens. As it is said: "The worst form of oppression is false ideas." Rehabilitation and restorative justice are revolutionary ideas. Contrary to popular belief in certain circles, they are also liberating for victims, perpetrators of crime, and society at large.

      Lastly, the timing. No one learns more about "time" than people serving it! Everything in prison (and life) is time oriented. After all, it is one of the very few truly non-renewable resources. Many of us incarcerated individuals failed precisely because of our poor usage of this precious asset. We can not mention enough how much our stories are filled with occasions of "missed opportunities". Most of us did not absorb the lesson that fortune favors the prepared. That is, until now!

      What you will read in this book (success stories all) are simply a product of all of the good people mentioned at the beginning of this introduction. Finding the initiative to change is a choice available in <u>all</u> places and times, as is taking advantage of the opportunities present all around us. History (and the future) is made by the right people, with the right ideas, at the right time. We are just privileged, and humbled, to be alive and a part of this great movement for personal, social, and political change. If you are not yet involved.... What are you waiting for? Time waits on no one!

Embodied within these pages are products of the minds of men who are currently incarcerated. There are several curriculums (empowerment documents) created by some of these man that have been approved as self-help programs (IL-TAG's) at High Desert State Prison. Several of these programs have been in operation for five years, or more (e.g. Life Choices, T.R.Y., and several others). We believe that, although they started in one prison, they are suitable for <u>any</u> person, or place, with an interest in self improvement and human development - free or incarcerated.

While our bodies are imprisoned, our minds are not; our brains are no longer behind bars. We offer these gifts, as best as we can articulate them, to the world. It is our hope that one day these curriculums will be implemented in various types of settings, prison merely being the stepping off point. The material in this book is useful for anyone, in any place.

If you are in prison (or transitional housing, youth facility, etc.) and desire to use these curriculums to set up, and organize, self-help groups where you are, then go right ahead! There are templates included for writing proposals to your Community Resource Manager's office for self-help group approval. You can even contact the Chaplain, or Warden, of your prison for guidance and support.* Included also are "chrono" formats for rewarding people for their participation in, and completion of, whichever group you desire to set up. There are proposals for pro-social events (tournaments, interfaithful religious events, talent shows, Pledge of Peace celebrations, etc.) as well. Pick your fruit!

---

*<u>Note</u>: If you are in a California prison, the title 15 gives instructions for setting up inmate leisure time activity groups (IL-TAG) - see section 3233-34. If you want rehabilitation access credits (RAC) approval for the group, the C.R.M. office, or Warden's office, can help you achieve that goal. We did it, and so can you!

Profiles in Rehabilitation is about just that: setting a model (a reproducible example) that is available for anyone who understands the value of....

People,

Ideas, and

Timing!

Don't miss your opportunity to join this great movement! As Muhammad Ali once said: "Don't do time. Make the time work for you."

Please accept this sincere, and humble, work from all of us involved, and those to come!

By: James Wilson
&
Donel Poston

2. Criminal Gangs Anonymous (C.G.A.)
3. Alcohol Anonymous
4. Narcotics anonymous
5. Leadership Workshops, Inmate Organizer
6. Reaching out from within, A group I Co-Founded
7. Pledge of Peace, Inmate Organizer
8. The Day of Peace and Reconciliation, Inmate Organizer
9. Stop the Violence Talent Show, Inmate Organizer
10. Staff Appreciation Day, Inmate Organizer
11. Cash Donation to Veterans Group, Inmate Organizer
12. Veteran's Walk, Inmate Organizer
13. Financial Literacy Class, Inmate Organizer
14. Path to Restoration, Inmate Organizer
15. Ironman Challenge, Inmate Organizer
16. Racial and Cultural Tolerance Class, Inmate Organizer
17. Various Book Reports
18. Received G.E.D.!
19. Lifer Support Group
20. Peer Health Course
21. GOGI – Tools for Positive Decision Making
22. T.R.Y.s' Advance class
23. NEW H.E.A.R.T.s' Self-Help Group, Co-Founder
24. Suicide Awareness and Prevention Week, Inmate Organizer
25. Alternative to Violence Project (A.V.P.)
26. Inter-Faith Religious Seminar, Inmate Organizer
27. Islamic Study Courses and Practices (from different Islamic schools of thought)
28. Purpose Driven Life Seminar (Christian-based study)
29. Study of the Human Brain Course
30. Initiate Justice Legal Conference and Workshop, Inmate Assistant
31. Initiate Justice Self-Help Class
32. Civil Rights Peace Project, Inmate Organizer
33. Black History Month Celebration
34. Cancer Prevention Walk
35. Self-Improvement and Human Development Class, Co-Founder
36. In-Cell Writing Activities Programs (promoted by the CRM's Office after Covid-19 outbreak)
37. I have received various Laudatory Chrono's, from Chaplain's and Free-Staff Self-Help sponsors.
38. Besides Co-Founding Five (5) Self-Help Groups (T.R.Y., new H.E.A.R.T.S., Reaching Out from Within, Self-improvement and a Sports Activity Group (G.A.M.E.), I have Co-Organized several community events, Such as:
    - ➢ Talent Shows
    - ➢ Pledge of Peace

> Sports Tournaments
> Facilitates Symposiums
> Inter-Faith Religious activities
> Staff Appreciation Day
> Racial Tolerance Conferences
> Iron-Man Positive Competition Challenge

39. Participated in writing a Victims Impact Anthology with several inmates (most of them Are included in this profile) with future hopes of publishing the project and donating financial proceeds to Victims Impact Inmates. (title: "Writing our Wrongs")

40. I paid off my restitution fees

41. I am a regular mentor of men of all ages in the prison.

42. I have a strong and long standing support base on the outside. All of my friends are career people and active in their communities.

I have been offered a place to live and a job by Nate Williams with his organization "Choices for Freedom."

Following this list is a short selection of my personal achievement chronos and certificates. A complete list is documented in my CDCR file for further review. Additional insight about me is inside my Bio-Sketch on: prisonfoundations.com, under: Brains Behind Bars. Author: Adrian Woodard and Christopher Compton.

Profile Presentation

Of

Doon Saetern

My name is Doon Saetern, BF9710. I am 30 years old. I am convicted for two counts of attempted murder, Inflicting Great bodily injury, personal use of a dangerous or deadly weapon, burglary in the first degree, as a habitual criminal with a strike enhancement. I have been incarcerated for four and a half years. Since being in prison I have completed the below listed academic, rehabilitation, and pro-social activities, seeking to amend for my crimes, improve my life and community.

They are as follows:

1. Alcoholic, Narcotics, and Criminal Gang Anonymous. (HDSP)
2. Won 2nd place in a state-wide poetry competition. (Union Supply)
3. Alternative to Violence Project. Basic and Advanced. (HDSP)
4. Completed 2019 Fall Semester with a 4.0 G.P.A. (Lassen Community College)
5. Gave a motivational speech and performed a song at the "Stop the Violence" talent show. (HDSP)

6. Participated and won 1ˢᵗ place in a poetry competition at the "Suicide Awareness and Prevention" event. (HDSP)
7. Shared life stories with juveniles and got it published.(The Beat Within) April-May (2019) and January (2020)
8. Gave a motivational speech and performed a song at the "Pledge of Peace" Ceremony. (HDSP)
9. Participated in a Community Religious event. (HDSP)
10. Participated in the "Day of Peace and Reconciliation" event. (HDSP)

Those are just some of the things that are documented, and are saved on record. However, I have been doing much more for my community behind the scene. As you can see, ever since arriving to High Desert State Prison, I have been using my gift for the betterment of society. I wrote a poem; '25 Hours a Day," not only as a reality check, but to inspire every incarcerated person to make the most out of life despite their circumstances. The poem "This Maze of Despair" that I wrote, and performed at the "suicide Awareness and Prevention" event, was to motivate everybody to never give up. The personal life stories that I shared with juveniles detained all access America who read "The Beat Within," was to inform them not to get complacent in life, and be courageous when it comes to their dreams. Everyone makes mistakes. We just have to learn from them.

As I was having these high light moments, "The Success" from doing the right thing caused me so much pain and suffering. It made me feel all alone in my struggles. I felt like I had no one I can go to, to talk about my problems. While I was experiencing many hardships, I continued to uplift people in my community, and in the process the love was reciprocated.

For about ten years of my life I've been in and out of jails and institutions. To be able to enjoy the remainder of my years alongside my family is a dream come true. I am awake... and as long as I am alive, I will continue striving for the betterment of society, regardless of my situation.

<u>Section: 4</u>

Profile Presentation

<u>Of</u>

Nathan Ramazzini

"Transformation comes from within'..."

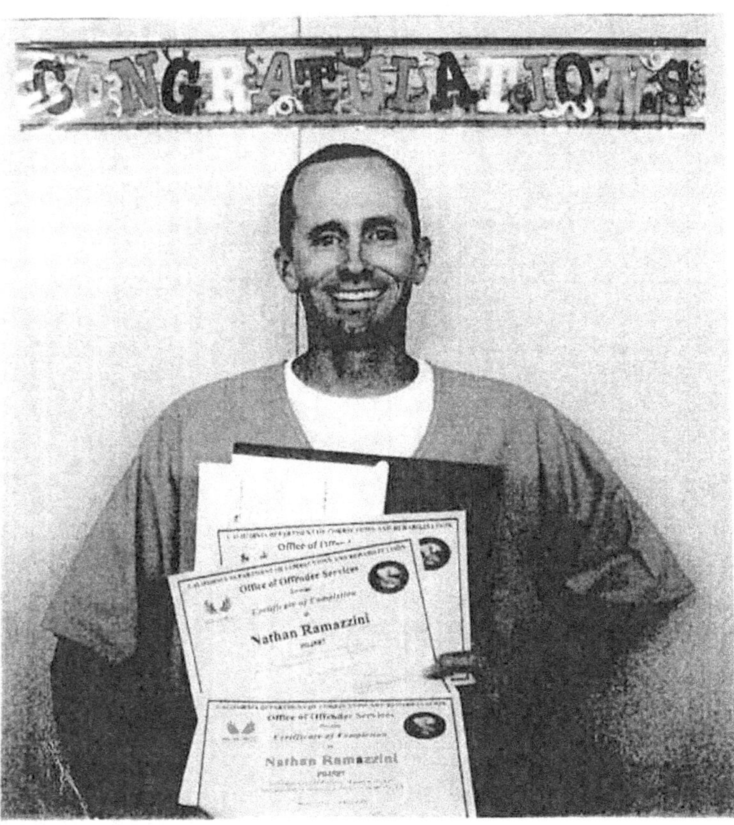

My name is Nathan Joshua Ramazzini, CDCR # P-04587. I am 39 years old. I was convicted of First Degree Murder. I have been incarcerated for 23 years. Since being in prison, I have completed the below listed academic, Rehabilitation, and Pro-Social Activities seeking to amend for my crimes, improve my life, and my community.

They are as follows:

1. G.E.D. Certificate
2. High School Diploma
3. AA Degree in Sociology from Lake Tahoe Community College
4. Entrepreneurship Certificate from Lassen Community College
5. Vocational Computer Literacy Certificate
6. Alternatives to Violence Project (AVP) Facilitator Certificate
7. Letter of recognition as an AVP team coordinator from AVP California High Desert State Prison(HDSP) coordinator Ann Boone
8. Laudatory Chrono from my supervisors Correctional Cook J. Riley and Correctional Officer T. Fountain
9. Laudatory Chrono from Correctional Lieutenant R. Gamberg
10. Laudatory Chrono from my building Correctional Officer S Parks

11. Letter of recognition from Long Term Offender Prrogram(LTOP) Counselor J. Smith
12. Letter of recognition from Warden M. E. Spearman, High Desert State Prison
13. Laudatory letter from founders of Place 4 Grace, K. McDaniel, and Choices for Freedom/Path 2 Restoration, N. Williams
14. Letter of recognition from Lassen Family Services for organizing the "Giving Back Hygiene Drive," W. Owen, Data/Office Coordinator

The following are my personal achievements, chronos, certificates, and letters from the short selection mentioned above. A complete list is documented in my CDCR Central File for further review. Additional insight about me is inside my Bio-Sketch at: PrisonFoundations.com - under Brains Behind Bars, Author: Adrian Woodard

<u>Section: 5</u>

<u>Profile Presentation</u>

<u>Of</u>

<u>Aaron Chandra</u>

"It is not the length of one's life that matters...
It's the depth of it that counts."

My name is Aaron Chandra AP0929. I am 29 years old. I am convicted for Second Degree Murder. I have been incarcerated 10 Years. Since being in prison I have completed the below listed academic, rehabilitation and pro-social activities, Seeking to amend for my crimes, improve my life and community.

They are as follows:

1. Completed 20 hour Basic Course in Non-violent Conflict Resolution (AVP)
2. Completion Chrono- Criminal Gang Members Anonymous (CGA)
3. Participated in First Annual Labor Day event. To show support for under privileged youth in the community
4. Participated in the essay project titled; "The positive Things I Have Learned In Prison"
5. Completion Chrono- "Choices" a Juvenile Diversion Program (JDP)

6. Completion Chrono- "Helping Everyone Articulate Through Storytelling" New Hearts
7. Participated in Talent Show
8. Participated in Suicide Awareness and Prevention Week
9. Made a Donation during the First Annual "Give Back" hygiene drive
10. Participated in the "Day of Peace and Reconciliation"
11. Earned G.E.D.
12. Lassen College "Presidential Honors" (3.8.GPA)

Following this list is a short selection of my personal achievement Chronos/Certificates. A complete list is documented in my CDCR Central File for further review. Additional insight about me is inside my Bio-Sketch on Prisonfoundations.com under Brains Behind Bars. Authors: Adrian Woodard and Christopher Compton

<u>Section: 6</u>

<u>Profile Presentation</u>

<u>Of</u>

<u>Lionel Shell</u>

"A second chance isn't given it's earned!"

My name is Lionel Shell (CDCR# G13733). I am 35 years old. I have been convicted of 1st Degree Murder. I have been incarcerated for the past 14 years. This is my first prison term.

Since being in prison I have invested in my future by seeking to make amends for my crimes, improve my life and community, and having completed the below-listed academic, rehabilitation and pro-social activities.

They are as follows

1. G.E.D.
2. 33 Units towards A.A. Degree
3. PHI THETA KAPPA Honor Society Member #20890771
4. Narcotics Anonymous
5. Alcoholics anonymous
6. Danny Trejo Substance Dependency Series
7. Anger and Stress Management
8. Pledge of Peace Event and Money Donation
9. Day of Peace and Reconciliation Laudatory Chrono
10. Initiate Justice Legal Conference and Workshops

This list is just a short selection of my personal achievement chronos and certificates. To view a complete list of these documents please feel free to look into my CDCR file for further review.

<u>Section: 7</u>

Profile Presentation

Of

Ray Bracamonte

"I can't control anyone else… but I can control <u>Myself</u>. <u>My</u> thoughts. <u>My</u> words. <u>My</u> choices. <u>My</u> reactions. <u>My</u> future."

My name is Ray Bracamonte (CDCR # K85547). I am 48 years old. I am convicted of Murder/Robbery of the 1st Degree. I have been incarcerated 25 years. Since being in prison I have completed the below-listed academic, rehabilitation, and pro-social activities, seeking to amend for my crimes and improve my life and community.

They are as follows:

<u>EDUCATIONAL ACHIEVEMENTS</u> * currently studying for my masters

- G.E.D.
- Associates Degree- Harvest Bible University (June 18, 2016)
- Bachelor's Degree- Harvest Bible University (June 22, 2019)
- Business Degree- Baylor University Hankamer School of Business and Career Readiness (August 21, 2018)
- Defy Ventures; C.E.O. of your New Life (August 21, 2018)
- Drug and Alcohol Treatment Specialist- (With Honors) Stratford Career Institute (November 17, 2018)

<u>VOCATIONALS</u>

- Janitorial (December 17, 2007) - Peer Educational Program, Infectious Disease Awareness.
- Graphic Arts (April 17, 2009)- Certified in Hep-C, HIV-AIDS, and Immune System (2015-2017)

<u>SUBSTANCE ABUSE</u>

- 1 year certificate N.A. participation (10/2011 – 10/2012)

- ➢ N.A. Chrono (6/10/09), N.A. Chrono (6/10/09),
- ➢ N.A. Chrono (8/4/10), N.A. Chrono (8/4/10),
- ➢ N.A. Chrono (2/12/11), N.A. Chrono (2/12/11),
- ➢ N.A. Chrono (6/10/11), N.A. Chrono (6/10/11),
- ➢ N.A. Chrono (12/22/11), N.A. Chrono (4/2/12),
- ➢ N.A. Chrono (7/23/12), N.A. Chrono (12/30/12),
<u>RELAPSE PREVENTION</u>
- ➢ C.G.A. Substance Abuse Workshop; *Facilitator* (8/12/19)
<u>CELEBRATE RECOVERY</u>
- ➢ C.R. Chrono (3/5/15), C.R. Chrono (7/3/15),
- ➢ C.R. Chrono (10/5/15), C.R. Chrono (1/1/16),
- ➢ C.R. Chrono (4/5/16),

<u>MASCELLANEOUS CHRONOS</u>

- ➢ Independent Study Program (1/16/09)
- ➢ Chapel Participation; *Laudatory* (6/18/08)
- ➢ Positive Prison Participation; *Laudatory* (12/20/19)
- ➢ Infectious Disease Awareness Support Group (10/15/15)
- ➢ Infectious Disease Awareness Support Group (4/15/16)
- ➢ Infectious Disease Awareness Support Group (7/15/15)
- ➢ Infectious Disease Awareness Support Group (7/15/16)
- ➢ Financial Literacy Class Completion (10/18/19)
- ➢ Business and Human Development Course Completion (12/6/19)
- ➢ Religious, Racial, Cultural Tolerance Community Event; *Participant* (6/18/19)
- ➢ Leadership Workshop Completion (12/6/19)
- ➢ Lifer's Group; *90 Day Participation* .(9/9/12)
- ➢ Lifer's Group; 90 Day Participation (1/6/13)
- ➢ Path 2 Restoration; *Laudatory* (2/25/20)
- ➢ B.P.H Question and Answer Participation (8/20/13)
- ➢ Staff Psychologist; *Laudatory* (4/20/16)
- ➢ Sports Certification Volleyball Champs (2016)
- ➢ Sports Certification Volleyball Champs (2016)

<u>FAITH BASED ACHIEVEMENTS</u>

- ➢ Baptized (5/29/09)
- ➢ Mount Zion Certificate **Look to Jesus* (2004)
- ➢ American Bible Academy **completed program* (2006 – 2009)
- ➢ Kairos **3.5 Day* (25.5 Hour*) Intensive Program*
- ➢ Kairos *<u>Inside Team</u>*
- ➢ Celebrate Recovery **6 month Participation* x2 Participation Chronos / 1.5 Years covered
- ➢ Signs of Life **12 week program completion* (2015)
- ➢ Self-Confrontation **24 week in-depth Biblical Discipleship*
<u>COLLOEGE CURRICULUM</u>
- ➢ Diploma – Biblical Theology, Israelite Heritage Institute (7/31/11)

> Walking the 12 Steps with Jesus Christ (7/14/14)

SELF-HELP REHABILITATION

> Stress Management – Transforming Lives Network
> (Multiple Certificates)
> Criminals and Gangmembers Anonymous (C.G.A.)
> *Continuous Participation since 2012*
> Alternatives to Violence Program (A.V.P.)
> Multiple Chronos and Certificates; (2014 – 2020)
> C.G.A. Workshops, Exploring Victimization (10/17/16);

Facilitated:

Substance Abuse and Relapse Prevention (3/6/17);
Conflict Resolution (5/3/17); Exploring the Root Causes of
Criminality (4/25/18); Domestic Violence (12/23/19); Beliefs
(1/14/20); R.A.R.A. Responsibility Accountability Remorse and
Amends *participated* (1/9/20); General Facilitator Chrono
(12/2018 – 3/2019); Facilitator Training Chrono (2014);
Substance Abuse and Relapse Prevention; *Facilitator* (8/12/19);
*Should be noted that Bracamonte participated in the creation of "The Domestic
Violence Abuse Workshop" (12/2019)*

> Anger Management – Transforming Lives Network (2009)
> Parenting Education Program – Friends Outside (3/27/09)
> Victims Awareness:

Transforming Lives Network (4/15/09); Office of Restorative
Justice (10/24/12); Exploring Victim C.G.A. (10/17/16); Violence
of Aftermath, 25 week course (2/12/15); Prisoners Educating
Prisoners (10/26/15) & (11/1/15); Stop the Violence (8/20/19);
Lifers Group 90 Day Victims Awareness Participation (9/9/12);
Victims Awareness (10/24/12)

> Breaking Barriers:

Program Completion *30 hours Personal Counseling* (9/12/14);
Exemplary Conduct Chrono from Program Facility -
52 hours Personal Counseling (12/9/14)

MENTAL HEALTH

> Emotional Processing Psychotherapy *6 month course*
> (5/21/12 – 10/5/12)
> Anger Management Therapy (10/2/12)
> Insight Into Overcoming Criminal Behavior (5/7/13)
> Impulse Control Group (7/12/13)
> Self Esteem (1/30/14)
> Violence of Aftermath *25 Weeks* (2/12/15)
> Conflict Resolution (7/2/15)

❖ *ACCI Accredited*

❖ Anger Management/Life Skills (12/9/15)
❖ Domestic Violence/Life Skills (2/24/16)
❖ Interpersonal Relationships (1/5/16)

- ❖ Offender Correction Life Skills (3/23/16)
- ❖ Contentious Relationships (2/24/16)
- ❖ Offender Responsibility Life Skills (3/23/16)
- ❖ Theft/Shoplifting Life Skills (4/13/16)
- ❖ Cognitive Awareness Life Skills (4/13/16)
- ❖ Substance Abuse Life Skills (4/19/16)
- ❖ Parenting Life Skills (4/20/16)
- ➢ Interpersonal Violence (4/19/16)
- ➢ Stress Management (4/18/17)
- ➢ Lifespan Development *12 Weeks Assisted Facilitation* (7/12/18)
- ➢ Suicide Awareness and Prevention Chrono (9/26/19)

LEADERSHIP & AMENDS

Fund Raising:
- ➢ Donation to Red Cross *Tsunami Relief* (4/4/05)
- ➢ Donation to World Missionary Press Inc. (8/12/06 - 4/27/07)
- ➢ Valley Children's Hospital Art Drive Participation (8/16/10)
- ➢ Self – Help Program Donation for At Risk You Tu (4/1/11)
- ➢ Donation Veterans Group (11/18/19)
- ➢ Donation American Cancer Society – Making Strides Against Breast Cancer Inmate Fund Raising Campaign (10/15/16)
- ➢ Donation American Cancer Society (12/15/16)
- ➢ Donation Lassen Family Services Hygiene Drive (12/21/19)
- ➢ Fund Raising Walk or Roll-A-Thon for The American Cancer Society (2/28/17)

Program Facilitation:
- ➢ Criminals and Gangmembers Anonymous (C.G.A.); *Facilitator* (2014 – present)
- ➢ Alternatives To Violence; *Facilitator* (2014 – present)
- ➢ Day of Healing Workshop; *Organizer* (2/2020)

Leadership:
- ➢ Laudatory Staff Appreciation Day; *Elected Speaker (3/6/20)*
- ➢ Iron Man Challenge; *Organizer Chrono* (11/16/19)
- ➢ A.V.P *Leadership/Facilitation* (3/3/17)
- ➢ Laudatory; "For his tremendous efforts towards serving his community and personal growth." (10/19/20)
- ➢ Laudatory for Selfless Acts, Leadership Ability, Community Building, and Continuous Social Development (2/26/20)
- ➢ Laudatory Recognized as a Positive Asset to the Community (8/20/19)
- ➢ Suicide and Prevention *Chrono (9/26/19)*

<u>C.D.C.R EMPLOYEE LAUDATORY CHRONO'S</u>

- Character Reference, Insight, Interpersonal Leadership Skills, Remorse and Continued Dedication to Growth.
  J. Dalgish, Psy. D (4/20/16)
- Work performance, leadership, attitude towards Officers, and skill set that allows Bracamonte to "Help me with inmates that are in the Development Disabled Program." (D.D.P)
  Sgt. G. Arteaga, D.D.P Sgt. (11/3/17)
- Character Reference, Above and beyond work performance, role model and overall leadership.   Correctional Officer, Moore (1/8/17)
- Work Performance (Clerk) recommendation, Staff assistance, trust worthiness and recognition for Self-Help program leadership. Noting inmate Bracamonte's work ethic and need for "little or no supervision".
  Correctional Officer, D. Aguilar (2/4/18)
- Supervisorial/Interaction Laudatory, Noting inmate Bracamonte's positive attitude and dependability as a "Critical Worker"
  Correctional Officer, H. Zakaryan (2/13/18)

<u>LASTING IMPACT</u>

- Helped to develop the Criminals and Gangmembers Anonymous 12 Week Workshop
- Founded and created "The Road to Redemption Project" with the input of four SB 260/SB 261 Juvenile Offenders who have all obtained their Freedom through the Parole Board Process
- Founded and Developed The <u>Building Individual Ownership</u> (B.I.O) Program. An in-depth topical workshop geared towards equipping men and women with the insight and skills necessary for personal accountability, growth, character development and responsible living.

Following this list is a short selection of my Personal Achievement Chrono's and Certificates. A complete list is documented in my C.D.C.R file for further review. Additional insight about me is inside my Bio-Sketch on: prisonfoundations.com, under: Brains Behind Bars, Authors: Adrian Woodard and Christopher Compton.

<u>Section: 8</u>

Profile Presentation

Of

Adrian Woodard

"Make your life the subject of intense inquiry, in this way you will discover its goal, direction and destiny."

~Kemetic Wisdom Teaching~

My name is Adrian Woodard CDCR #K-03214. I am 48 years old. I am convicted of Attempted Murder of a Police Officer (664-187). I have been incarcerated for 25 years. Since my incarceration I have completed the below listed Academic, Rehabilitation and Pro-Social Activities in an effort to make amends for my crimes, improve my life and make Positive contributions to my Community.

They are as Follows:

1. High School Diploma
2. N.A. (Narcotics Anonymous)
3. Anger Management
4. Victims Awareness

5. Building Resilience
6. A.V.P. (Alternatives to Violence Program)
7. Turning Point (Correspondence Modules)
8. A.R.C. (Anti Recidivism Coalition) – *Avatar BPH Prep*
9. A.R.C. (Anti Recidivism Coalition) – *Youth Offender Mentoring*
10. Gang Awareness and Recovery
11. G.O.G.I. – Getting Out by Going In
12. LTOP – (Long Term Offender Program) – Victim Impact Class
13. LTOP – Substance Use Disorder Treatment
14. LTOP – Criminal Thinking Class
15. LTOP – Anger Management Class
16. LTOP – Denial Management Class
17. Family Relationship Class
18. Self-Improvement Class
19. C.G.A. – (Criminal Gang members Anonymous)
20. PREP – Domestic Violence Modules

Following this list is a short selection of some of my Personal Achievement Chrono's/Certificates. A complete list is documented in my CDCR file for further review. Additional insight about me is reviewable in my Bio-Sketch on PrisonFoundations.com – Under: Brains Behind Bars. Author: Adrian Woodard.

<u>Section: 9</u>

<u>Profile Presentation</u>

<u>Of</u>

<u>Steven Allee</u>

"I am change..."

My name is Steven Drew Allee (CDCR #BA8058). I am 37 years old. I was convicted of First Degree Murder. I have been incarcerated for 5 years. Since being in prison I have completed the below listed Academic, Rehabilitation, and Pro-Social Activities seeking to amend for my crimes, improve my life and Community.

They are as follows:

1) Article posted on the CDCR website by High Desert State Prison (HDSP) Staff: Recognition as model inmate and returning Camp Grace Dad.
2) Letter O recognition from Lassen Family Services for planning and organizing the 1st Annual "Giving Back Hygiene Drive".
3) My personal record of phone call with the Secretary of CDCR, Mr. Ralph Diaz.
4) Laudatory Chrono from my Supervisor in the Law Library, Ms. Jenkins.
5) Laudatory Chrono from my building Officer, Ms. Parks.
6) Laudatory Chrono from my Building Officer, Mr. McGinnis.
7) Letter of recognition as a Positive Programmer and Role Model from H.D.S.P. Community Resource Manager, Ms. Speers.
8) Laudatory Chrono from Clinical Psychologist, Dr. Spencer.
9) Laudatory Chrono for Facilitating Narcotics Anonymous.

10) Laudatory Chrono for recognition of long standing member and participant of Narcotics Anonymous group on the yard.
11) Laudatory letter from the Founders of Place 4 Grace and Choices for Freedom Path 2 Restoration.
12) Cover page and table of contents of the H.O.P.E. Project I created for long term offenders that are new to the system or for any inmates wishing to change.

Following this list is a short selection of my personal achievements. A complete list is documented in my CDCR file for further review. Additional insight about me is reviewable in my Bio-Sketch on PrisonFoundations.com. – Under: Brains Behind Bars. Author: Adrian Woodard.

<u>Section: 10</u>

<u>Profile Presentation</u>

<u>Of</u>

<u>Brett Richardson</u>

"The ultimate measure of a man is not where he stands in moments of comfort and convenience. But where he stands at moments of challenge and controversy."

M.L.K. JR.

My name is Brett Richardson (CDCR #AL4303). I'm 41 years old, and I was convicted of First Degree Murder. I have been incarcerated for 11 years.

Since being in prison I have completed the below listed Academic, rehabilitation, and Pro-Social Activities, seeking to amend for my crimes, improve my life and Community.

They are as follows:

1) Narcotics Anonymous
2) Alcoholics Anonymous
3) Criminal and Gangmembers Anonymous
4) Pledge of Peace Event

5) Pledge of Peace (Cash donation)
6) Self-Improvement Class Workshop – A Day of Healing
7) 4-month Workshop for Project Avary
8) Individual Self-Improvement Laudatory Chrono
9) Initiate Justice – Legal Conference and Workshop
10) Mind over Matter Seminar

This list is a short selection of my Personal Achievement Chronos/Certificates. A complete list is documented in my CDCR file for further review.

<u>Section: 11</u>

<u>Profile Presentation</u>

<u>Of</u>

<u>Christopher Compton</u>

"We are greater than our worst acts."

My name is Christopher Compton (CDCR #AW6959), I am 26 years old. I am convicted of Second Degree Armed Robbery and First Degree Murder. I have been incarcerated for 8 years. Since my incarceration I have completed the below listed Academic, Rehabilitation and Pro-Social Activities in an effort to make amends for my crimes, improve my life and make positive contributions to my community.

They are as follows:

1. First and foremost, I have attained my G.E.D. while in prison, something I took for granted.
2. I participating in Criminal and Gangmembers Anonymous (C.G.A) and it helped me understand why I thought and felt the way I did. I was able to confront my criminal mind-set, walk away from gangs and prison cliques and find legal and legitimate solutions to my person-to-person conflicts rather than result to violence or the wolf pack mentality.
3. Through my Academic and moral growth in C.G.A., I took advantage of the self-improvement class offered here which provided the Community setting to exercise all that I've learned before. The motto in this class is: "Self Improvement is the basis for Community Development."

4. Having all the above experiences obligated me to share this progress with the Prison Community. I became a Co-Organizer in "Pledge of Peace", "Day of Peace and Reconciliation", and the "Stop the Violence" Talent Show at High Desert State Prison (HDSP).

5. Last but not least, T.R.Y – Truly Redefine Yourself, Has been a consistent motivating factor in my life. Its core Philosophy is: "Life is business, manage it well". The individual life (business) is weighed against the entire progress and well-being of the Community (economic system). Without gangs and crimes (CGA) the Community can progress, schools can play their role in people's lives and peace is the result.

That is what I have learned, despite some of my mistakes in prison. I came in a simple-minded boy, and I am emerging as a thinking man.

For further review of my achievements, see my CDCR file and my Bio-Sketch on PrisonFoundations.com. Title: Brains Behind Bars, Authors: Adrian Woodard and Christopher Compton.

<u>Section: 12</u>

<u>Profile Presentation</u>

<u>Of</u>

Donel Poston

"Tough times don't last, tough people do!"

(Me in the center)

My name is Donel Poston (AT-2512). I am 44 years old. I am convicted of second degree murder, under the Provocative act Doctrine. I have been incarcerated for seven years. Since being in prison, I have completed the below-listed academic, rehabilitation, and pro-social activities, seeking to make amends for my crimes and improve my life and community.

They are as follows:

- ❖ 12/17/15 AVP Participation Chrono/Certificate
- ❖ 01/16/16 AVP Advance Workshop Chrono/Certificate
- ❖ 03/17/16 Training for Facilitators AVP Workshop
- ❖ 04/20/16 Criminal and Gangmembers Anonymous (CGA) Chrono
- ❖ 06/08/16 Strong Man Competition Chrono
- ❖ 06/15/16 CGA Parenting Workshop Certificate
- ❖ 08/01/16 CGA Facilitator Chrono
- ❖ 09/07/16 Field Day Event Chrono
- ❖ 12/16 Certificate of Completion/Entrepreneurship
- ❖ 04/17/17 Juvenile Diversion Program (JDP) Membership Training
- ❖ 05/27/17 Houses of Healing, A prisoner's guide to inner power and Freedom
- ❖ 06/15/17 Donated a Book I authored to The Library
- ❖ 08/18/17 The positive things I learned in Prison Chrono
- ❖ 08/20/17 AVP Facilitator Chrono

- ❖ 11/18/17 Fatherhood Focus Parenting Program Certificate/Chrono
- ❖ 11/25/17 30 hr. Positive Parenting Program Certificate/Chrono
       Victims Impact Workshop Certificate
- ❖ 01/21/18 AVP Facilitator Basic Chrono (Facilitated a Group)
- ❖ 01/24/18 RAC Credit
- ❖ 04/15/18 AVP Facilitator Chrono (Facilitated a Group)
- ❖ 05/08/18 RAC Credit
- ❖ 05/17/18 Facilitator Completion Chrono/Certificate
- ❖ 05/25/18 Presidents Honors GPA 3.75 or higher
- ❖ 10/31/18 Individual Works Initiative from Chaplin
- ❖ 05/13/19 Pledge for Peace
- ❖ 06/03/19 Life Skillz Facilitator Chrono
- ❖ 06/03/19 JDP Mentorship Chrono
- ❖ 06/18/19 Organized Structured and Prticipated in Community Event
- ❖ 07/18/19 AVP Facilitator Chrono (Facilitated a Group)
- ❖ 07/25/19 TRY Advanced Chrono
- ❖ 08/06/19 New H.E.A.R.T Co-Founding and Facilitating Chrono
- ❖ 08/07/19 RAC Credit
- ❖ 08/20/19 Organized Stop the Violence Talent Show
- ❖ 08/27/19 Talim Chrono
- ❖ 08/31/19 Ramadan Chrono
       Path 2 Restoration Chrono
- ❖ 09/07/19 Night of Power Chrono
- ❖ 09/26/19 Suicide Awareness and Prevention Week
- ❖ 10/06/19 Path 2 Restoration
- ❖ 11/18/19 Path 2 Restoration
- ❖ 11/18/19 Cash Donation
- ❖ 11/18/19 Veterans Walk Certificate
- ❖ 11/27/19 Reaching Out From Within Co-Founder/Facilitator Chrono
- ❖ 12/21/19 Giving Back Hygiene Drive/Donation
- ❖ 12/06/19 Leadership Workshop
- ❖ 01/06/20 Reaching Out From Within
- ❖ 01/28/20 Day of Peace and Reconciliation
- ❖ 02/16/20 AVP Facilitator Chrono (Facilitated a Group)
- ❖ 02/25/20 Path 2 Restoration Chrono
- ❖ 03/12/20 Staff Appreciation Day Speaker/Organizer Chrono
- ❖ 02/12-3/11/20 Mind Over Matter Seminar Certificate
- ❖ 03/17/20 Initiate Justice
- ❖ 04/27/20 In Cell Covid 19 Packet Chrono

I haved also earned three degrees, including AST: Business Administration, AS: Social Science, AS: University Studies. I am currently in my second semester at Adam's State University, looking to achieve a BA Small Business Management in two more semesters. I have published three books, all available at Barnes and Noble or on

Amazon. I have Co-written several Self-Help groups and have completed an unpublished book, Co-written with 11 other inmates.

Following this list is a short selection of my personal achievement Chronos/Certificates. A complete list is documented in my CDCR file for further review, additional insight about me is inside my bio-sketch on: prisonfoundations.com – under: Brains Behind Bars. Authors: Adrian Woodard and Christopher Compton.

Profile Presentation

Of

Jose Duarte

"A gem cannot be polished without friction, nor man perfected without adversity."

My name is Jose Duarte #AI-5098. I am 33 years old. I am convicted of Murder and Arson. I have been incarcerated for 12 years. Since being in prison, I have completed the below listed academic, rehabilitation, and pro-social activities seeking to amend for my crimes, improve my life and Community.

They are as Follows:

- A.A. Social and Behavioral Sciences(Degree pending due to COVID-19)
- A.A. Arts and Humanities (Degree pending due to COVID-19)
- A.A. American Studies(Degree pending due to COVID-19)
- A.A. Sociology (Degree pending due to COVID-19)
- Vocation Completion – Office Services and Related Technologies
- Self-Reconstruction Therapy
- P.A.S.S. – Personal Psychological Development

- Alternatives to Violence Program (AVP)
- Day of Peace and Reconciliation
- Suicide Awareness and Prevention
- PREP Turning Point – Domestic Violence
- GOGI – Tools of Choice
- GOGI – Tolls of the Body
- Criminal Gangmembers Anonymous (CGA) (HDSP)
- Lifer's Group (HDSP)
- Reaching Out From Within
- Iron Man Challenge
- Donation – "Giving Back" Hygiene Drive
- Leadership Workshop
- Donation – Pledge of Peace
- Human Development Causes
- Lifer's Group – (KVSP) Gang Awareness
- Lifer's Group – (KVSP) Conflict Resolution
- Lifer's Group – (KVSP) Insight
- Lifer's Group – (KVSP) Re-entry in Society
- PREP – Insight
- HDSP in-Cell Program Packet #1
- HDSP in-Cell Program Packet #2
- January Positive Prison Participation
- February Positive Prison Participation
- March Positive Prison Participation
- Pledge of Peace Event
- November Positive Prison Participation
- Ugly Sweater Participation
- Cookbook Participation
- December Positive Prison Participation
- Initiate Justice Legal Conference and Workshop
- Black History Participation (HDSP)
- Self-Improvement Class – Peace Project
- Self-Improvement Class Workshop – A Day of Healing
- Mind Over Matter Seminar
- Path 2 Restoration
- Coastline Community Scholarship
- Facilitator of Lifer's Group (HDSP)
- Facilitator of Criminal Gangmembers Anonymous (HDSP)
- Facilitator of PREP Turning Point – Anger Management
- Facilitator of PREP Turning Point – Domestic Violence
- Facilitator of PREP Turning Point – Victims Impact
- Staff Laudatory Chrono Allan, K.

- Staff Laudatory Chrono Rodriguez, t.
- Staff Laudatory Chrono Vargas, J.
- Staff Laudatory Chrono Cochrane, K.

Following this list is a short selection of my personal achievement Chronos/Certificates. A complete list is documented in my CDCR file for further review. Additional Insight about me is inside my Bio-Sketch on: prisonfoundations.com – under: Brains Behind Bars.

Section: 14

Profile Presentation

Of

Albert Sandoval

"Freedom is not free."

My Name is Albert Sandoval (CDCR #AZ7789). I am 27 years old. I am convicted for Home Invasion and Robbery and have been in custody almost 7 years. While being Incarcerated I have been on a mission to transform my life and prepare myself for Societal Re-entry. To accomplish this goal (and several others) I Have done, in short order, to increase my chances for success.

They are as Follows:

1. Received my G.E.D
2. Enrolled into College
3. Reconciled with my Parents
4. Completed Criminal Gangmembers Anonymous (CGA)
5. Participated in Alternatives to Violence Program (AVP) and got Completion Certificate
6. Completed Narcotics Anonymous
7. Participated in Pledge of Peace
8. Cancer Prevention Walk
9. Suicide Prevention Class
10. Initiate Justice Workshop
11. T.R.Y.'s Sports Tournament Event
12. T.R.Y.'s Basic Class – Completed
13. T.R.Y.'s Advanced Class – Completed
14. Peer Health

Following this list is a short selection of my personal achievement Chronos/Certificates. A complete list is documented in my CDCR file for further review.

LIFE CHOICES

<u>LIFE CHOICES</u>

<u>PROGRAM OUTLINE</u>

<u>WEEK 1</u>

- Introduction
- Facilitators tell their stories
- <u>Questions for participants</u>:
    - Tell us about yourself.
    - What do you intend on accomplishing in this group?
    - Where do you see yourself in 5 years?

<u>WEEK 2</u>

- Introduction to timelines
- Facilitators read their timelines
- Week 2 discussion questions
- <u>Homework</u>:
    - Create a timeline beginning with your earliest memory up to the time of your arrest.

<u>WEEK 3</u>

- Read timelines
- Do victims workshop #1:
    - "Can we become victims?"
- Pass out emotions list
- <u>Homework</u>:
    - Attach emotions to timeline.

<u>WEEK 4</u>

- Facilitators connect emotions to their timelines - **No Fluff Events**
- Week 4 Discussion Questions
- <u>Homework</u>:
    - Continue to work on attaching emotions to timeline.

<u>WEEK 5</u>

- Do victims workshop #2:
    - "Exploring The Impact of Crime"
- Facilitators discussion on extracting fluff from timelines

- Homework:
    - Refine timelines with emotions attached, extract fluff events.

WEEK 6

- Do victims workshop #3:
    - "Victims Impact and Collateral Damage"
- Facilitators discussion on progress of timeline events and your emotions
- Homework:
    - Begin to think about your stories from your earliest memory up to age 10 - 5 to 10 years old.

WEEK 7

- Facilitators read their stories ages 5 to 10 years old
- Do victims workshop #4:
    - "An in-depth look into victimization"
- Homework:
    - Do your stories ages 5 to 10 years old.

WEEK 8

- Read your stories ages 5 to 10 years old

WEEK 9

- Continue with ages 5 to 10 years old stories, if needed
- Facilitators read their stories ages 10 to 15 years old
- Week 9 discussion questions
- Homework:
    - Do your stories ages 10 to 15 years old.

WEEK 10

- Read your stories ages 10 to 15 years old

WEEK 11

- Continue with stories ages 10 to 15 years old, if needed
- Do victims workshop #5:
    - "Pain, Anger, and Resentment"
- Homework:
    - Do your stories ages 15 years old to time of arrest.

WEEK 12

- Everyone reads their stories ages 15 years old to time of arrest

<u>WEEK 13</u>

- Continue with stories ages 15 years old to time of arrest, if needed

<u>WEEK 14</u>

- Facilitators tell their full stories again
- Open discussion of facilitators full stories
- Do victims workshop #7:
    - "Healing is a Process"
- <u>Homework</u>:
    - Continue to work on full stories.

<u>WEEK 15</u>

- Full stories begin

NEW H.E.A.R.T.S

"If the eye (heart) is dark then the entire body (actions) will be too."

-Jesus

New Hearts Introduction

This program places, at it's core, one of the human being's most vital organs: the heart.

The heart is not just central in physical anatomy; this organ has earned a central role in almost every significant area of study and practice - religion, psychology, biology, romance, and symbolism.

The heart is also the focus of many of the great world teachers of humanity, and the main subject of discussion regarding transformation in prominent religious texts. Several of these teachers and books will be quoted throughout this curriculum. We will rely on science, spirituality, history, law, and common knowledge to engender a new mind, or way of thinking, into people.

We believe that in order to effect a quality and lasting change in people's lives, we must go to the "heart of the matter" - the stories behind each person's upbringing. Our goal is to discover those crucial events that worked to develop and shape the "old hearts" that brought us to our lowest point and/or prison.

Hence, the meaning behind our curriculum's title and acronym: New Hearts. We interpret the word H.E.A.R.T. to mean:

H - Helping

E - Everyone

A - Articulate

R - Rehabilitation

T - Through

S - Story-telling

While the word "Rehabilitation" has become only a catch phrase in prison jargon, the word has great meaning and importance for changing human lives. The word actually means: "the process of bringing one back to proper habits or civility." Basically, regaining our humanity. Therefore, when we are truly rehabilitated, our every day words and actions "articulate" - or speak for - the rediscovery of the good that exists in each one of us. New hearts are basically good hearts. So, the rehabilitated person seeks to live an honest, peaceful, and productive life. Yes, the good life! That is the "art" (creative power) that comes from articulating our story. There is a saying which goes like this: "the distance between a person and a changed life, is a story."

And that is what the program New Hearts seeks to help each participant

with: crossing that distance, closing that gap, in order to realize our heart's
desire of being better men, and better citizens, through self-examination
and story-telling. Basically, taking a hard look at our past negative development
and reshaping that past into a positive present and future.

Out with the old, and in with the new.

We look forward to embarking on that journey with each of you; the most
rewarding journey is the one to find our true selves. But, the "journey of
a million miles begins with the first step". Let's take that step forward!

- New Hearts Members

"There is no need to run if you're on the wrong road."

- German Saying

Chapter 1

Facing the Old Heart

The first step of change is to realize that something is wrong. Only when we acknowledge that our lives are "broken" will we find the courage and help to fix them.

Let us admit: we have done tremendous wrong and our lives are broken!

The hard answer has now been stated. However, the hard work of self-examination and change is yet to be undertaken and completed.

By willingly enrolling in this class, we have all volunteered to face the hard facts of our past misconducts, and the present need to begin the hard work of: (1) self-examination, and (2) individual and cooperative work to change our lives no matter how challenging or difficult.

The gauntlet has been thrown down. We are all here to accept the challenge!

Brief Definitions of the Heart

The heart has been defined in many ways, A few of these definitions are provided below.

The Heart is:

1. the seat of human intelligence.
2. The center of the human mind.
3. The third-eye.
4. The spiritual essence of humans.
5. The core of the soul and human passion.
6. The well-spring of life.
7. The core of a matter or desire.
8. The light of our being.
9. The inner (or spiritual) ear.
10. The organ responsible for pumping blood throughout the human body.

Despite which definition one selects, it is obvious that the heart, and it's meaning, has been given some weighty appraisal.

Examining the Old Heart

In the New Testament of the Bible, it is said that "out of the heart proceeds defilements", such as:

- **Evil Thoughts** - Negative mind state.
- **Murders** - All forms of violence.
- **Adulteries** - Unfaithfulness.
- **Fornications** - Promiscuity, even sex crimes; and pimping women.
- **Thefts** - Robbery, burglary.
- **False Witness** - Not being honest.
- **Blasphemies** - No respect for what is sacred, or divine law.

This seems to be the "penal code" of the heart, categorizing the crimes of a sick and misguided mind.

So, an examination of the old heart begins at the top of the list: **Evil Thoughts**. Criminal thoughts begin in our heart or mind - the source from which our actions spring. Once our minds have been contaminated with bad thoughts then the actions that stream from that source will certainly be polluted (defiled).

For us, the old heart is all things evil. And evil is anything that threatens or damages the life, liberty, property, and pursuit of happiness of human beings, including ourselves.

The word evil, spelled live in reverse, seeks to ruin lives in any way it can. An evil mind, a corrupt and depraved heart, can commit crimes with impunity. It has no respect for law or life. Even crimes that are "accidental" or "unintended" ruins lives.

The old heart is what led us to rebel against legitimate authority figures, like our parents, teachers, and law enforcement; who are put into our lives, and society, to instill and enforce moral standards of beliefs and conduct.

The old heart brought us to accept illegitimate authority, such as gangs, and prison codes of conduct. A lawless form of life-style.

The old heart justified all forms of stealing, burglary, and robberies.

The old heart permitted us to sell drugs and alcohol to others, and abuse them ourselves.

The old heart motivated us to inflict various acts of abuse and violence on other people, for whatever reason we used to justify them.

The old heart would abuse others, male or female, sexually, emotionally, or mentally.

The old heart centered our passions and desires on all the wrong things; so, our core philosophy became destructive. Our old heart and it's history is written in blood, tears, and pain.

The religious text for Muslims, the Holy Quran, says: "Blind is not man's eyes, but blind is his heart." The same book also says that man's hearts have become like animals. Basically, following pleasure and living by the "law of the jungle" instead of higher human reason and civility. A blind heart moves through life wrecklessly and with no regard for others.

Further noting the importance of guarding the heart from passions, the Hindu avatar, Krishna, warned his followers: "Plunge into battle, but leave your heart by the lotus plant." The lotus plant is the symbol of purity in Hinduism and Buddhism. This is a basic instruction to all human beings: life's battles, struggles, or a hard life is no excuse for an impure or evil heart. The battle between good and evil is constantly present and we are challenged to make a conscious choice: guard our hearts and actions against what we know is wrong. Do the right thing, even when it hard to do.

Louis Eugene Walcott said: "There is a connection between the mind and the heart; if you affect the heart it will reflect in the way a person uses his mind."

The heart is a significant feature in the Judgement Day scene of the Ancient Egyptians. On this most important day, the heart of every human being is weighed on a scale against a single feather. Nestled at the center of the scale is the Egyptian Neter[*], Thoth.

Thoth, the origin of our English word "thought", appears as an animal. The symbolism is revealing: the human intellect has two polarities: one higher and the other lower, like animals. But to enter paradise, the intellect must be light (humble and pure) as a feather! The feather in Egypt was symbolic to the Law of Ma'at (righteousness).

---

[*]Neter - the term the Greeks translate as 'God'.

The Old Testament and the Quran describes an unruly and prideful heart as a stone; it is heavy and hard to move (motivate) in the right direction! A hard heart, like a hard head, resists change. The old heart does not want to do right.

After examining the above insight into the human heart, it should be obvious that what we are facing is a great challenge; a challenge to win back our souls and free ourselves from harming others and future adverse "judgements" (R.V.R.'s and prison sentences).

This is the good fight, so let's plunge into it and purify our hearts from all forms of evil.

<u>Questions</u>

1. Which definition of the heart best reflects your view of the heart?

2. Socrates once said: "The unexamined life isn't worth living." What is your take on the quote?

3. Do you agree with how the old heart is described? **Yes / No.** Explain.

4. Give your input on the phrase: "Blind is not their eyes. Blind is their hearts."

5. How do we guard our hearts from evil?

"We can turn our mess into a message."
                                    - Rick James

"The ink of the scholar is more important than the blood of the martyr."

- Prophet Muhammad

Chapter 2

Finding a New Heart

Many of us have written our entire history with the blood and tears of other people. But, at this crucial interval in our lives we have made a conscious choice to reflect on all of our past wrongs, amend them, and begin the process of re-writing our history - not in blood, but with the ink of love and a renewed heart.

The ancient leader Jeremiah had a vision of a time when human beings would receive a new heart, and upon that heart would be written the law of God. Many religious scholars say that this new heart would be a reflection of the love of God; the highest law being the law of love.

There is an old song: "Love Lifts Us Up Where We Belong."

So, what is love?

<u>Love</u> is the enactment of righteous principles carried into practice.

"I have never seen someone wake up happy, then go out and hurt someone", one quote says. A happy person is usually a safe person.

When our hearts have been infused with the love of righteous law and respect for authority, then we are not so inclined to the pull of the old heart; we are lifted above the drives of our animal nature, into the domain of our higher nature (our better selves) where crime is not our first instinct.

Crime, like sin, simply means to break the law.

We must fall in love with all that is right. In order to hurt other people, to rob other people, and to live a totally dishonest life, we first had to commit to <u>breaking the law</u>: the laws of God and the laws of man.

What is law?

<u>Laws</u> are rules put in place to govern the behavior of a person, place, or thing.

Although the law itself can not change a person, the love of the law will!

The law says: "do not steal...", "do not kill", etc. The law sets boundaries to protect people's property and life.

But, what animal respects boundaries?!

There must be a point where the animal in us ends and the human begins. This process begins with respect and ends with love.

How many times have we heard: "It is all about <u>respect</u> in prison"? But, the moment we are angry or feel slighted we throw respect out the window and elect violence. It was a conditional respect, a political form of respect.

While respect is a good place to start, it is still not the end game. Because the prisoner's mind would rather be 'feared' than 'loved' anyways.

Imagine if we started saying: "It is all about <u>love</u> in prison." What affect do you think that would have on people's thinking and behavior?

We hurt less those we love the most, or so we should. It is so much easier to fight someone I say I respect than a brother I love.

Love would say: "I won't steal that, not because it's not mine or because I don't want to get caught"; love won't do it because it is wrong and will injure some other person.

Love, unlike evil, has respect, appreciation, and a promotion of life and human success at it's heart.

Love is creation, not destruction; it elevates human instinct to the promotion and protection of the general welfare of all human beings.

Our English word respect is really a compound word with latin roots. In English, respect means to: "hold someone in high esteem or regard." But, the latin origin is more telling.

The word "<u>re</u>" is a prefix which means: "to do again"; the word "<u>spect</u>" means: "to see", like the word 'spectate'.

So, when you put the two meanings together you get: "to see again." Basically, when we truly respect someone, we do things that ensures we will see them again!

In a genuine and rightful relationship people want to see us again because, while in our presence, they experience (amongst other things) love.

When we both respect and love people, then we respect not just their lives, but their rights, their property, and their boundaries. I don't cross the line because my heart won't let me. There is a moral voice in my head which condemns my negative thoughts. In psychology it is called "conscience". This word means "the ability to distinguish between right and wrong".

This moral mind is called the <u>"self-accusing spirit"</u> in the Holy Quran.

There is something developed inside our minds helping us to overcome what is called man's "inclination to do evil". When the self-accusing spirit is developed, "good triumphs over evil".

The Buddha called it "<u>Right Thought</u>".

the Christian Bible declares our right conduct to be 'Fruits of Spirit' that spring from the law of love. We don't do what is right for the fear we have of the consequences for breaking the law; we do right simply out of love for what's right.

The new heart is a restored conscience that encourages Right Thought, instead of the evil thoughts mentioned in Chapter One.

The Ancients used high art forms to express man's potential to rise above his animal passions and drives. Prophet Muhammad rode a horse from Mecca to Jerusalem on, what the Quran calls, the night journey and ascendancy. In India, the Hindu's created images of the spiritual figures, Krishna or Vishnu, riding upon an elephant; an animal. The Buddhist's mirrored this imagery with Buddha atop an elephant as well. Jesus rode into Jerusalem, the city of peace, on a donkey in a chapter of the Bible, calling this: "the triumphant entry".

In ancient Mexico this expression of human maturity is codified in the deity Quetzalcoatl, who is called the "feathered serpent". This figure is a composition of a bird, a symbol of spirituality, and a snake, the symbol of lower nature.

The imagery is more powerful when we understand that snakes only eat "living things". Snakes don't eat carrion (or dead flesh) like vultures.

It is not surprising that the early Hebrew people depicted the devil, the personification of evil, as a snake. The serpent ruined the life of Adam and Eve, and ushered in a world of disobedience, death, and darkness, according to the text in the book of Genesis.

The Ancient Egyptians (and the Greeks in their writings) depicted the <u>Sphinx</u>. The Sphinx is a large architectural structure in Northern Africa with the head of a man erected upon the body of an animal, a lion. In the adjoining structures of the Sphinx, the incription reads: "Man, know thyself." This is the same message written in Greek over the Oracle Temple in Greece.

The knowledge of self is man's ability to rise above his lower nature and put the animal mind under the direct control of the higher mental, moral, and spiritual nature.

The higher nature is the journey we are on to achieve moral ascendancy.

It is love that will lift us up where we belong! "To fall in love with ourselves (and others) is a life-long romance", it's been said.

This is a picture and insight into the new heart. With it's development we can rise above, or ride upon, our old heart.

Let's begin to re-write our future with a heart that beats (or pumps) love.

Questions

1. Have you ever thought about writing a book about your life? What made you want to do so?

2. Why do you think a happy person is less inclined to hurt another person?

3. Do you agree with the definition of the new heart presented here?

4. What is the relationship between law and love?

5. Have the entire class write down 5 things the lower nature reflects and 5 things the higher nature should reflect below. Discuss these developments in open class.

> "Love is the fulfillment of the law."
>   - The Bible

Chapter 3

Writing Our Wrongs

This is a writing class, so we have relied on ancient illustrative imagery to paint a picture, or convey concepts, of what the new heart actually is. Images are vehicles to transmit ideas and messages. But, scientifically speaking, human vision is actually made possible not simply because we have eyes, but due to light and it's reflection off of things (and people) in our physical environment.

This is why, morally, one can have physical eyes and still be spiritually blind. Because spiritual light isn't present to facilitate moral vision. We had eyes, but we did not see the error of our ways! This is one reason The Ancients described the heart as "the third-eye"; a non-physical agency. The third-eye is, basically, the spiritual eye.

This should give more validity to the assessment that, "we don't see the world as it is; but we see the world as we are."

What kind of world have we created from our inner image?

From our warped and defected minds, we projected on the world a savage-like terrain where the rules of the jungle - dog eat dog - was the order of the day. Then, we rationalized and committed acts of cruelty against other people, having minimized the value of human life in general. We brought the world, in our own hearts, down to our level of moral immaturity. People simply became like other "things" which have no real intrinsic value.

After we used, or destroyed, them we could care less if we ever saw them again. We had no love or respect for human dignity, or human life.

Now is the time, like Shaka Senghor, that we <u>write our wrongs</u>, by highlighting aspects of our old heart (our past) that we would like to "write out" of our current lives today. We can transform tragedy into an art form - a new life.

Writing Exercise - Scenario 1: Past Life

Going back as far as you can remember, write a short story about where you believe your heart went wrong. The story should include:

1.   When the incident occurred.
2.   Where it occurred.
3.   How it occurred.

4. Who committed the act.

5. Why you believe it happened.

(write story below)

<u>Note</u>: Every one in the class shall get an opportunity to articulate their back story with the participants.

"Our greatest glory is not in never falling, but in rising every time we fall."
                                                    - Confucius

"If you think you're good or bad then, you're right."

Chapter 4

Imagine That!

In the book, 'Care of the Soul', Thomas Moore writes: "Tradition teaches that the soul lies mid-way between understanding and unconsciousness, and that it's instrument is neither the mind, nor the body, but imagination."

Much of who we are, or want to be, is stored up in our minds, our imagination. The imagination is the main feeding pipe-line to our hearts. If we are receptive, visually and audibly, to a daily curriculum of negativity, then we begin to feed from that slop-trough of degenerate knowledge.

I believe that it is no coincidence that the word 'heart' has both the words hear and ear as part of it's spelling. The inner-heart, like the third-eye description, has ears - it hears!

As our five senses are our connections and receptors to the outside, physical, world; there is an inner-world of activity that takes place within us; that "feeds" from every idea, experience, or vision we take in.

We have already described the workings of physical vision, and how it is facilitated by the eye's sensitivity to light. In the back of the eye-lid is a lens which receives images we see, and projects them like a film projector onto our retina, before the signal is transmitted to the brain for interpretation.

The ear has a similar mechanism. Sound reaches our eardrums in the form of vibrations. Once these vibrations are received they travel into, what is called in anatomy, the inner-ear. The brain receives these vibrations and translates them into words or other sound-types (music, etc.).

Basically, we are wired for images, whether they are received from sound or light.

Our self-concept (the internal image) we have of ourselves that translates how we think, or feel, about ourselves, is not a personal inventory that we are born with. We are made into "bad people", not created that way.

Here it is important to state that vast numbers of people in our culture encounter negative music, violence, movies, and have bad personal experiences without turning into "bad people", or people who do bad things. However, it is much easier to succumb to this negative imagery if, for some reason, you've "accepted" this input as who you are, or who you want to be. Basically, you've imagined yourself to be a certain way and enhanced that image through your daily companionship and behavior.

That is why one sociologist said: "you can not think yourself into new forms of behavior. You can only behave yourself into new forms of thinking."

The same applies to negative thinking patterns. Every one has negative thoughts. But, in order to manifest them, a person must behave them into reality, or existence. Once you have imagined yourself a certain way, and accepted that role for yourself, then acting on it seals the deal. The formula is:

1. <u>Input from external sources</u> (environment).
2. <u>Images</u> (generated in the mind).
3. <u>Acceptance</u> (believing it's you).
4. <u>Behavior</u> (daily reinforcement).
5. <u>Consequences</u> (a life-style of criminality, hurting people, prison-terms, or untimely death).

<u>Writing Exercise - Scenario 2: Best-Life</u>

Write a short story about your imagined "best-self":

1. Who would you want this person to be like (someone you admire, or an imaginary person, etc.)?
2. How would you want this person to behave?
3. Why have you chosen this person / image as your ideal self?
4. When is this occurring in your life (now or in the future)?
5. Where is this ideal tranformation taking place (in prison, in the free world, a particular place you want to live, etc.)?

(write story below)

Nothing is good or bad except thinking makes it so."
                                    - Abraham Lincoln

"When you let go of what you are, you become what you might be."

- Lao Tzu

Chapter 5

Examination

The sound heart is understood to be free of character defects and spiritual blemishes. Somehow, we have managed to stray from our natural self. When we were children, fresh out of the womb, we were free from blemishes. Not until we were shown otherwise did we adapt to whatever outside influences that disrupted the soundness of our hearts, as mentioned in Chapter 4. The infusion of corrupt beliefs has tainted our hearts.

According to traditional Chinese medicine, the heart houses what is known as Shen, which is spirit. The Chinese characters for thinking, thought, love, the intention to listen, and virtue all contain the ideogram for the heart.

The physical heart, which houses the spiritual heart, beats about 100,000 times a day, pumping two gallons of blood per minute, and over 100 gallons per hour.

Coincidentally, we have not been taking good care of our physical heart or spiritual heart. Our physical heart, as well as our spiritual heart, needs exercise. A sedentary heart, alongside bad eating, can cause plaque to develop around the heart, which may cause heart disease. In order to keep the physical and spiritual heart pure, we have to consistently do acts (exercise), big or small, that will keep the physical and spiritual heart conditioned.

It's like waxing a floor. You can apply a single coat of wax on a floor and it may shine nicely, but if you consistently apply a new coat of wax it will have an intense shine. However, if you leave it unattended, then it becomes crusty and dull, just like your heart. Unwholesome deeds will accumulate and take the purity away from your heart.

Furthermore, there is a dormant element within the human heart that, if nurtured and allowed to grow, can damage the soul and eventually destroy it. This unseen aspect of the heart contains a bad seed that has the potential of becoming like a cancer that can metastasize and overtake the heart.

This "disease" of the heart is manifested in such actions as:

Hatred: Prejudiced hostility, or animosity. This part of human nature causes people to desire harm to befall their enemies, and to discriminate against those who are unlike them (in creed, color, or character). Although hatred is not necessarily negative. It is commendable to hate corruption, evil, murder, lewdness, and anything that your higher power has exposed as despicable.

<u>Envy</u>: Painful or resentful awareness of another's advantages; which is said to be the root of all diseases. In the Abrahamic religions, "nothing prevented Satan from bowing down except his envy of Adam, for God chose Adam to be his vicegerent on earth instead of him". The envious develop a mindset that makes it impossible for them to admit they are wrong. Moreso, they despise others who excel.

<u>Ostentation</u>: Pretentious or excessive display. This disease is rooted in desire. It is astonishing how much energy people expend seeking the pleasure of others, trying (for example) to seek prestige or promotion by pleasing someone. Ironically, when a person finds himself with great wealth and fame, friends start to appear everywhere. But, if he were to lose his wealth and standing, those friends disappear.

<u>Vanity</u>: Undue pride in oneself or one's appearance. The word "vanity" comes from the latin word 'vanus', which means empty, implying that the source of our vanity is void of substance and will vanish. When the Roman Emperor triumphed in a battle, he put on a victory celebration in which the general of the battle paraded through the street. Behind him, or his chariot, a slave would hold a victory laurel and whisper in the general's ear, "all is vanity". Reminding the general of the perils of vanity. It is part of ancient wisdom to remind people that all accomplishments people praise and admire will perish until no one remembers them.

<u>Boasting & Arrogance</u>: To praise oneself; to mention or assert with excessive pride. No one likes a boaster, one who walks with swank and swagger, and one who cannot be in the company of other people without speaking about himself, or drawing attention to what he has done.

Arrogance means, offensively exaggerating one's own importance. When it comes to arrogance there are different qualities, and types, of arrogance.

The first type is when a person deems himself superior to others. Imam al-Ghazali said, "people of knowledge are in greater danger of arrogance than anyone else"; this is because the knowledge they have attained may lead them to feelings of superiority.

The second type of arrogance is in displaying contempt and scorn towards others. For example, a loud and obnoxious person graces your presence, and when you see them you are poorly tempered and annoyed.

The third type of arrogance is beauty. Conceit is displayed by being snobby or stubborn, because of how a person looks. Beauty does not last; it will dissipate as time and age tirelessly run down the flesh. All that remains is what one should have been concerned with in the first place: the content of one's character, personal beliefs, and one's deeds.

The fourth type of arrogance is due to possessing an abundance of something. Example: having more canteen, cars, family support, or love.

The focus here is recognizing these diseases, and having the sheer ability of owning them, and ridding one's character of them. At some point in our old heart, one or more of these qualities have appeared, causing us to be impulsive and inconsiderate.

Each of these diseases are rooted in man's self-satisfaction. Likewise, the root cause of all good qualities is the lack of self-satisfaction. The origin of either of these states relates to the company one keeps, "for a man's character is that of the company he keeps". Because, if a man achieves any state, inevitably his companions will be affected by it.

<u>Writing Exercise - Scenario 3: Examining my own Diseases</u>

In three paragraphs (introduction, a body paragraph, and conclusion): Which of these diseases are you most affected by, and how has this disease hindered you from accomplishing something?

"Rudeness is the weak man's imitation of strength."
- Eric Hoffer

"There is a single, albeit incomplete or broken, chain of mental association that defines the identity of each person."

        - Sigmund Freud, Interpretation of Dreams

Chapter 6

Interpretation

In nearly every culture in the world, people use metaphors that directly or indirectly allude to the heart.

- We call certain types of people "hard-hearted", usually because they show no mercy or kindness.
- People are said to be "cold-hearted", and yet some who are "warm-hearted".
- We speak of people wearing their heart on their sleeves because they do not (or can not) conceal their emotions from others.
- When someone's words or actions penetrate our souls, and affect us profoundly, we say that this person "touched my heart".

In our daily lives, most of the time, we let our emotions decide how we act. These actions are detrimental to our well-being because all actions have consequences.

Consequently, in prison, we are often faced with situations that prod our pride, and/or egg on our emotions. Depending on how our old heart was nurtured, and the nature in which it was nurtured (substance abuse, domestic violence, family dysfunction, mental health, and/or anger or defiance) we have developed our own solutions for dealing with our problems.

Oftentimes, depending on the situation, we choose fighting, drugs, or violence in order to rectify the problem that we are faced with. Seemingly, the problem still awaits us when all is said and done.

In a valiant attempt at resurrecting a new heart, we need to find solutions in lieu of the attempted solutions that we held in the past. While building this new heart, unlike the old, it should be nurtured in an environment that's in accordance to sustaining a healthy new heart.

First, we need to figure out how we are to sustain a healthy new heart.

1. We have to guard our heart. Let's not be so quick to invest in bad, or negative, protection. What we need is:

   a) Protection from bad or old beliefs.
   b) Protection from negative environments and information.
   c) Protection from bad company and relationships.

2. The heart needs to be exercised, just as we go through our day taking care of our body's cleanliness, we must tend to our new heart with daily routines that ensure that the heart grows with enthusiasm, and is nurtured in an environment that allows optimal growth.

   a) Spend time with energetic and healthy people.
   b) Attend and participate with others (family, groups, friends, or sports) in discussions or groups that may prevent you from crashing.
   c) Daily meditation, prayer, or quiet time in order to allow yourselves to decompress.

3. In sustaining the new heart, we must feed the heart with healthy information, hearty company, and wholesome thoughts which will eventually stimulate growth that leads to a better belief system, well thought out actions (instead of impulsive and irrational), and reputable relationships.

4. **List 3 additional things you could do to "feed" your new heart to nurture it to health:**

   a)
   b)
   c)

As we grow, we must interpret our past actions, not as failure, but lessons. As with rebuilding, we don't necessarily have to 'replace' as much as we need to 'redesign'. Those past failures will help us succeed in the future.

In the past, we were afraid. Fear has a way of making people vulnerable to acting irrationally; making terrible mistakes. As mentioned aforehand, the new heart will be protected, conditioned, and nurtured with elements that will help you face your fears.

James Baldwin once said, "not everything that is faced can be changed; but nothing can be changed until it is faced."

There is an acronym for F.E.A.R.: False Evidence Appearing Real. The only way to dispute this false evidence is to confront it with truth. The truth is, the way we were living was toxic; our thoughts, beliefs, the company we kept, which led to bad choices, costly decisions, and unfavorable actions.

Group Discussion

Now that we understand the different interpretations of the heart, can we think of some ways that we can condition, exercise, or nurture (feed) the heart?

How would you help your children develop healthy interpretations of a heart?

>"Not everything that is faced can be changed; but nothing can be changed until it is faced."
>
>— James Baldwin

"The ultimate measure of a man is not where he stands in moments of comfort
and convenience, but where he stands at times of challenge and controversy."

- Dr. Martin Luther King Jr.

Chapter 7

Hardship

Thus far, we have surveyed the heart, assessed it's many afflictions,
and recognized some general interpretations. We now know that our old heart
is ailing, and it's subject to hardships.

Hardship is defined as: something that causes suffering. The diseases
and afflictions that have caused us to live a toxic and destructive life have
also caused us to suffer, such as: spending time in jail, not being able to
raise our children, missing out on important dates or events (birthdays, anni-
versaries, and graduations), and oftentimes death. This immense suffering
only adds pressure to a feeble heart. This pressure is often said to burst
pipes (arteries) or make diamonds.

Here, we are trying to make diamonds as the only other option is to
succumb to the pressure and let it break us. But, this only lets everybody
down that is depending on us to pull it together, including ourselves.

Once we have assessed the damages, and we are about to partake in a
surgery that is so complete, yet vital, to our well being, we need to enlist
some help that may benefit us before, during, and after the surgery.

Prior to surgery, it's good to establish a support system; people around
you that you can lean on. Also, we need to get a proper understanding of why
we're having surgery in the first place.

To elaborate: "Understanding is to see the knowledge underneath where
we currently stand. A process of seeing through our toxic ways to what is
below the surface", or our natural state of being. Presently, we can't see
that far. It may require an endoscopic camera; better yet, some basic self-
reflection in order to prepare ourselves for this new heart.

As we have discovered, we need surgery because we have detected a terminal
illness that has invaded our own well-being.

During this surgery, we must take into consideration our experiences,
what they have made us, and why we're presently in surgery. Substance abuse
is not only physically harming our heart, it's destroying our relationships.
The criminal thinking has removed us from thinking like a law-abiding citizen,

which has moved us to criminal behavior, instead of earning an honest living.

Had we been mindful of our actions, prior to contracting said diseases, we'd be better positioned in protecting our heart. Therefore, since we'll be undergoing surgery we'll need a watchful eye. Someone to hold us accountable while the surgery is taking place. People such as: teachers, mentors, counselors, and loved ones willing to help during this crucial time.

There will be pain, but know that the pain will subside and the healing will begin.

Post-surgery, you may be prescribed an antibiotic to keep the infection from resurfacing. That antibiotic may come in the forms of:

- <u>Spiritual Medicine</u> - Having faith in your higher power, confiding in your loved ones, and/or visualizing a healthy future with your new heart.
- <u>Physical Healing</u> - Which may be accomplished by exercising, drawing, and/or writing.
- <u>Emotional Healing</u> - Building healthy relationships with kids, significant others, as well as rebuilding old relationships that were ruined by your old heart.

Seemingly, "truth has no consciousness of error. Love has no sense of hatred. Life has no partnership with death. Truth, life, and love are a law of annihilation to everything unlike themselves, because they declare nothing except God [or your higher power]." - Mary Baker Eddy

This is because there is no compliment to life; there is no anti-life. Death is simply the end of life's cycle, not an opposite reality.

Just know, suffering comes before success in life. Take your hardships one day at a time because the healing is on the horizon.

<u>Exercise</u>

Free write about a hardship that has changed the course of your life, and tell us about how you intend on getting over it.

"The heart is the book of everything the eyes see."

- Sahaba Ali

Chapter 8

Open Heart Surgery

One of the leading causes of death in America is heart disease, or heart failure. Heart attacks take thousands of lives each year. Genetics, poor diet, and personal and environmental stress are listed as main causative factors for this disease.

The Quran calls spiritual disruption "quakes", as in a heart (or spiritual) attack. We have talked a lot about the physical and spiritual heart in this curriculum. We have also discussed some of the conditions and activities that ruin the heart, and others that improve it. Basically, there are solutions for our problems.

The spiritual and physical life are connected. So, an untimely physical death could be the result of spiritual corruption inside of us. "The fish", it is said, "rots from the head down." There is a heart and head connection. Carl Jung put it this way: "Every psychological problem is ultimately a matter of religion." So, a spiritual life of some kind is necessary for psychological health.

This is why in Greek literature the following medical terms held religious significant:

1. In Plato's writings, Socrates says that <u>therapy</u> refers to "service to gods".
2. <u>Nurse</u> happens to be the early meaning for therapeia (therapy in Greek).
3. <u>Cura</u> (or care of the soul) meant: Attention, devotion, hubandry, adorning the body, healing, managing, and - worshipping the gods.
4. <u>Observance</u> - A word from ritual and religion. It means to "watch out for", but also to keep holy. "Serv" meant to tend the sheep. Jews "observe" Passover. Muslims "observe" Ramadhan. Christians "observe" Easter. So, the soul is not a thing, but a quality of dimension of experiencing life and ourselves. It has to do with depth, value, relatedness, and personal substance.

The word for success and Arabic is synonomous with the word farmer. A farmer not only tends the "sheep" (a humble heart), he also cultivates the "land" (spiritual and physical body).

In order not to fail in life, we must cut disease out of our hearts. Jesus and Muhammad are both recorded to have said: "there is a lump of flesh in you and he who cultivates it succeeds, and he who doesn't, fails."

That lump of flesh they're referring to is the human heart.

The Quran is called a "healing" and Jesus once said, "physicians, heal yourself". It is also recorded that he said, "the doctor only comes to the sick".
Surprisingly, the word doctor originally meant "teacher". Healing begins with learning what is wrong. We are sick with many problems, but we can be our best doctors too!

We must "examine", look into, and work on our hearts. So, in this lesson we want to do an Open Heart Surgery; or, what is called in the medical field, a 'bypass'. Let's take an honest look within. We need a heart transplant!

Now, we want to "open our hearts" for corrective surgery, and the scalpel for this procedure is decision-making. The word decision is a compound word. De means: from. Cision is related to the word "cisors", an instrument used 'to cut'. The two words together then mean, "to cut from".

So, after we make a decision to change, we must begin to cut ourselves away from:

1.   Old Thoughts
2.   Old Habits
3.   Negative Friends
4.   Negative Environments
These 4 things corrupt the heart from which all life issues from.

<u>Exercise – Open Heart Surgery</u>

1.   I have opened up and looked into my heart and found ________________ (What bad trait), and have decided to ____

____________________________________.

2.   I have examined this old habit; ______________________________ (list the habit), nurtured in my heart, and I've decided to change it for this new habit: __________

____________________________________.

3.   I have observed the company I've kept near to my heart (interest) and I've decided today that ____

____________________________________.

4.   I have realized that "home is where the heart is", and since I no longer desire a negative heart, I want an environment that reflects a peaceful condition.

So, I have decided that my ideal home would be ___________________________
____.

Only when we are "open" and honest about these matters of the heart can it "beat to another drum of life".

Interestingly, the only full word we can get if we unscramble the word 'heart' is, 'Earth'. Most ancient scriptures say that man was created from the Earth, the land, and a spirit from The Creator was breathed into him, and the man became "a living soul". This emphasizes the physical and spiritual connection of life. The heart is instrumental with maintaining health and progressive existence.

Cultivate your land! change your heart!

"We can not think ourselves into new forms of behavior,
we have to behave ourselves into new ways of thinking."

Chapter 9

Rehabilitation

There is an old adage that goes, "what is real speaks for itself". change can not be faked. Eventually, who you truly are will show through.

In this last chapter, we would like to bring our study to a "head" by emphasizing that transformation is a language of it's own, and it will speak (or be "articulated") through every aspect of human behavior. That is, mentally, spiritually, emotionally, and verbally.

Furthermore, having come this far in the curriculum, it should not be difficult for any of us to express how we have changed our hearts. The work has been put in!

Exercise - Heart of the Matter

Write one paragraph (3 sentences) on the following topics below:

1.   My spiritual heart can be articulated in these words:

2.   My mental heart can be articulated in these words:

3.   My physical heart can be articulated in these words:

4.   My emotional heart can be articulated in these words:

<u>Remember</u>: No matter what we wrote, our actions will speak louder than our words.

Finally, each participant is expected to express (articulate) their heart (personal dispositions and findings) with the group. In doing such, we have helped each other articulate rehabilitation through telling our stories - the journey of our heart - to maturity and progress!

REACHING OUT FROM WITHIN

REACHING OUT FROM WITHIN

Transforming pain into power and success

"Be a real man, not a prison man."
- Former Warden (M.E. Spearman)

By: Donel Poston and James Wilson

"I want to do on the outside the things I've done on the inside."

                                       - Alice Marie Johnson

Reaching Out From Within Introduction

In recent years there has been a spirit of liberation sweeping across the country, particularly in California. While there are still grave problems in the criminal justice system, no one can deny that each year, old links on the chains of bondage are being broken. We have seen new laws signed into effect by the last two Governors (Jerry Brown and Gavin Newsom) and multiple assembly and senate bills giving inmates a second chance at freedom, either through the courts or rehabilitation initiatives. To frame this discussion, I will list just some of the progress made thus far. To name a few:

- SB260-261 - Giving long-term youth offenders early parole dates.
- Prop 57 - Reducing 85% to 80%, and providing inmates access to earn time off their sentences through rehabilitation program participation.
- SB1437 - Reforms to the felony murder rule.
- SB1391 - No longer can 14-15 year olds be charged as adults.
- SB620 - Judges now have discretion to strike gun enhancement sentences.
- SB1393 - Judges have discretion to strike enhancements for prior violent prison commitments.
- AB2845 - Makes it easier for rehabilitated inmates serving long terms to apply for a Certificate of Rehabilitation (Commutation) from the governor.
- SB439 - Ends prosecution and detention of juveniles 12 years and under.

These are a summary of California's criminal justice reforms, but around the country there has been similar progress:

- 20 states have now dropped the death penalty (more will follow!).
- The Los Angeles District Attorney is seeking radical changes in the law.
- A bi-partisan bill - called the "1st Step Act" - was signed into law providing parole for federal prisoners serving life sentences for drugs, and other non-violent offenses. Matthew Charles was the first inmate released under this law. He was even invited to President Trump's 2019 Inaugural Address to Congress and the nation.

The Commutation of Cyntonia Brown's prison term (31 years-old today, having been in prison since age 16) is another such example of the above progress. The most popular clemency case, however, is that of Alice Marie Johnson, who was serving a life-sentence for drug trafficking. After 21 years in prison the President, via the advocacy of Kim Kardashian, Van Jones of Cut 50, and

CNN; granted her clemency. She was also invited to the Inaugural Address of
the President.

These cases prove true the saying of Solomon (over 3,000 years ago)
that: (1) a person's talent can bring them before Kings, and (2) a man (or
woman), can walk out of prison and become a King (or Queen)!

Believe me, these men and women did not receive their freedom by hanging
out in prison, doing nothing. While incarcerated they completed school, attended
religious services, graduated from self-help groups, and were active leaders
in their prison communities. Further, they "reached out from the inside" so
the world could know about their lives and talent, and since they were faithful
in governing their lives in prison they earned the opportunity to be in charge
of (rule) their lives outside of prison!

By reaching out and helping others, other people (Kim Kardashian, lawyers,
advocacy groups, etc.) reached in and helped them.

There is an old saying that says: "Some of our solutions are for other people's
problems."

Alice Marie Johnson couldn't begin to help people on the outside if
she hadn't first done the work on the inside - inside of her own heart and
behind the walls.

Shaka Senghor, another former prisoner, belongs to the organization
Cut 50 which advocated for Ms. Johnson's freedom. Mr. Senghor served 19 years
in prison for murder in Detroit, Michigan. While in prison he applied himself
to studying, organizing, and educating people. Now that he is out of prison,
he is a book author ("Writing My Wrongs"), a prison reform advocate with [*]Cut
50, and now hosts a show on Oprah's 'OWN' network called "Released".

His talent brought him before Kings (Van Jones) and Queens (Oprah Winfrey)!
He is out of prison and ruling (governing) his life properly.

But, what they have accomplished is not exclusive; yes, it is extraordinary,
but it is an end game that is available to anyone who wants to do the hard
work. The heart work. It begins from within!

That is the working definition of this program: reach out to help others,

---

[*]Cut 50 is an organization founded by Van Jones and Jessica Jackson whose
goal it is to cut the prison population in half (cut 50) by 2024.

but first begin reaching within yourself to mine those great treasuries inside
in order to have somewthing of value to share with others.

You can't give what you don't have!

<u>Forward</u>

The goal of this program is geared towards accomplishing three primary things:

1.   To [INFORM] you of the good you have within;
2.   To [INSPIRE] you to look within to discover the good; and,
3.   To [MOTIVATE] you to bring out the good to help yourself and to serve others.

Let's begin to do the work on the inside (our hearts and in prison) so we'll qualify to do it on the outside, in the prison community, and the free world.

Opray Winfrey has a famous saying about success: "Success is when preparation meets opportunity."

Don't miss your opportunity by being unprepared!

By: James Wilson

"The enemy is fear. We think it is hate; but, it is fear."

- Ghandi

Chapter One

Re-Think Your Story, change Your Future

Frederick Douglass, a former slave who became an abolitionist, a leader for powerless men and women, and a book author, has this opening tale at the beginning of his book:

> "Do you remember the old fable of 'The Man and the Lion' where the lion complained that he should not be so mis-represented 'when lion's wrote history'?"

We tend to be our own worst critics. Scientists speculate that human beings are genetically wired to look for the 'worst case' in every scenario. They claim that by doing so we heighten our awareness against possible dangers, and therefore increase our chances of surviving. This interprets the human experience as "fear-based". I was glad to have sought a second opinion on this topic because I encountered an opposing view. It is summed up in the excerpt below:

> "The truth is, humans can change, and change fast. Our hall-mark is adaptability. Long ago, we looked out from the trees and savannahs. Beyond the savannahs we glimpsed further fron-tiers. History proves that when we behold a better world, we move towards it - one person at a time - leaving behind what no longer works."

This quote interprets human experience as optimistic and courageous... Human history, including our own personal stories, can tell us alot about how most of our growth came from moving beyond fear and limitations. Dana Car, the famous martial arts expert, teaches that if we want to grow we must do two primary things:

1. Overcome our self-limiting stories; and,
2. Increase our tolerance of pain.

Part of the reason we find it difficult to progress is that we "author" self-defeating interpretations about our past experiences, even after we try to edit out all the painful things that may cause us ridicule or embarrassment.

No matter how we re-write the story, it has a "bad" ending.

We have all heard the saying that change is always resisted. Do we ever ask why? Change is resisted because: (1) we grow content with how we are; and (2) it becomes difficult (or painful) to undo what we've already accepted. Plus, we fear the work that comes with this entire process.

I believe it is time for a new approach to change. The old methods of fear, guilt, and shame no longer work. Martin Luther King Jr. once said: "Darkness can not drive out darkness; only light can do that. Hate can not drive out hate; only love can do that." And I will add: "Fear can not overcome powerlessness; only courage can do that. Criticism can't drive out self-doubt; only love and acceptance can do that."

Self-hatred will not produce the desired result of self-love. James Baldwin put it this way:

> "I imagine one of the reasons people cling to their hate so
> stubbornly is because they sense, once hate is gone, they
> will be forced to deal with pain."

Basically, we learn to hide our stories of pain behind veneers of hatred. "I hate society." "I hate authority." I hate.... I hate.... that sounds more powerful than saying: "I am in pain. I am hurt here. Can you help?" Pain is personal. It puts the spot light on us, not society or external authority figures. We are afriad to face the truth, to face our own vulnerability.

We are basically shaped by experiences, usually contrary to our desire, to prepare us to render a great service in the future. To make us leaders for ourselves and others. Vulnerability ripens us to find security in ourselves, and to create safe and secure environments for others.

Prison is a dark and dangerous place. We can't overcome prison with a prison mentality. We need a freedom thinking mind to do that! We need good mentors, optimism, and courage. We need light. Then, we must overcome the fear of change and begin re-thinking our past experiences - re-writing our stories with a positive, non-fearful, approach to surviving life's challenges. We must add hope and courage to our past stories. I have looked back in order to find the "gifts" in my experiences. Have you?

We must reach out to help other people even when we have very little matieral possessions ourselves. We must know the fight isn't material really, but it's all those intangible values: love, generosity, courage, selflessness, and optimism that we can offer others during the winter of their discontent.

We must be a shelter of love to warm and thaw every cold heart.

Questions

1. What is one thing you have criticized yourself most for?
2. What do you fear most about change?
3. Looking back on your life story, what are 3 things you once thought were bad, but now you can find the gift of good in them?

Chapter 2

Cylindrical Pattern of Behavior

Word Definitions

<u>Fear</u> - A distressing emotion aroused by impending pain or danger.

<u>Anger</u> - A strong feeling of displeasure.

<u>Hatred</u> - Prejudiced hostility or animosity; intense hostility and aversion, usually deriving from fear, anger, or a sense of injury.

Do you see the connection between fear, anger, and hatred?

Write a scenario below where fear and anger turned into feelings of hatred in your life:

<u>Note</u>:

Discuss in group how you could re-think and re-write the scenario in a more positive light. How could you have went about it differently? Each person will get an opportunity to share their insight with the class.

<u>Questions</u>

1. What comes to your mind when you think of hatred, and why?

2. Why do you believe so many people are filled with anger?

3. **Class Activity:** Each participant should finish this statement:

   "I will not fear ____________________________ anymore."

"Someone has been hurt before you; wronged before you; hungered before you;
humiliated before you; raped before you; yet, someone survived."

- Maya Angelou

Chapter 3

Turning Pain Into Power

Life expectancy in the United States, according to the Center for Disease
Control, has declined by several years recent studies have shown. Two main
reasons cited for this tipping point: (1) overdoses related to the recent
opioid crisis; and (2) an increase in suicides.

Unsurprisingly, both drug addiction and suicides have been linked to
personal pain. The book "Pain Killer", written by Barry Meir, explored this
phenomenon and details how large pharmaceutical companies like Purdue Pharma
make billions of dollars from exploiting human pain and offering chemical
relief for it in the form of pills. This has also been a recent subject addressed
on PBS, 60 Minutes, and even prison Wardens took up the issue of the harmful
effects of Fentanol in institutions.

All across America, including prisons, men and women of all ages are
succumbing to the quick fix of drugs, which is simply suicide by another name.

While many states have legalized the use of marijuana, high doses of
Fentanol have been traced even in commercial weed products. It is no secret
why a report was published recently expressing how, even low doses of marijuana
are having severe damaging affects on teenagers' brains.

While weed has become widespread in our communities, popularized by
celebrities and music, we are paying a human cost by it's usage. Remember:
there is nothing more valuable than developing brains. The brain is our most
important organ, but we tend to protect it and exercise it less than others.

One of the amazing features of the brain is it's ability to reduce the
affects of trauma in the conscious memory of humans. When we experience a
traumatic event, the brain, to save us from overwhelming shock, pushes most
of the memory from the event into our subconscious mind.

While this makes sense as an immediate and temporary plan-B strategy,
the consequence is that we rarely want to bring those memories to the forefront
of our minds to deal with them, so they remain in our "closet memory", festering
and combining with other suppressed painful experiences. This pain becomes
a living creature of it's own, taking control over our lives from the inside

out. Pain grows off of what it feeds on: (1) more trauma; and (2) more temporary relief.

The cause behind suicide has eluded researchers forever, and while there is no single definitive explanation for why people take their own lives, a theory has been proposed: People do not dislike living, they don't want to actually die. However, they want to escape a particular life-style, or experience they feel trapped in. The easiest way to escape a tragic experience is simply to end the life that gives expression to it. (Note: If you are having thoughts of harming yourself, please tell someone).

One historian opined that gang-banging, one of the most dangerous activities, was a form of suicide by another name. A slow death for generations of kids who could never find meaning, or escape from poor and depressed communities. No wonder studies have shown that kids who live for long periods in drug and gang-infested neighborhoods show signs of P.T.S.D. (Post-Traumatic Stress Disorder). This level of stress is most common in war veterans who have served in combat zones. Many of these veterans return home and turn to opioids (pain killers) and hundreds of vets commit suicide every year.

We are well aware that a painful family upbringing drove us to seek relief in gangs, drugs, alcohol, early sexual activity, and even sports. Sports historians have even admitted that scouts find their best athletes in communities where kids experience the most adverse conditions, and therefore, pain. Study some of your best players and you'll discover two fairly consistent factors: (1) they grew up in rough environments, and (2) they experienced a lot of pain.

Here is the bright spot though: Someone stepped in to help them transform their pain into power! It can actually be alleged that the NFL and NBA - like Purdue Pharma - is exploiting the pain of human beings! Obviously, however, the results are far different.

Believe it or not, gangs and violence are vehicles, not of power, but of pain. The gang is a master at harnessing and focusing the pain of it's members towards a specific agenda. The gang phenomenon gives many over-looked and insecure people a sense of belonging, and voice.

Remember the movie "Man on Fire" with Denzel Washington? In it, there is a caption that reads: 'Fear has a voice'. Well, so does pain, anger, and self-hatred.

But, we can transform our victimization into victory like Lebron James,

Dewayne Wade, and Shaka Senghor, and now ourselves.

As young men, we experience emotional, mental, physical, and even sexual abuse. Hurt people will eventually hurt other people, unless they transform their pain into the power to help themselves and others. So, instead of allowing pain to turn us to a permanent life of self-destructive behavior, let's find ways to express our pain with a positive and transformative voice; not drugs, gangs, and violence. As we heal, we can create healthy environments and friendships that make the community safe and compassionate.

It has been said that "every one has a song inside them, all they need to do is find their voice."

No matter what your song (story) is, it is up to you to discover your own voice and how you intend to share it with the world.

Curiously, another study weighed in on the issue of human life-expectancy. The study was called: <u>School or the Streets</u>. Here is what it found for people who lack a high school diploma; they will:

1.   Have high health costs;
2.   Average lower incomes;
3.   Experience welfare dependancy; and
4.   Have a lower life-expectancy!

This adds new meaning to the saying: "live and learn". According to this report, if we're not learning, then we will live shorter lives! If you thought that education was expensive, then try ignorance. It can cost you half of your life-expectancy! Perhaps, we should instead be "learning to live".

There is something great inside every one of us (first our brains) that have the ability to transform our pain into power! Reach not for drugs and weapons, but deep inside of yourself for tools of change and solutions.

Questions

1.   Have you ever used drugs or alcohol to escape your pain?
2.   What is your "go-to" when you find yourself under stress?
3.   List 3 ways you can transform your pain into power. Explain.
4.   What would you like for your song (legacy) to be?

"To the man who only has a hammer, everything he encounters begins to look like a nail."

- Abraham Maslow

Chapter 4

Some Brief Facts on the Brain

There are times when a conflict between the high road of <u>controlled reason</u> and the low road of <u>automatic emotion</u> occurs. Brain functions can be divided into two processes:

1.   Controlled
2.   Automatic

Controlled processes tend to use linear, step-by-step, logic and are deliberately employed, and we are aware of them when we use them. Automatic processes operate unconsciously, nondeliberately, and in parallel. Controlled processes tend to occur in the front (orbital and prefrontal) parts of the brain. The <u>prefrontal cortex</u> (PFC) is known as the executive region because it integrates the other region for long-term planning. Automatic processes tend to occur in the back (<u>occipital</u>), top (<u>parietal</u>), and side (<u>temporal</u>) part of the brain. The amygdala is associated with automatic emotional response; especially fear. During extreme and unusual events there may be a competition between these controlled and automatic brain systems. During fight or flight, the high road of controlled reason begins to shut down due to oxygen deprivation, sleep deprivation, extreme temperatures, starvation, exhaustion, etc.; The body powers down higher functions in order to preserve the lower functions necessary for basic survival. During normal situations, these controlled circuits of reason keep our autonomic circuits of emotions in check, and we don't just give in to every whim. But, remove the rational governor and the emotional machinery begins to spin out of control.

The brain is not only an organ of intellect and logic, it's also the source of emotion. Emotions are brought to life in what is known as the "limbic system". The limbic system is a collection of parts that constitute approximately 20% of the brain's area. <u>The forces of pride</u>, <u>fear</u>, <u>joy</u>, <u>grief</u>, <u>anger</u>, <u>lust</u>, <u>hatred</u>, <u>envy</u>, <u>jealousy</u>, <u>etc.</u>, <u>arise from this region of the brain.</u>

The limbic system is found surrounding the most primitive part of the brain and is found in almost thet same form in all mammals. It is that part of man that is hardly distinguishable from beast. <u>The limbic system works with both the cerebrum above and the brainstem below. Its connections with</u>

the brainstem help maintain a state of emotional balance and alertness. Its connections with the cerebrum allow a person to temper emotion with reason.

The goal is for the two processes to work in harmony, but the balance can be easily upset. The limbic system can become so highly activated that it overwhelms rational thought, making a person speechless with anger, or joy. On the other hand, through conscious effort, a person can resist the natural urge to eat or drink, can fight back tears, or suppress sexual desire.

Brain Chart 1

Fill in the blanks with emotions from your old, or current, brain (what emotions dominate your thinking on a consistent basis?).

Brain Chart 2

Fill in the blanks for the brain you are building; your work in progress. What emotions best fits you going forward?

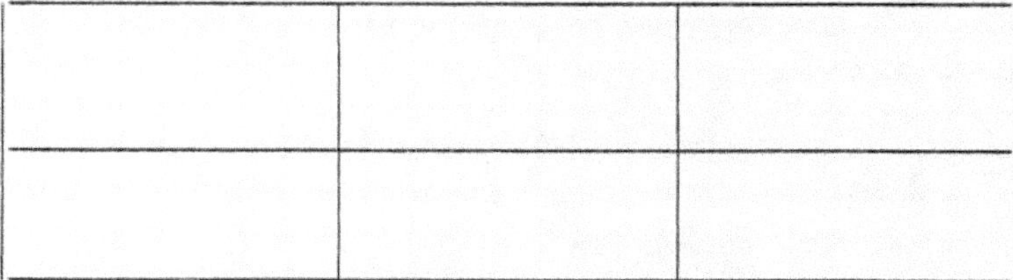

Allow every student to discuss their charts.

Questions

1. Fear is a natural reaction (emotion) of the brain. How do you deal with fears in your personal life?
2. Anger is natural. What is one thing that angers you? How do you handle that anger when it arises?
3. If the lymbic system represents our animal brain, then what aspect of our brain determines our humanity? what word would you use to describe

that part of the brain?

4. Knowing what you know about drug usage and gang-banging, what emotions will you say characterizes those activities, and why?

5. What are some things we can do to achieve self-control? List them and discuss them in class.

Chapter 5

Catch Up With Yourself

"All my life I had been looking for something and everywhere
I turned someone tried to tell me what it was. I accepted
their answers too, though they were often in contradiction
and even self-contradictory. I was naive. I was looking for
myself and asking everyone except myself. Questions which
I, and only I, could answer. It took me a long time and much
painful boomeranging of my expectations to achieve a realization everyone else appears to have been born with. That
I am nobody but myself."

- Ralph Ellison (The invisible man)

We are not a one story person. So many different impressions and influences
have gone into the so-called individual we call "me". Some of it is good,
and a lot is bad, and most of it we wouldn't miss if we discarded. The lineage
of our personhood is quite lengthy.

While it is an acceptable fact that throughout our lives - and naturally
so - we will have to assume different roles based on a process called "socialization", or the way we learn appropriate behavior.

When we are young, we are socialized into the role and expectations
of a child. This role changes as we enter school and later our teenage, and
then early adult years. Our roles continue to expand and complicate as we
enter new experiences (like work, or religious and social organizations) and
relationships like marriage and fatherhood.

These are normal multi-faceted transformations in a single person, like
a larvae that evolves into a tadpole that later metamorphasizes into a frog.
Same "person", but acting out different roles depending on which stage of
growth is appropriate. So, it would be "inappropriate" for me to play the
role of child with my wife. The appropriate role is man and husband for that
relationship. So, in context, multiple roles for a single person is well established and acceptable according to normal social standards. that is, when
we are privileged to enjoy a normal upbringing.

Most of us have adopted abnormal sets of behavior from an illegitimate
sub-cultural world. For instance: gang, criminal, and prison mentalities,
and codes of conduct that become deeply rooted into our personalities, even

distorting normal roles of relationships, like parent - child, husband and wife, and youth and elder status. I have heard of men and sons who were the pimps of their mothers; and fathers who were the drug clients of their children. These young eyes have seen a lot, if not, far too much for my precious years.

But, some of the greatest damage I've seen to this generation is, the lack of knowledge of self. I think some people call this dilemma an identity crisis, or even worse, multiple personality disorder. Decades ago, society called people unsure of themselves "Generation X" (an unknown, or lost, generation). We are still lost and seeking an identity that truly fits us. But, when a person doesn't know his history (himself) then anyone's history will do. So, growing up, people have presented us with a spectrum of "false identities" which we have sought to assume as our own. Some of us have claimed to have been playas, pimps, and gangsters on one end and on the other end of the spectrum: fathers, husbands, and children of God!

Obviously, we have been confused and lived lives of self-contradiction.

It is time that we've committed to the hard work of clearing our heads of all the garbage we've dumped into it, and rebuild our self-image on healthy and noble principles of conduct.

Since being in prison, I've had so many people try to impose, or insert, their opinions of "who I should be" on me. They say that since I grew up over here I am 'this' or 'that', when the real me is better than the fake somebody else! True empowerment comes from being one's authentic self - or original - not a carbon copy!

One of our gravest "crimes" is simply wanting to be ourselves. But, we are ridiculed for being "us". Taylor Swift has a famous quote which goes, "they laugh at me because I'm different; but, I laugh at them because they are all the same."

There is nothing wrong with being an individual, being different. We are all born unique and with a purpose, but if we have no clue of who we are then how are we to nurture ourselves to our fullest potential? You don't feed a dog bird food. If we are to perform the appropriate roles, we ought to know who we are, and what expectations come with those particular roles.

Don't ask anyone else who you are. Today is the day you do your own work, and ask yourself: "who am I, and what is my purpose in life?"

Once you discover who you are, it will be easy to decide what you are to do. The brain has a name and comes with a function (or purpose). So does a heart, lung, or liver. They know what they are, and perform their function. Now we can mistreat, or damage, these organs. That is our choice. But, in their proper state of existence, they function accordingly.

So can we. but we have to first drop all the "extras" from our lives.

I want all of us to write down 5 things we need to drop from our lives, whether they are self-imposed or adopted from others:

1.

2.

3.

4.

5.

Now, write down 5 positive qualities you would like to pick up and implement into your life:

1.

2.

3.

4.

5.

Let's begin to catch up with ourselves (our authentic selves) and get rid of the masks we've picked up from distorted beliefs and outside influences.

NOTE - Your purpose is usually:

1.   Something you are good at.

2.   Something you enjoy doing.

3.   Something that can bring you a livelihood; and

4.   Something that can bring glory to your Creator.

Quotes to Remember

- Any dead fish can float down-stream, but it takes a living fish to swim upstream.

- In order to lead the orchestra, you must turn your back to the crowd.

- Kites rise by going against the wind, not with it.

- One man with truth is a majority.

•   Don't follow the crowd, move it.

Leave other people's negative and useless views behind. Catch up with yourself because that is when you're really going places; getting somewhere.

Once you find out who you are, only then allow other to add (what is positive and strengthening) to who you are.

Chapter 6

A Letter to All You Men

Greetings to you all! We are honored to have you men read this curriculum, and take the "Reaching Out From Within" course. This program is for all races, and ages.

One of the authors (James Wilson) is a co-founder of T.R.Y. (Truly Re-Define Yourself), a self-help program that started in High Desert State Prison (H.D.S.P) in 2016. One of the unique aspects about T.R.Y. is that the idea for the group came from the mind of a young person (when he was 23 years old). Donel Poston's group he co-authored (Life Choices) started as a juvenile diversion program. James is in his mid-40's but he never hesitates to give credit to young people for their potential, progress, and personal accomplishments. Recently we had a discussion, and he told me: "sometimes it takes a young person to demonstrate to the older guys what progress truly looks like." Then, he shared with me something an older mentor told him when he was about my age: "If you get the young, the old will come through shame."

James and Donel have been guest speakers in a Transitions class, and after they finished speaking, one of the youngsters approached them and said, "I wish we had more O.G.'s around like y'all to share that kind of knowledge."

It is something I have wondered myself before; why there are not more O.G.'s doing this? James told me that many of the O.G.'s have given up on the youngsters, believing that most young people lack respect for their elders and resist sound advice and leadership from older people. But, as I said before, he is convinced that younger guys are capable of achieving great things if older gentlemen would put their pride and propriety to the side, and give them a chance. He and Donel serve as mentors for this purpose.

Further, if those of my generation would bring their game up and break away from peer influence, seeking out older mentors, they would find them. I have several.

Many of these older men came to prison at our age and were once called "youngsters" themselves, and how they have lived long enough to be called "O.G.'s", so they have seen a thing or two, and qualify to teach us something. No tree flourishes without it's roots; we are all chips off the same old block! We came from somewhere. We should respect and honor older people, whether we agree with them or not. "Don't throw away the wisdom with the wise man!"

Similarly, older men should set a better example for youngsters. It is difficult to respect an old fool (smile). Muhammad Ali once said: "If a man is 40 years old and acting like he's 20 then he's missing out on 20 years of life." An O.G. should be distinguished by, not just his age, but his conduct! "The wine gets better with age", or so it's been said. But no one, especially an energetic youngster, wants to be dampered by a sour old grape (a grumpy old man). So, be smooth when you mess with us!

That's pretty much all I'd like to share with all of you, young and old!

Writing Project

(A) Write a letter to your younger self. What advive would you give to your teenage self?

(B) Write a letter to your ideal adult self. How do you see yourself 5, 10, or 20 years from now?

Each participant will get a chance to share their letter with the class.

- Written from a youngsters point-of-view

Chapter 7

Finding Our Formula For Success

There is a story told about three gods who were creating a man, and they were undecided as to where to place the man's treasures for his personal benefits while on Earth. One god said: "Put the treasures on top of a mountain. Maybe he'll find them one day. Maybe not." The second said: "No, place them at the bottom of the sea. He'll certainly appreciate them more if he finds them way down there." But, the last god, being more clever said: "No, place the man's treasures within him. Certainly, he won't look inside himself to find them."

People used to say that the best way to hide knowledge from us is to put it inside of a book. To an extent there is a lot of truth to this statement. But, I think it was St. Augustine who said: "Life is like a book, and he who doesn't read travels very little."

So, we are all living books, full of treasures of insight and personal gifts. Much of our greatness lies dormant or untapped, but it's there if we do the hard work and dig it all out, refine it, and put it to use.

Life is the travel-journey that we are on, and every day we should be turning new pages and learning new things. In the last chapter we expressed interest in reading books, but as this curriculum shows, we must be smart enough to surround ourselves with people who are smarter than we are, so that way we will learn more. Ray Lewis, the former Ravens line-backer, once said: "Nothing prevents a pigeon from flying high as an eagle" (or something to that effect). We ponder greatness yet we are unwilling to flap our wings (use our minds more) to reach a new height. Get up earlier. Find new friends. Do more self-help groups. Turn off the T.V. and pick up a book. Or look within to discover what lies beneath all the rubbish we've piled into ourselves.

We don't say this to put anyone down. We have problems of our own. We are not saying that we are the great eagle, flying at our fullest potential; but, we're the pigeon willing to get to that next level of our game!

In this last chapter of the curriculum, we want to come up with a formula for success. There are many, so ours may not look exactly like yours, or the next persons, but we should all have some vision (or formula) for what we conceive of as success.

Here is ours (as an example):

1.   We have a vision of where we want to go in life. Not only do I want to be a better man, I want to be a better father to my kids. A better leader in my community. A business owner. A book author. A better citizen. Basically, I have a vision and plans (goals) towards reaching them.

2.   We believe in sacrificing to achieve our goals. They say if you're not giving up something then you're not sacrificing. So, I give up my "play time", recreation, extra sleep, hanging out, to have the time to put in the work required to achieve what I want.

3.   Consistency. I take no days off. Every day I try to learn something, and push towards my goals.

4.   Companionship. I surround myself with people who support my goals and reinforce my values and aspirations. I don't need weeds in my garden, or haters knocking my hustle!

5.   We are optimists. I never block the sun. I try not to despair of the next possibility for success or opportunity, no matter how dark or unfortunate the circumstances might be. "Today's failures can be tomorrow's successes." I don't have to win by a touchdown. I can succeed with a field goal. Just as long as I win!

Those are my 5 elements of success. Below we would like for everyone to take some time out of their day to figure out a success formula. It doesn't take anything to fail, but it takes work to succeed! If you're not planning to succeed, then you're planning to fail; period.

Remember what James wrote in the introduction about Alice Marie Johnson, Shaka Senghor, and Matthew Charles. They put in work on the inside, in prison, in their own hearts, and now they're successful on the outside; in their daily lives, and in the free world.

What are your treasures; your gifts?

List 5 things that you believe are your treasures:

1.

2.

3.

4.

5.

Now that you see the good inside of you, it should be much easier to develop
a plan of success.
List the formula of your success below:

<u>Success Formula</u>

1.

2.

3.

4.

5.

It is not supposed to be easy. The best things come with trial and difficulty.
Remember: don't be afraid to ask for assistance. That is why we have mentors,
and that is how we are able to be skilled enough to articulate our words on
paper. But, we had a <u>vision</u>. We had to <u>sacrifice</u> time to sit and write. We
had to be <u>consistent</u>. It was not hard to do because we are <u>companions</u>, and
we support each other's goals and aspirations. Even when we find it difficult
to articulate our vision, we encourage each other to remain <u>optimistic</u>; to
see the plan all the way through.

So, you see how this formula for success works? They are the above 5 underlined
words!

We are all works in progress. But, in order to see the masterpiece fulfilled we have to see it all the way through! We have to put in the work, time, and effort.

There is no life-sentence, disability, program status, criminal charge, or lack of funding in your way. Nothing can stop you, but you. If you remove your feet out of the way, everyone else's feet will move!

Dana Car, the martial arts expert mentioned in Chapter One said: "the only thing that separates a Corvette from a Toyota is that a Toyota's engine has governors on it that regulates it's speed." It has self-imposed (engineered) limitations installed within it.

This isn't about appearances. We are speaking of performance. If you remove your limitation (governors) from your mind, you can escalate your activity. We are limited by the concepts of our own potential. A thugs self-image doesn't include a vision to be a doctor, a lawyer, a community leader, or a great father. A thug sees the world outside of him from the lens he has inside of himself. His ideas are drawn from that image. So are his words, dress code, companionships, and daily routines. If the image changes, so does everything that flows from it. We see, and move, in the world as _we_ are, not as the world actually is. We dealt with the identity crisis issue _in Chapter 5_. We are far greater than we have been led to believe. If only we had the true knowledge of ourselves! That is what this journey is about. All our trials are to teach us something. To assist us in locating that great treasure hidden, not from us, but actually for us. But, we have to reach within to get it out. Only then can we perform like champions on the world stage!

It begins with each of you; one person at a time; improving yourselves and moving toward a better world.

"Be a real man, not a prison man."
- Warden M.E. Spearman (H.D.S.P.)

Chapter 8

"The unexamined life isn't worth living."
- Socrates

"The spirit is upon me to free the prisoners."
- Jesus

"I put prison second to college as the best place for a man to get an education."
- Malcolm X

"If you wanna change your life, read a book. If you wanna change the life of others then write a book."

- Nelson Mandela

"I went from ex-con to icon."
- Danny Trejo

"Our goal is to tranform the criminal mind into a revolutionary mind."
- G. Jackson

"The knowledge of self is the most important education."
- Elijah Muhammad

"Getting off parole was the hardest fight I experienced as a champion."
- Bernard Hopkins

"Prison was my monastary."
- Ghandi

"Prison is the place, even for a righteous man, in a society that imprisons anyone unjustly."

- Henry David Thoreau

Class Exercise

There are 10 quotes above from former prisoners. Each class participant must select one to write, and/or speak, about in open class.

Questions

1. Why did you choose that quote to speak on and why?
2. What, if anything, do you know about any of the men mentioned above? How do you think they survived prison?
3. How do you plan to contribute to prison reform and changing lives?

Afterthought

A Prisoners' Success Story

My name is Donel Poston. I first entered the prison system in 1996. After three commitments and currently serving a sentence of 72 to life, I have learned a valuable lesson about the misuse of time. Every time I entered prison on a violation, or a new term, I let prison become an experience that was not only unhealthy to my future development, but not conducive to what I wanted to be, and who I eventually would become. Fortunately, through trial and error, I have learned to take advantage of situations like this, and utilize my experience as a gift, as opposed to treating it like a curse.

Prison is an institution, as is college. In both instances, you can go or grow. Most men and women go to prison, mill around until a release date, and go home; released from prison without a plan, or any substantial growth that they may account for during the time they spent absent from society. I am guilty of doing this on numerous occasions.

Currently, I have been incarcerated for five years. I have published several books, earned two degrees, and have created and facilitated a plethora of self-help groups. I am 44 years old. I have done more in five years than I did in the previous 39. Growth is a slow process, and life is a marathon. The past is where you learn the lesson; the future is where you apply it. Albert Camus once said, "Freedom ain't nothing but a chance to be better." Understand that your potential must lead to action, and your action to progress.

Furthermore, don't go through life, grow through life. Help yourself become successful by putting your best foot forward. Stop standing in the way of your own success. MLK said, "Faith is taking the first step, even when you don't see the whole staircase."

Moreso, find a balance and implement a routine. Results are best achieved by consistency. Everyday you wake up, work on you. In reaching your true potential, expect to fail. Fail fast, and bounce back even quicker, better, and stronger. Be resilient.

Lastly, if you're following your calling the fatigue will be easier to bear, the disappointment will be fuel, the highs will be like nothing you ever felt. Focus, and don't let off the gas until you get there.

T.R.Y

T. R. Y.
(Truly Redefine Yourself)

T. R. Y.'s 8-Week Basic Curriculum

Self Help Through Self Knowledge

SELF-IMPROVEMENT IS THE BASIS FOR PERSONAL AND COMMUNITY DEVELOPMENT

T. R. Y.

(TRULY REDEFINE YOURSELF)

THE MODEL FOR PERSONAL, SOCIAL AND COMMUNITY DEVELOPMENT

SELF-HELP GROUP WORK PRODUCT

T. R. Y.
(Truly Redefine Yourself)

T. R. Y. 's 8-Week Basic Curriculum

Self Help Through Self Knowledge

Summary of T. R. Y.'s 12-Week Curriculum

Business Class and Training Courses 1-12

First Week: Life as a Business

Using traditional business concepts this lesson teaches our members the necessity of planning, organizing, fulfilling, and managing their lives as business men.

Second Week: Economics as a Lifestyle

A lesson based on personal life management concepts and discovering one's natural talents for earning a legitimate livelihood.

Third Week: Work in Progress

Teaching the science of work and the work ethic, this lesson emphasizes the necessity of hard work and personal improvement as a means of progress, socially and personally.

Fourth Week: The Noun Factor; Life as an Education

Drawing from the rules of grammar in academics, this lesson exhorts one to see everyday life, people, and experiences we encounter as part of the larger textbook of our education and learning.

Fifth Week: A New Education

This lesson delves into the etymology of education and uses the true meaning behind education and intelligence to teach people about self-empowerment and social and ethical responsibilities.

Sixth Week: True Leaders are Problem-Solvers

Leadership is defined in terms of solving problems and fulfilling primary needs of the individual self and society and seeking to eliminate problems that hinder human progress and personal growth.

Seventh Week: Methods for Solving Problems

The traditional scientific method is used to teach people a systematic method for solving everyday problems they experience in life.

Eighth Week: Brand New; Control Your Image

Encourages the proper development of self-image and promotion of it in the best way, by incorporating better habits and character into people.

Advanced Program: 12 Week program. Will consist of four additional weeks of workshops, teaching and training for leadership and community building. These training courses are:

1. Being a good citizen
2. Freedom from within
3. Living freedom
4. Leading the charge

T. R. Y.'s Class Schedule

Public academic and business class meetings

- T. R. Y. Factor: T. R. Y.'s Pledge is read and recited by all participants.

- Round Table: A session where all participants are asked to give their opinion or insight to a question, idea, or quote put to them.

- Food for Thought: One person is selected weekly to prepare a 3-5 minute lesson to share with all participants.

- Goal Instructor: This instructor is called a "Career Coach". The goal instructor teaches the set curriculum.

- Closing Remarks: At the end of every class meeting each participant is asked if he'd like to make a general, or specific, comment.

T. R. Y.'s Pledge

The T. R. Y. Factor

T = Trying to teach ourselves a better way.

R = Redefining ourselves as men through a new education.

Y = Yearning to become better men for the good of our future.

<u>T. R. Y.'s Group Rules</u>

- Participants must promptly arrive to each group fully dressed in their blues.

- Only Career Coaches for the day, and those specifically elected, should be standing at meetings.

- Participants must come prepared to learn; bring T. R. Y. materials, and pen and paper.

- Horseplaying, side-talking, and excessive movement is prohibited. No disruptions!

- Career Coaches and participants will respect one another's privacy - what is said in group, stays in group.

- There will be no debating. Participants shall respect one another's views and opinions.

- Participants must be open to integrated seating - no grouping up with only people you know.

- Participants will save their questions until the end of that evening's Career Coaches presentation.

- Everyone will follow that evening's Career Coaches instructions.

NOTE: Violation of any of the above rules will subject any participant to group suspension, or termination.

* Missing two meetings will result in termination (unless absence is excused by that evening's Career Coach).

____
Participant's Signature
____
Date

"The unexamined life is not worth living."

- Socrates

Introduction

Overview of T. R. Y.'s Program

The overall mission of T. R. Y. is to make better men and citizens out of our group members by encouraging them to invest their time, while incarcerated, into pursuing academic, economic, and self-help education as a basis for personal, social, and future financial growth and progress.

A View of the Problem

While we accept accountability for our negative behavior, and crimes, we also believe that at least three consistent factors are associated with why many people find themselves incarcerated, and these factors are:

1) Poor education
2) Poverty
3) Poor social conditioning

A Focus on Solving the Problem

By integrating basic academic, economic, and improved social behavior concepts into our curriculum, we believe that we will be deliberately and effectively confronting the many conditions which lend themselves to poor choices and criminal behavior. At it's core, T. R. Y. is a solution-oriented program.

The Negative Self-Image

The T. R. Y. program teaches that the combined effect of poor education, poverty, and poor social conditioning has created a negative (or poor) self-image within many people, and that "prison life" can further enhance such a negative personality. So, it is T. R. Y.'s aim to work as a daily force to assist our fellow inmates with redefining this poor and negative mental conditioning by engaging them in a daily process - and program - whose core philosophy is that "life is a business, manage it well."

Management implies taking personal accountability for our past criminal behavior, and the responsibility required to redefine a new positive and productive lifestyle for the future.

Why Businesses and Citizens Fail

T. R. Y. is not simply a class for learning academics, economics, and social change. T. R. Y. teaches it's members to look at their lives as a business, and themselves as the sole proprietors over it; including it's personal and social assets and liabilities. It is a general truism that most businesses fail for three main reasons:

1) Lack of capital
2) Poor management
3) Inadequate planning

So, it is our belief that many peoples' lives fail to achieve the possibilities of success for many of the same reasons: lack of investment in social capital (or; the social contract), poor life-management skills, and the absence of realistic, worthwhile, and attainable plans or goals. So, in addition to encouraging a "business model" for personal change and success, a lifestyle of daily education and goal-setting is stressed at T. R. Y.

The Need to Redefine Ourselves

Further, T. R. Y. is a pure self-help group that teaches it's members the importance of the knowledge of self. The "self" being one's gifts, talents, and possible skills that can only be realized through self-examination, study, and application. The "R" in T. R. Y. - Redefining ourselves - means that we are seeking "reeducation" about who we truly are, and educing that new insight out through accepting a positive self-image and a new set of assertive, effective, and non-violent behaviors for our lives and managing this new lifestyle wisely, as "business men" in our everyday thinking and practices. "Reeducation is a tranformed lifestyle."

Further Teachings at T. R. Y.

T. R. Y.'s naming of it's weekly meetings as "business class meetings", and it's instructors as "career coaches", is to instill and reinforce a strong work personality, ethic, and attitude of service within it's group members because we believe "hard work pays off and harder work pays off even more," a phrase we at T. R. Y. coined for ourselves. By holding ourselves to a higher standard, we can instruct others toward the same goal.

By teaching "self knowledge" at T. R. Y. we're encouraging people to do better because they know better and therefore much more is required of them in light of a better assessment of their self-worth, and the responsibility that comes with being better men, inmates, and future citizens. Investing in ourselves, and serving others, makes us "social entrepreneurs" and assets to society.

At T. R. Y. we teach that "man means mind", and we are the principal steward of it's magnificent potentials. It is our duty as improved men to invest, discover, and educe (short for education!) the valuable treasures stored within our minds for our everyday "living expenses" of being responsible HU-MAN beings, personally and socially.

Freedom is not free! Our rights come with responsibilities, and it's an expense we are all beholden to. As human, and social, stakeholders in life and our everyday environments, our investment must begin now.

T. R. Y. places great emphasis on brotherhood and mentorship. We leave no one behind. We make it our duty to make contact with all of our members regularly to assess their well-being, their personal needs, and educational growth and development. We at T. R. Y. are not a 'meet and greet' program, but a brotherhood of personal and social entrepreneurs who believe the highest investment we can make is in human beings. Our profit philosophy is: peace and progress among men.

All T. R. Y. members are encouraged and required to read, write, and speak at business class meetings. Those who find it difficult to read, write, and speak are encouraged to spend time with those who are qualified to assist them with learning academically. Most of our core members have either G.E.D.'s, High School Diplomas, or are enrolled in adult basic education or college classes.

We also encourage learning auto-didactically, that is, being self-taught. We provide a variety of books in our group library.

T. R. Y. is a self-initiative self-help group whose emphasis is on self-knowledge. We require that men join our group voluntarily without the intentional incentive for a "certificate". We hold weekly scheduled business class meetings with our participants, and additional Career Coach meetings during our own dayroom time; sacrificing recreation, and so-called "free-time", to invest in our human, informational, and social capital.

T. R. Y. is an "on the job" life training process. Experience, time-management, knowledge, and friendship are some of our greatest resources and rewards for seeking positive change.

Please give T. R. Y. a try! Gain control, and run the greatest business you'll ever have. The business of your life. That is the business!

T. R. Y. Core Group Members

Business Course #1

Life is a Business

In this lesson we will be looking at some key components of business, and how they relate to maintaining and managing a positive and productive life. We all know that business requires education, effort, and hard work to truly become successful. Moreover, it requires planning, organizational, and effective leadership skills.

Business Defined

Business as the word is defined means: "an organized effort of individuals to produce and sell for a profit, the goods and services that satisfy society's needs." Looking at this definition and how it relates to life, we know that everybody needs to plan ahead and put forth an organized effort before figuring out how they fit into the social needs of a community and the larger society. The goal is to return the good of one's life into the service of the community. First, however, we need to look at what an organized effort is. An organized effort is the gathering of knowledge, ideas, and skills for a purpose, plan, or goal. It is through hard work and effort that one might achieve these aims, and ultimately become successful. All great businesses and all great minds were not created on the backs of people who were lazy and unmotivated. Like our motto says at T. R. Y.: "Hard work pays off and harder work pays off even more." However, it all begins with the knowledge of self, a good idea, and skills to work it all out.

Applying Skills to Life

Next, we need to ask what a need in society is. To know what this is, all you have to do is look around and see all of the things that people rely on every day. You might see maintenance workers outside, or cashiers in a grocery shop. By observing these things you will better understand what needs to be done, and what you can do to get it done. But, you must have a business plan (a life's plan) prior to executing your idea of a successful life (or career).

It is well known that the beginning of all great and successful businesses start with an idea and a plan. A plan is an organized course of action that one must take in order to truly manifest an idea. To have a plan in life one must know the following things:

First, you must know what you want to do in life. Then, you must figure out the nature of how to do it. This process can take some time as it requires some deep thinking and self-analyzing. It is not always easy to pinpoint what you are skilled at, but consider the following questions: "Am I good with my hands?" "Do I know how to use a computer?" "Am I a good team player, or do I work better alone?" This method of self-discovery is outlined in several of T. R. Y.'s business courses, especially the math and scientific methods used to solve everyday problems, even the problem of not knowing the purpose, or plan, for one's life.

After you have figured out what your skills are, and what you want to do in life, you must have a course of action to utilize your skills; to satisfy a need in society. For example, I met a man who took a welding class in high school and developed a unique skill for it. As he got older he figured out that he could use this skill to satisfy society's need for welders. To do this, he knew he needed to become certified, so he took a welding class. After he became certified, he got a job as a welder. He knew the course of action that he needed to take in order to utilize his skill. Do you?

In order to find one's purpose (or career in life) it is important to take the proper course of action (procedure) to arrive at it. It is a problem-solving process. Remember, T. R. Y. has a solution-oriented philosophy at it's core.

However, the business plan doesn't stop here. Now we are talking money. All successful business know how to keep track of, and manage money. They do this through using Income Statements, Cash Flow Statements, and Balance Sheets. In life it is extremely important to have a balance of mind, body, and soul, and of course money. Without a proper balance one can get lost and unorganized in the everyday struggle of life and business. Money needs to be balanced, and keep in mind that money is not just a currency; it is also applying yourself to a certain goal or task. Time is also money, that is why it is just as important to manage your time as it is your money. We all know the people down the street who have nice clothes and fancy cars, but no food in the refrigerator, and no money in the bank. They are poor managers of their time, and money, and in most cases they rack up credit card debt, and are forced to default on loans. That is why it is extremely important to keep a monthly Income Statement to gauge any future and present expenses.

There is also a need to utilize time management skills as a way of maximizing one's ability to get the most out of everyday life, and each opportunity.

Questions

1. What is the meaning of "life as a business"?

2. How does "business" relate to serving the community?

3. Why is observation important in the process of discovering one's goal?

4. Why are the expressions "figure out" and "course of action" used?

5. Why is balance, time, and money management important?

"Get what is yours, and give back."

Business Course #2

Economics as a Life-Style

The word 'economics' has it's origins in a Greek word that means "Home".[*]
People who are "economical" are those who are prudent and not wasteful with
money. They are efficient when it comes to managing wealth, and therefore
they are not only good money managers, but great home managers as well. They
know how to "keep up their home" and everything related to it, especially
their lives.

The American Heritage Dictionary defines economics as: "The science
that deals with the production, distribution, and consumption of goods and
services."

It is our intent to take the term and function of economics and apply
it to our everyday lives. Economics is a lifestyle. Home is where the heart
is, and at T. R. Y. our heart is in the business of making better people;
better lives. It's a lifestyle.

It is the intent of parents to raise their children and one day see
them leave the home of their upbringing to go off and establish a HOME of
their own; complete with a family and livelihood to manage it all. Life, like
business, is about management.

Many of us come from "broken homes" and never received a productive
model of what it should be like to go out into the world, pursue an honest
living, and establish a good home and healthy family life. For many of us,
"the system" raised us. These combined experiences have shaped our thought
process and behavior.

Growing up in broken homes and destructive environments, including poor
communities and prison, have worked to reinfoce a poor self-concept within
ourselves, and the combined effect of lack of personal self-worth has reflected
in the way we see money, how we use it, and even pursue it. Further, these
processes have diminished our view about the true worth of human life.

One of the urban synonyms for financial destitution is the slang term
"broke". When a person has no money, the words "broke" and "poor" are commonly

---

[*]Greek word "Oikos", meaning 'house' or 'home'.

used to describe one's economic conditions. Words have power, and behind them lie some of the reality we consciously and deliberately try to "edit" from our own personal stories when we talk, or present, ourselves to other people. Even our "dress code" becomes a surface philosophy encoding who we want people to believe, and think we are. The purchase of fancy clothes, jewelry, and expensive cars is an attempt to compensate for the lack of personal self-worth. So "things" become the outer garment to substitute for the lack of inner content. We find ways to mask or disguise our deficiencies, to compensate for areas we lack in.

We risk our lives to chase after money. We even take penitentiary chances and rob and kill innocent people for their hard-earned money. By destroying lives we ruin homes and also possible bread-winners, and pillars of families and communities.

The lack of money is not the root of our evils, neither is the simple love of it. However, the root of our condition is the lack of self-love and self-worth as it has been said: "The lack of money has never prevented anyone from achieving anything. But, the lack of creativity has." Where the knowledge of self is absent, the love of self will not be present.

We lack the proper "picture" (or self-concept) of ourselves which would be worth a thousand wonderful, wholesome, and creative words and ideas from which to produce external conditions that mirror the inner conditions of a complete man, not a poor, or broken, man. Our life's art imitates a tragedy inside, depicted without. We experience economic poverty and social brokenness from the poverty of our minds, broken spirits, and crippled manhood. Broke pocket books are the manifestation of broken wills, and shattered dreams. This is an extension of the poor education, economic, and social poverty that facilitates our incarceration.

The first home we have is the body our soul-life inhabits. This body, human life, comes with power and talents naturally endowed within it. It is created with dormant wealth. Wealth, however, that requires cultivation and planning to educe, or bring out. It is raw material in need of conversion into useful productive service, as mentioned in Business Course #1.

Inside of every human being is the means for economic survival, called talent. A talent is not only a natural skill, but also a unit of money. Cultivated talent is the ability to earn one's living, but without the knowledge of self, Knowing who we are, what we possess inside, it is impossible to engage in

the proper practice of self-help and personal and social entrepreneurship.
Working for ourselves, our community, and society is a citizen's job. It is
a lifestyle.

Each of us are born to do something for ourselves. As long as we are
alive we should never be "unemployed" because there is always work for us
to do on ourselves, our environment, and also "getting our house in order".
Self-improvement is the basis for home and community development.

Further, there is something called a dormant ledger at banks. It's a
place where forgotten money is placed from people who deposited it, and never
withdrew it. This reality is tantamount to all the forgotten, and therefore
unwithdrawn talent and ability lying dormant in every human being unknown,
and therefore untapped and unused.

Sadly, this is "poor economics" and a waste of the use of productive
human potential which can not be distributed and consumed by you, nor members
of your community and society at large. You can offer no "good service" to
yourself or others who are in need of it. Many homes - both human beings and
households - live below what is called the 'poverty line', subsist on welfare,
and despair not because they are unemployed by some brick and mortar business
structure, but because of a lack of prudence, and the abundant waste of non-
renewable resources like time, vitality, opportunities, and talents that have
legitimate personal, community, and marketable potential. This dilemma must
be rectified if we are to discover, manage, and maintain a positive and productive
"business" (life).
People cannot do for self where they lack the true knowledge of self. The
word "self" has it's origin in the words 'psyche', 'soul', and also 'ego'.
One's individual and collective consciousness and worth. It is imperative
that we grasp the meaning of economics as a lifestyle, know our self-worth,
and employ that knowledge and self-appraisal toward the betterment of our
lives, our environment, community, and society. That is good economic sense,
and as you've learned in Business Course #1 you know that life is a business,
and like time, and wealth, it must be managed well.

Questions

1.   Can you see the connection between the word economics and the word home?
     Explain.

2.   Name two things that you've learned from the knowledge of self that
     has helped you to do better for yourself. Explain.

3. What are you doing to improve any negative self-images you've imposed on yourself as a result of personal and economic deprivations?

4. What measure of wealth (talents) do you believe you possess that can help you earn an honest living?

5. Do you see your life as a business with economic features? Explain.

"A man plans his work and works his plan."

Business Course #3

Work In Progress

Work is a scientific term and is based on a measurable formula. The equation for work is: $F \cdot D = W$.

Force multiplied by distance equals work. The idea of work is obviously progress. So, no matter how much effort you might apply to a task, if no distance (progress) is achieved, then effort has been exerted but no actual work has been done.

In order for a "Business Person" to be successful he must make progress, and that is only possible if one works. The "work personality" has already been discussed in the introduction section.

This is our mission at T. R. Y.: to put in work. We are work men, and business men. That must be reflected in our input and productivity. As stated before, T. R. Y. is a self-help group. So, everything we do from writing curriculums, collecting and producing stories for our S. T. E. P. and Food for Thought booklets, to conducting our classes and running libraries are all self-ran by T. R. Y. members. T. R. Y. members understand that when we wake up in the morning, and throughout our day, we are to be engaged in some form of social, or personal, work that will improve our environment, and ourselves. We do not believe in "unemployment". We teach that every man is "employed" to naturally work, and do something for himself, whether or not he has a "9-to-5" job. Work is a lifetime process, and progress should always be underway. That is one reason we call ourselves "social entrepreneurs" and invest good within ourselves as input for the service of helping self, and our community.

We teach that every day without progress is a day of regress. Because we believe that there is a Solution To Every Problem (S. T. E. P.), we accept no unjustified excuse for lack of effort to achieve our model of "life as a business". From beginning to end, T. R. Y. is a solutions-oriented program.

T. R. Y.'s work ethic is preparation for a lifestyle of social and economic success, and a preventative measure against laziness, excuse making, and blaming society and others for our continued failures to be productive, and worthwhile, human beings and citizens because we grew up uneducated, poor, and/or in bad neighborhoods - the three consistent factors mentioned in the Introduction section.

The buck stops at T. R. Y.

We are to look at each other and our community service as "work in progress" and understand that the job is never over. There is always more to do, as Martin Luther King Jr. encouraged: "No man should die before he's done something for humanity that he could never be repaid for."

We are measured by our service; as we teach at T. R. Y.: "Hard work pays off, and harder work pays off even more."

Work harder and harder each day!

Questions

1. What does hard work mean to you?

2. What comes to mind when you read that phrase: "Every day without progress is a day of regress"?

3. Give an example of a time in your life where you have hindered your own progress by laziness or excuse-making.

Business Course #4

The Noun Factor: Life as an Education

As a teaching concept, and device, the "Noun Factor" represents the process by which we learn, understand, and apply information. That is, new ideas and beliefs, within one, or several environmental contexts.

Academically, in English rules of grammar, a <u>noun</u> is defined as a <u>person</u>, <u>place</u>, <u>thing</u>, <u>idea</u>, <u>feeling</u>, or <u>quality</u>. It is from this definition that the elements for the noun factor are derived.

Education as a process of learning and application takes place within a total sphere of interaction(s) between <u>people</u>, their <u>ideas</u> (beliefs), specific locations (<u>places</u>); and this sphere of human activity is infused by the <u>things</u> individuals value, their <u>feelings</u> about themselves and life, and the total <u>quality</u> derived from this daily social curriculum.

There is a connection between people and the ideas they learn, the places they learn at, and the things they learn from. The by-product of this learning process gives each person their unique feelings and qualities (values) about the world they live in and how they share their "education" with other people they meet and interact with.

Life is "school" and we're all both students and teachers.

The <u>Noun Factor</u> within the T. R. Y. educational program is intended to redefine, that is, re-educate and improve the way we view and experience our total learning environment as human beings in a "global village" (world). Even if we live locally, we must think globally because we live in a very diverse and multicultural world. Think about this: when the Greek philosopher Diodenes was asked what city-state he belonged to, he said, "I am a citizen of the world". This response is similar to a quote from Minister Farrakhan: "He who gives you the diameter of your knowledge prescribes the circumference of your activities." It is time to think big, and play big.

It is our aim to introduce life as an education. Every day, school (learning) is in session, and we are all students and teachers of those we encounter in the social classroom of life. This philosophy of life is not a new teaching. The ancient Egyptians had this belief at the center of their education. They called their people <u>Rekhytes</u>, which meant "learning beings", and they called their schools "houses of life", drawing a direct connection between the human being, learning, and life.

The essence of T. R. Y.'s teaching method is: "each one, teach one"; to become better people on the pathway of life.

Questions

1. What does the phrase, "life as an education" mean to you?
2. Minister Farrakhan once said, "he who gives you the diameter of your knowledge prescribes the circumference of your activities". How do you interpret this quote?
3. Do you see yourself as a citizen of the world? Explain.
4. What is the connection between life and learning?
5. Is your life rooted in education? Explain.

"We change your outlook. You change your life."

Business Course #5

A New Education

The American Heritage Dictionary defines the word educate as: "To provide with formal knowledge or training; to provide with information." Education is defined as: "The act, or process, of educating or being educated; the knowledge or skill obtained; the field of study concerned with teaching and learning."

The brilliant scholar, Naim Akbar, teaches that the basis of the word education comes from ancient Kemet, and is based on the understanding that all one needs to know is inside the self. This view of education recognized the structuring of an environment to educe (bring out) the higher potential of that person.

His research also concluded that the "logos" (meaning) of the "psyche" (soul; mind) is the concept that the Greeks learned from their teachers in Kemet. This is how the Greeks received their word "Psychology". They were instructed to view the objective of psychology as the object of life: To gain awareness of the full dimensionality of the soul.

The word "self" in self-knowledge and self-help has it's roots in the word 'soul' or 'psyche'. In Kemet, it was written 'Sakhu'. Within the self, like a multidimensional seed, is everything one needs to achieve life's success. Although the dictionary defines education as a formal process by which the student is "provided" information from some external source; providing individuals with "facts" and simply requiring them to receive, retain, and recall them when needed; is not true education, but instead 'memorization'. This brand of education is partially inefficient because no two people receives information in the exact same way, and peoples' memory often fail them. There is a discrepancy between reception and application that can only be connected through a careful study of who we are as individual persons, and our goals and plans. So, the knowledge of self (self-awareness) is highly necessary.

The word 'education' comes from a prefix, and a latin word: "E" and "duco". 'Duco' means "to lead" and the prefix 'E' means "out from". So, when one is truly educated, they are led out from darkness into light; from weakness into strength; from powerlessness into power.

'Education', by it's root definition, is the process of empowering, and usually this empowerment is based on what is educed (brought out) of the person from the awareness of self-knowledge. Human purpose is built on this awareness, and once purpose is discovered, the proper procedure (Plan and Method) must then be applied in order to achieve it. This is why T. R. Y. seeks to create a daily learning environment from which it's members (and other non-member inmates) can find the structured setting necessary to discover, and bring out, their innate talents and skills to apply to a self-help vision based on what one learns about themselves (self-knowledge), and their purpose in life.

The Problem Within

In business we are taught that a problem is really an opportunity, and at T. R. Y. we teach (through our monthly S. T. E. P. booklets) that there is a Solution To Every Problem. A problem is defined in business C100 as: "The discrepancy between an actual condition and a desired condition."

If you look closely at the word 'problem', you can see the word "probe" within it. To probe means to examine something from within. "The solution", stated by the ancient poet Rumi, "is in the problem", and (I believe) it was Socrates who said that, "the unexamined life is not worth living". The problem of working out one's purpose, and plan, for life requires a critical examination of oneself. After purpose is understood then proper practice (application) must follow.

The knowledge of self is an education about "looking within" to examine ourselves, to discover both our problems and the solutions to them (proper practices that are also called 'habits').

A problem is like a question, as a solution is an answer. Each of life's problems contain key information, that if intelligently examined, would help one decide what to do about it. Life is like a big "word problem" (a word picture) to be figured out.

The word 'intelligence' is defined as: "The capacity to learn and to solve problems and difficulties. It also means the capacity to learn."

An intelligent man is a problem solver, like a doctor, who examines his patient in order to fix his dilemma. That makes every leader a natural learner and fixer of problems. At T. R. Y., we teach that people are their first and best "doctors"; doctors of prevention and cures via self-knowledge and self-help. This concept is addressed in T. R. Y.'s Advanced Curriculum.

According to one etymological book source: "There are people who are educated and intelligent, although these two words can have widely different meanings. There are educated men and women who could not be called intelligent.

When one is educated in the sense described above (educe) it means that a
teacher by the discipline of school, or college, has "led" or "drawn out"
the innate qualities and abilities of a pupil. Even then, though, the pupil
may not have inborn skills that are worthwhile. The word 'intelligent', however,
finds it's original source in the Latin "intelligens", from "intelligo", which
splits up 'inter' (between) and 'lego' (choose), and this gives us a rather
nice distinction. After all, every success in life, whether in business, the
professions, or the arts, is based on "choosing"; on the skillful choice of
what to leave out and what to keep and use, and the intelligent person knows
how to select and choose."

T. R. Y.'s view of education helps it's members "choose" between those
behaviors and traits that are worthwhile, and those that are not. Like "medicine",
T. R. Y. is mental and social intervention, separating people from actual,
and "contrived" problems.

In academics, we are taught six methods for solving "word problems"
in mathematics, and they are:

1. Understand what the <u>question</u> (or situation) is asking.
2. <u>Select</u> important information to use in solving the problem and organize
   it.
3. <u>Choose</u> the correct operation: add, subtract, divide, or multiply.
4. <u>Estimate</u> an answer. For some problems an estimate is all you need.
5. <u>Calculate</u> the problem accurately.
6. Reread the problem and evaluate your solution to make sure it answers
   the question sensibly. Use your estimate to check whether your answer
   makes sense. Basically, "re-check" your answers.

So, "problems" are like equations; they have some formula, or make up,
and must be understood. Understanding problems requires asking questions,
selecting or choosing the correct information about them, and then choosing
the appropriate operation.

Problem-solving, like business, is an "organized effort". To achieve
one's goal of creating a desirable person, and condition, sometimes requires
help from other individuals, and that is why T. R. Y. is at it's core a
mentorship-oriented group. Every core member is a teacher, and counselor.
It is our trusted duty to help others discover and select those worthwhile
talents, and skills, useful for taking care of their business (plan) of life.

So, every day is "school" for T. R. Y. members. We consistently learn to enable us to solve problems within ourselves, our situation, and our business plan (vision) for life.

We encourage men to think, a word that once meant "to add up the numbers and re-check them". 'Think', like the word 'reason', has mathematical origins (mathematikos; the order of numbers). Thinking and reasoning allow us to examine and calculate what our best option is from a range of alternatives (operations) given the situation we are confronted with. We must think (calculate) before we act, and know that in acting there are always favorable alternatives, especially against violence.

Teaching ourselves a better way through a new education will result in creating better men; better products. It is about redefining (re-educating) ourselves by transforming the negative self-images we've imposed on ourselves due to negative environments, and negative thought patterns (habits) developed from within them, both socially and from prison experiences.

Our word "habit" comes from a word that once meant "hat", and as a hat is something worn over the head, a person's habits are worn over (or selected by) person[ality]. Habits are selected for personality (our brand). But, it begins in our heads, our brains, our education, and from environmental and personal sources.

The word 'personality', from "persona", means both <u>mask</u> and <u>sound</u>. It is what we wear, or send out, about ourselves; our broadcasting, or advertisement. It is our encoded social philosophy, surface and in-depth. If our personalities are negative (bad for business) so will our habits (ethics) be. Without good ethics (behavior), a business is destined to fail. The new education is about both internal (mental), and external (behavioral) change.

'Personality' means: "The quality or condition of being a person; the totality of distinctive traits of a specific person; the personal traits that make one socially appealing." Undesired personalities are part of the condition we must change in ourselves. Businesses (people) succeed by promoting desirable products; positive results.

T. R. Y.'s business is personal! We are judged by our numbers (progress), as it's said in the business world. However, in order to be socially appealing we must work on creating a better brand of men. Men who can be "led" to believe that they have great qualities that are worth being "drawn out" through a daily informational and social curriculum based on education, business, and management as a total lifestyle. Make sure that your business is handled ethically and that your service is worthy of the brand you represent.

Questions

1. Give us a definition of what education means to you.

2. Give us an explanation of how the words 'education' and 'self-help' relate to each other.

3. Socrates once said that, "the unexamined life is not worth living". What does this quote mean to you?

4. How does personality and the word 'mask' relate? How are the two related to the expression "surface philosophy"?

5. How is the word 'problem' related to self-examination?

6. What is the connection between 'think' and the six methods of math in word problems?

Business Course #6

True Leaders are Problem-Solvers

Leaders are born and raised to do two primary things: (1) to fulfill one, or more, of the human needs; and (2) to solve one or more of the problems that affect the human condition(s). The roles are intricately connected. A business man is a leader in the sense that businesses are organized to satisfy human needs, as shown in Business Course #1.

Societal and Human Needs

- Food
- Clothing
- Health Care
- Proper Housing
- Proper Education
- Employment

- Love
- Belonging
- Respect / Dignity
- Social Progress
- Safety & Security
- Spirituality

Since there are a range of things that can interfere with the fulfillment of human needs (for instance: greed, injustice, and inequality), people are selected (or elected) to ensure that there is a fair distribution of resources to members of the human family to fulfill their needs. Fulfilling human needs are the duties of leaders in communities and societies. The leadership spectrum includes, but is not limited to:

- Parents
- Teachers
- Career Coaches
- Life Coaches

- Elected Officials
- Ministers
- Social Advocates
- Business Men / Women

Human Problems

Parents, social advocates, and teachers respond, and work, to solve some of humanity's problems that result from human, social, cultural, or political reasons. It is correct to state that the human being will always have problems, and human history is a record of how human beings have went about solving their particular problems. History is about problem-solving, to say the least. Solving problems requires effective leadership. History is replete with examples of persons, and groups, who sought to increase the level of problems for members of other groups and nations through means listed, but not limited to:

- Racism
- Nationalism
- Fascism
- Colonialism
- Classism
- Prison Politics
- Government Corruption
- Terrorism
- Religious Intolerance
- Homophobia
- Sexism
- Individualism
- Imperialism
- Gangs
- Drugs
- Religiosity
- Fear
- Bullying
- Xenophobia

This is why the T. R. Y. program has sought to make it a core belief for it's members to be solution-oriented thinkers. In the last Business Course (#5) you read about "the math method" of problem solving. In Business Course #7, the "scientific method" is further provided for the same reason. Interestingly, throughout every period of historical crisis, there has been men and women (leaders) who have emerged to resist, challenge, and change unfair and unjust beliefs and policies promoted by those seeking to create problems, rather than eliminate them.

Remember: True leaders are <u>problem</u> <u>solvers</u>.

At T. R. Y. it is our aim to build a community and a brotherhood that works daily to fulfill the needs of human beings, and reduce various problems, through helping people discover their true purpose; the need to know why they exist. It is the lack of knowledge of self that is one of the gravest problems human beings face, as is taught in T. R. Y.'s Teachers Guide: The more we know who we are, the more we can do for ourselves and others.

Be a leader! Educate yourself! Be a problem solver!

<u>Questions</u>

1. Do you believe you are a leader? Whether yes, or no, explain.
2. List three problems in society you would like to eliminate, and how.
3. List three historical problem-solvers (male or female) that you admire. What problems did they solve?

"The significant problems we face cannot be solved at the same
rate of thinking we were at when we created them."

- Albert Einstein

Business Course #7

Methods for Solving Problems

As human beings, we all face problems in our day-to-day lives. Some
problems are much more difficult to solve than others, but there is always
a way in which we can solve them. In school, we were taught the six steps
of the scientific method, and how these steps are used as a process for answering
some of the most difficult questions in the world. The six steps in the scientific
method are:

1. Observation
2. State the Problem
3. Analyzation
4. Hypothesis (educated guess)
5. Experimentation (test)
6. Collecting the data and reporting the results

We teach at T. R. Y. that these six steps in the scientific method can
be utilized in our daily approach to problem solving. So. let's look at each
step individually.

First is _observation_. We must look at the problem in totality. Then,
we must examine every aspect of the problem that we are faced with in order
to get a better understanding of it.

The next thing we do is _state the problem_. Stating the problem means
that we are presenting it based on our observations of it. Realizing what
the problem is gives us the best possibilities of figuring out how to solve
it.

The third thing we do is _analyze_ the problem. This is when we study,
in closer detail, all the aspects of the problem or situation we're faced
with. The goal here is to figure out the most logical approach to solving
the problem as indicated throughout T. R. Y.'s curriculum.

Now we have our fourth step, which is coming up with a _hypothesis_ (a
proposed explanation) for why something is taking place. This step sets us
up for further investigation into a particular matter in our quest for understanding the problem, and any set of resolutions for it.

Our fifth step is the next logical step to take after hypothesis. This is the step in which we begin applying everything we've previously learned in order to test whether our research into the situation, or problem, is correct or not.

Finally, our last, and final, step is to collect our data in order to see if we are getting the desired results we hoped for. If we have not, then we must go back to the third step, and try again. As it has been said: "If at first you don't succeed, then try and try again." The goal is to never give up on our search for solutions in ourselves, and in problems faced in our communities and society.

As Einstein stated (see above quote), it is easier to solve problems once we've changed the "thinking" which created them. A point similarly made after the discussion of the math method in Business Course #5: we must "re-think" every situation. If, as leaders, we are to solve problems and get the desired results, producing desirable conditions and people, then there is a critical need for us to be both educated _and_ intelligent. Our rate of thinking must change! We must be effective leaders, counselors, parents, and Career Coach teachers because at T. R. Y. we believe wholeheartedly that there is a solution to every problem, and that is the message behind our monthly publication (S. T. E. P.) as well as the problem solving "steps" presented in this course.

<u>Questions</u>

1. Give one example of a problem that you have had a struggle with solving.
2. Now give one example of how you could have used the Scientific Method to solve your problem.
3. Do you see any connection between the Scientific Method and the Math Method in Business Course #5? Explain.

"Control your image."

Business Course #8

Brand New!

What is your brand? How do you advertise your brand? In this course we will be discussing the parallels between developing, marketing, and distributing one's personal brand. Moreover, we will delve into what it takes to be a good manager, and how the proper communication is needed to promote one's brand.

To develop something means you recognize it's potentialities. As discussed in other courses, the human being comes equipped with a full set of potential capabilities and talents that are in particular need of cultivation from simple "raw material" to marketable potential. To develop also means that after you've recognized the potential of a product you begin a process of bringing that potential into being, or existence. This process is what we call progress in business and in life. To produce means "to bring forth" as mentioned in the root word for 'education'; to educe.

There is a saying: "The world is your stage, perform well upon it." Everywhere we go, and whatever we do, is part of our marketing efforts, because whether we like it or not, our personalities are "sent out", or distributed, when we encounter other people. So, as managers of our business, we are to take specific charge over how we are communicated (how we "sell ourselves") and how we are received. This process is referenced in the course called the "New Education" and it's the basic idea that cuts through our entire philosophy at T. R. Y., that: "Life is a business, manage it well." Bring out the good that lies withint you, manage and maintain it, for personal service, and service to the community.

If a business is to be successful it must be known to it's community (customers) and it's products and services respected. We learn in business that there are three important factors for establishing and operating a successful business, and they are:

1. Having a good location
2. Having a desired product
3. Having a customer traffic for your product(s)

The importance of location was addressed in Business Course #4, Life as an Education. Location can mean more than just a physical place. A location is also a reference point, a place one discovers, or a position that is established. Where are T. R. Y.'s beliefs and practices located within your mind and heart? Are you settled in your beliefs, understanding about yourself, and your newly growing or established self-concept and image? This interpretation represents "good location" at T. R. Y.! Are you well grounded? Do you frequent areas (school, chapel, library, T. R. Y. meetings, etc.) that are productive for your growth and development? Locations that you frequent are vital for your character building because "bad company destroys good habits". There is a . quote which captures this process: "Words shape thoughts. Thoughts shape actions. Actions shape habits. Habits shape character, and character shapes destiny."

Our character, and it's traits, are the product of the person (our brand), and how well it's developed and promoted will depend upon one's individual commitment to excellence. Do you desire to work hard? Do you care about how you're received? do you want to be a "desirable product" (person) and be of service to yourself, your environment, and your community?

A person's "customer traffic" is the accumulation and retention of good, productive, and beneficial friends "because counting friends isn't as important as having friends that count". Can you make good friends and keep them? Do your friends see your value and draw upon it? This is called consumption in the idea of business as previously taught in Business Course #2, Economics as a Life-Style.

To oversee the proper development, marketing, and distribution of one's personal brand, good management skills, and leadership is required. A point firmly established in the first Business Course of T. R. Y.'s curriculum.

Are you being a good marketing manager, an excellent leader, and promoter of a re-educated man? Are you communicating T. R. Y.'s teachings and beliefs to its highest standards?

Think of your advertisement method, and find ways to communicate it upon the stage of life. Perform well! the future of your life, and business, depends on it!

Questions

1. Explain what the phrase, "bad company destroys good habits" means to you.
2. Give your definition of the word "brand".
3. What do you think about the T. R. Y. program?
4. Has the philosophy "Life is a business" taken shape in you?

"Service is the expense we pay for space on this earth."
- Muhammad Ali

<u>T. R. Y.</u>
(TRULY REDEFINE YOURSELF)

The Teacher's Guide for Understanding T. R. Y.'s By-Laws,
its Pledge, the T. R. Y. Factor,
and its Basic 8-Week Curriculum

(Revised and Updated 2017)

"Self improvement is the basis for community development."

Prologue

Insight Into T. R. Y.'s Bylaws

At T. R. Y. we believe in adding by subtracting. This methodology is outlined in the by-laws of our orientation guide.

While we are not opposed to others religion, race or political beliefs it is our historical understanding that the above three categories have mostly operated as divisive measures against producing a universal brotherhood among all cultural and religious groups of the human family.

So, the first thing we do at T. R. Y. is subtract what divides us and then begin the more useful practice of adding those common factors that are unique to all human beings.

T. R. Y.'s first three bylaws are that which we are not. We are not:

1. Religious based
2. Race based, or
3. Political based

These are the factors that act as barriers against unity. Therefore, they are eliminated as criteria for participation in T. R. Y.

Since at T. R. Y. we encourage what is positive and productive we begin our mission having acknowledged that which can be negative, eliminating it, and building on that which is positive. Hence our next three by-laws at T. R. Y. We add:

4. Implementing T. R. Y.'s program into one's daily life and then taking a new step forward beyond the things that act as barriers in our lives

5. The participation and pursuit of academic and self-help knowledge and as a result arriving at a new level of thinking and understanding permitting us to enjoy the next condition, which is

6. The promotion of universal brotherhood

With these three positive additions we are able to achieve our vision statement outlined in our vision's seventh by-law, which is:

7. Creating an environment conducive to peace, growth and progress

T. R. Y.'s teachings further enhance this mission in its Food for Thought booklets. Further references to brotherhood in T. R. Y.'s teachings can be found on pages: ii, 6, 8, 15 and 16 of its Basic Curriculum. See also T. R. Y.'s "Family Affair" pamphlet. Business Course #6 of T. R. Y.'s Basic 8-Week Curriculum provides additional insight as to why religion, race and politics are eliminated as a basis for membership in T. R. Y.

"Empty pockets have never held anyone back.
Only empty heads & hearts can do that."
                              - Vincent Peale

T. R. Y.'s Overall Mission
INTRODUCTION

The T. R. Y. Factor
The T. R. Y. Factor promotes T. R. Y.'s ultimate objective
to make a better way for ourselves by seeking a new education
and as a result allowing us to discover the good within ourselves
which becomes the bridge for building a better future.
In T. R. Y.'s introduction (page i) to its curriculum this
core vision is expressed in the following words:

"The overall mission of T. R. Y. is to make better
men and citizens out of its group members."

A quick review of the following curriculum passages will
further enhance this message (see pages i, ii, 3, 8, 13).
To make better men and citizens we must acknowledge and
confront those conditions that are barriers towards our goals.
From reading T. R. Y.'s orientation guide we specify in our mission
statement that our goal is to redefine the negative self images
that we have imposed upon ourselves through past experiences.
At T. R. Y. we acknowledge that three factors have mainly
shaped our lives and they are:

- Poor education
- Poverty, and
- Poor social conditioning

The evidence is clear from the outcome of our lives that
our environment & our experiences within it has produced within
us a negative & poor self-image. T. R. Y.'s curriculum mentions
this mindset on the following pages: i, 3-5, 6, 8, 10-13.
Several other conditions are specified as being barriers

to our mission and they are listed but not limited to: domestic (pages 2, 3-4, 15); social (pgs. 3-4, 6, 8, 13); political (pg. 15); economic (pgs. i, 1-2, 3-5, 15, 19-20); educational (pgs. 1, 8, 10-13, 15); mental (pgs. i, 3-5, 6, 8, 10-13).

T. R. Y. has outlined the following remedies for overcoming the above barriers and relieving the human being from the problems that obstruct the pathway of progress:

1. _A new education_, as mentioned in the T. R. Y. Factor and the curriculum (pgs. i, 8, 10-13);

2. _Developing a business_, _work_, _and service mentality_ (pgs. ii, 1-2, 3-5, 6, 19-20);

3. _Effective leadership_ (pgs. 1, 11, 15-16, 17).

Further, T. R. Y. has designed its program to confront poor education, poverty and poor social conditioning by encouraging its members to:

1. Seek academics to improve their education

2. Study & apply business & economic principles to improve their past life of poverty, and

3. Raise their social consciousness and behavior

This is a summary view of how T. R. Y. members seek to confront and change the three consistent factors which created the environment out of which we developed poor choices and criminal behavior, and ultimately, a negative and poor self-concept that is commonly referred to in psychology as a socio-pathic mentality (or a criminal mentality).

"Hard work pays off and harder work pays off even more."

Life as a Business

T. R. Y.'s Study Guide for Business Course 1
The word business is defined as:

"An organized effort of individuals to produce & sell for a profit the goods & services that satisfy society's needs."

Business as defined can be broken down into three factors supported by an organized effort, encouraging the accomplishments of:

1. Productivity
2. Goods and Services, and
3. Satisfying social needs

According to Business Course 1, business is related to maintaining and managing a positive and productive life. This comports with business because to produce goods within ourselves and society is the highest service and profit one could attain.

In Business Course 6 (page 15) where true leaders are called problem solvers the business man operates as a leader by solving one or more of the human needs, which when unmet creates human problems and negative conditions. So, the word problem is defined as: "The discrepancy between an actual condition and a desired condition."

The actual condition of individuals may vary as described by the barriers aforementioned. But, it is the removal of these actual barriers or conditions that allow T. R. Y. members to produce more desirable conditions and people, as outlined also in Business Course #5 (page 12 of the curriculum).

Another aspect of life as a business is putting people in charge of their daily lives and all of its aspects: mental, physical, spiritual, social, domestic and economic. Teaching business as a lifestyle is to incorporate the idea of personal responsibility and accountability into peoples' lives by encouraging them to recognize their need to:

1. Work & earn an honest living by investing their time into social capital (school, work, community service, etc)
2. Manage their talents, gifts and life skills, and
3. Organize and plan their lives around a worthwhile goal of satisfying their own purpose-related societal needs

This is a summary of life as a business according to T. R. Y.'s message and mission.

"Get what's yours & give back."

Economics as a Lifestyle

<u>T. R. Y.'s Study Guide for Business Course 2</u>

Understanding Business Course 2 has its basis in Business Course 1. Business Course 1 deals with the individual and his efforts to establish his personal life and pursuits on a business model as it relates to satisfying his goals as an individual and one or more of society's needs. Business Course 1 is to be seen through the eyes of the particular as it relates to the general. This is why Business Course 1 ends speaking in terms of family life and home and those members of families who have been poor managers of their time and money.

Then, Business Course 2 begins where Business Course 1 leaves off. It relates the concept of economics to the general premise of home and community. While not overlooking the value of the individual person, economics actually represents the broader systems in which individual business practices occur. Basically, the individual business person in the larger economic structure of the community and society.

This course teaches us how our individual beliefs about ourselves and our behavior has implications on the larger community and society.

The concept of the broken home, the general basis for human growth and development, reflects directly upon the individual and the concept he or she has of themselves. But the reverse is true as well:

"Self improvement is the basis for home and community development."

James Baldwin once said that "It is easier to raise strong children then it is to repair broken adults." So many of us are broken and poorly endowed personally, socially and economically because we spring from poverty of education, the poverty of finances, the poverty and lack of social upbringing.

It is the intent of this lesson to instill the concept of social entrepreneurship and self-knowledge into the self-concept of people in order that they may recover a more wholesome and useful picture of themselves & their community & be of good service to all.

The concept of good service is related to the definition of business which is to produce goods and services for a profit and that profit is personal & social rewards.

The idea of economics is also related to the production of our personality (Brand), the distribution (communication) & consumption (acceptance) of our truly redefined self.

"Every day without progress is a day of regress."

Work in Progress

T. R. Y.'s Study Guide for Business Course 3

As we teach in Business Course #1, work is one of the components of a successful business man as no progressive entity can be built with lazy or unmotivated individuals. Business is an organized effort and effort requires the exertion of energy which no work can be done without.

As social entrepreneurs and advocates we understand that our efforts fall squarely within the idea of a social worker, so in essence T. R. Y. is a social program. We teach in T. R. Y. that there is no such thing as unemployment because our life is a business and our work is always essential and required for personal progress as the curriculum teaches: "Self improvement is the basis for home and community development."

Therefore, the work on self is the first line of business and the model for success elsewhere. Part of our work effort is solving the problem of not knowing who we are...and this is why we acknowledge in the introduction specific factors consistent with why people fail in society, but in Business Course #3 we make no excuses for our failures. T. R. Y. is a self-help group & as we teach in our S. T. E. P. publications: "There is a solution to every problem," even the problem of discovering the knowledge of self. An organized work effort is part of arriving at that solution. The solution will produce the model upon which one can build his success. So work is an exact "science". As it is said: "Life is a just employer. You will only get out of it what you put into it."

Business Course #3 begins with the scientific formula for work (FXD=W) and the scientific method discussed in Business Course #7 demonstrates that progress is a step-by-step process requiring work. The same method is important in life, T. R. Y. business and community and social service.

Further, work is the bridge between both business and economics, the previous two study topics. However, it takes social and personal education to run a _business_, to operate _economically_ and to _work_ so this brings us to Study Guide #4, Life as an Education, and the importance of people, places and ideas etc, as the nexus for success.

Work transforms you and it is one of the main reasons T. R. Y. has a "business model" focus as its model for self-improvement and change.

As a business oriented group, T. R. Y. members can testify that our daily work in the prison environment has helped us come together and build brotherhood and community as it's said: "Those who fire together, wire together."

This process of living out the Noun Factor, uniting people and ideas in this place has helped us to achieve our Bylaws vision of implementing our program into our daily lives, achieving brotherhood and beginning the process of creating a more positive, peaceful and progressive environment.

"We live and we learn."

The Noun Factor: Life as an Education

T. R. Y.'s Study Guide for Business Course 4

This study guide gives us the functional definition of what true education is as represented at T. R. Y. in the following three words: Learn, Understand, Apply.

There is a familiar quote that says, "The true aim of education is not knowledge but action." To learn, understand & apply is the aim of T. R. Y. and it is the antedote against the rote learning process as mentioned in Business Course #5 - Education by Memorization. The teaching philosophy in T. R. Y. can be further emphasized by understanding that education is a method of living that is:

1. Strengthened by experience
2. Broadened by continuous learning, and
3. Governed by intelligent and judicious thinking

Education is a method of living, like the science and math method, and the leadership method taught in the Advanced Curriculum. T. R. Y.'s brand of education encompasses the traditional concept of teaching, coupling academic education with the more important education called the knowledge of self. The two knowledges must be present.

The Noun Factor teaches us that the entire life spectrum is part of the larger textbook of learning and life itself is that education we live, we learn, and we teach, which makes everyone a student and a teacher simultaneously. "Life is like a book," it's been said, "and he who doesn't travel turns very few pages." That is the message offered by the well traveled Greek philosopher, Diodenes, when he stated that he was a citizen of the world and the reason historians are requested to discard books and put on boots. Meaning, travel to the places they write about.

Life as an education encourages us to "travel read" - study - and understand that our environment is equally a part of our learning process as books are. This study sets the stages for understanding the next process in our education, the knowledge of self, as taught in the new education.

"We change your outlook. You change your life."

A New Education

T. R. Y.'s Study Guide for Business Course 5

The new education begins with understanding the "self". The self in T. R. Y. is defined as the knowing of one's gifts, skills and talents and bringing them out through cultivating them and applying them for one's livelihood. Therefore, education in T. R. Y. is directly tied to economic and personal growth and development, because "the self" includes the human soul. When you know who you are you can help yourself. Each person comes into the world with the ability to do something for themselves, but the problem lies in not knowing what it is one is born to do! This is why it is said that there are two types of education: 1. one that is taught to you and 2. another that you teach yourself. Most of us have been taught to be what others thought we should be (the first knowledge) but we lack the knowledge of who we are, our true purpose, in the latter sense - the knowledge of self, which is the true education. The "mask" of false knowledge is the living of a lie (personality means both mask and sound).

Once we know who we are our purpose is discovered and the only thing needed is to figure out the method to apply to reach that purpose - a course of action, a plan. This ties education (the bringing out) with choosing the method or plan for accomplishment with intelligence (the ability to solve problems and choose). This is why we have to be thinking people, giving us the ability to select from various alternatives, and what the math method instructs.

From understanding the definition of personality we see that it is a condition that can have either positive or negative associations - like add and subtract operations in mathematics. So, personality "disorders" are what T. R. Y. is organized to remedy. Some of these personality traits are:anti-social behavior and socio-pathic behavior, both are included in what we refer to as "the negative self-image," the part of us that has been shaped by poor social conditioning.

These problematic mental conditions are part of what's called "the criminal mentality" and presents one of the first personal barriers we need to overcome before we can advance in other areas of our social work and our improved social life, in and outside of prison.

Since every person and mind is different we are apt to use the math and scientific method to select the correct individual information before choosing our method of operation, selective approach for change, a subject briefly addressed in T. R. Y.'s Advanced curriculum, freedom from within, where non-traditional methods for healing are broached. This ties our belief that we are our best doctors to the various methods for healing.

Healing in T. R. Y. isn't just a physical remedy; actually, we believe true healing comes with knowing oneself, aligning with one's purpose and living a sincere and balanced life. This is captured in Business Courses 1, 3 and 5 of T. R. Y.'s curriculum, where the psyche, soul and self of the human being is discussed as being equivalent and in need of balance. The personality, the mask, we're wearing now has veiled our true identity, the true essence of who we are.

In T. R. Y.'s Advanced curriculum we teach that we are to:

1. _inform_, reference to the psyche, mind
2. _inspire_, reference to the soul or spirit (_spirit_ and _inspire_ come from the same root word), and
3. _motivate_, reference to the self, part of the will, an aspect of the physical and mental person

Without proper knowledge (information of who we are) we will not be inspired (encouraged) nor motivated (empowered) to transform our lives and do something good for ourselves and our communities. "Know thyself" said Socrates and all the wise men before and after him.

That is the New Education, true education.

"Leaders are readers."

True Leaders are Problem-Solvers

T. R. Y.'s Study Guide for Business Course 6

There are many types of leaders as mentioned in Business Course #6, such as: parents, teachers, ministers and Career Coaches. The role of leader as defined in T. R. Y. even includes "Business Men" because businesses are set up to satisfy "societal needs". And a quick reference to Business Course 1 would support this conclusion seeing that one of the key components for establishing life as a business was that one had to accomplish this in the capacity of an "effective leader". The business of change and social service requires leadership, simply.

So we teach in T. R. Y. that leaders do two things: 1. They seek to satisfy one or more of the human needs and 2. They work to solve human problems in the personal and social sectors of life. Many of our problems, the cause of them, derive from this corrollary: <u>we lack the things we need and what we lack creates problems in our lives</u>, our homes and our communities. This is evident from the 3 consistent factors which are found in most prisoners' lives and as described in the introduction of T. R. Y.'s curriculum.

In the new education, Business Course #5, the definition of a problem is not some horrible thing but actually an opportunity simply wanting to be changed. This is why we are encouraged to ask questions, seek advice, and use our intelligence in the process of problem-solving.

A problem is defined as: "The discrepancy between an actual condition and a desired condition." Simply put: you desire more but the actual condition of your situation is that you lack the education or skill-set to warrant a better job and with it a higher income, for instance.

Therefore, in order to solve the problem the actual condition (lack of education, etc.) must be removed by additional learning & new opportunity(s) will emerge and with them the many things one desires, even the desire to be a better person, a more socially appealing person.

The words that encaption Business Course #6 are testimonial as well: "Leaders are readers." So one of the key components for becoming a successful business person in Business Course 1 was: education. A leader must be educated. Even deeper as we teach in T. R. Y., the root word for education is "duco," a word meaning "to lead". So an educated man helps lead people out of their problems into the solution of them and that begins with knowing what people need and satisfying those needs. The first need is the need to know who we are - everything revolves around this vital knowledge.

Methods for Solving Problems

T. R. Y.'s Study Guide for Business Course 7

The methods for solving human problems will vary, but T. R. Y.'s teachings would be incomplete if we acknowledged that human beings have problems and did not provide a problem-solving system or method.

Business Course 7 can actually be ran alongside Business Course 5, especially page 12 where the method for solving "math problems" is described. The two methods work together if understood.

The science & mathematics of a problem have deep roots in medicine, chemistry & philosophy. So it has been said that, "Every musical problem has a musical cure." Aligning every problem with an achievable solution. We teach in T. R. Y. that everyone's problem is different. As problems vary, they are like formulas proportionate to the individual and, therefore, one's approach must acknowledge that there are a range of options or alternatives from which to choose from in discovering a solution. Both the math & scientific methods express the need to be selective and analytical in one's solution method. We also teach that we are: counselors, teachers and doctors and that T. R. Y.'s teachings, like medicine, are designed to perform an intervention between people and their problems - like medicine intervenes between a person and an ailment.

In order to effect change in peoples' lives we must know them, their problems and their needs as the word science is built on a word that means "to know". (Scientia is Latin for knowledge, the root word for science and similar to the root word that forms conscience).

So at T. R. Y. we stress mentorship and brotherhood. During daily interaction with our brothers we learn things about them and with this knowledge comes some unique perspective as to where we can be of greater service to individuals and our community as a collective.

The scientific method, as the math method, is an instrument to help remove many of our actual conditions to arrive at our desired condition, our goal, our purpose, that can only be attained with the accomplishment of the knowledge of self. Do your science, do your math!

Our ultimate goal is to arrive at our best self, our desired person, and that is dealt with in the last Business Course, course #8: The New Brand.

The New Brand is a new identity, a new self, based on proper character building.

"Control your image."

T. R. Y.'s Study Guide for Business Course 8

Brand New!

The final course in T. R. Y., Business Course #8, is the ultimate goal of T. R. Y.'s mission: to correct the poor and negative self-image and replace it with a more positive and productive one. We call the renewed image, in business, one's brand, as first discussed in Business Course #5 in conjunction with personality, our advertised self.

From Business Course 1-7 the entire aim is to arrive at the desired goal of a better man, a better person and therefore a better image (brand). A business will not be respected if it produces and markets a poor product (person), image and repre- sentation of themselves to the community and society.

In Business Courses 1 and 5 when we discuss "Goods & Services" (or no good service) we are not speaking of a particular merchandise. We are talking about the person and the good we've discovered and cultivated within ourselves and now can apply to the service of others and the good of society. Those who do not cultivate their goodness cannot serve properly. It begins with knowing who we are, the knowledge of self, transforming ourselves into our best self and then employing that to everyday life as a self-help tool to acquire a livelihood. It is called "character development" and rebuilding positive and productive relationships in order to accomplish the goal of succeeding as a business. So, Business Course 8 juxtaposes the 3 reasons businesses fail by describing the 3 reasons business succeed and they are:

1. Good location
2. A desired product, and
3. Customer traffic

Location is not just physical places as taught even in Business Course 4. It is about ideas & their place or "location" in our hearts. How are you set up? Once we have productive knowledge and apply it then we can arrive at the desired condition or be the desired product (person) we've set out to become. Our minds change, our habits change and therefore our brand (image) changes. It is a step-by-step process.

With a new brand, new friends and new network base (one's customer traffic) we will have access to better human material, financials, and informational resources. Our playgrounds, our playthings, and our playmates change when our mindset does.

"When you put the man together," it is said, "the entire world comes together."

Note: T. R. Y.'s Advanced curriculum goes more in-depth with the concept of how businesses, people, succeed.

T. R. Y. Core Group Members

<u>T.R.Y.'s Advanced Class</u>
<u>Operational Structure and Guide</u>

<u>Material Needed by All Participants:</u>

1. T.R.Y.'s 8 Week Basic Curriculum
2. T.R.Y.'s Teacher's Guide
3. T.R.Y.'s Advanced Curriculum
4. T.R.Y.'s Reference Guide (for Chrono Format)

<u>Note</u>: Please bring all material to class.

T.R.Y. Sponsored Group

Welcome to T.R.Y.'s 12 Week Advanced Course!

Class Introduction

<u>M.C.</u>
<u>T.R.Y. Factor</u>
<u>Words From Our Sponsor(s)</u>
<u>Opening</u>

Introduction

1. Facilitator speak about the goals and visions of the class and the T.R.Y. program.
2. Next, permit everyone to introduce themselves and express what they'd like to get out of the group.

Selected Reading

- Introduction to Basic Curriculum
- Introduction and Preface to Teacher's Guide

Readers

1.   3.
2.   4.

Facilitator should select certain main idea passages to elaborate on and/or ask new participants questions about.

<u>Closing</u>:

<u>Week 1</u>

<u>M.C.</u>
<u>T.R.Y. Factor</u>
<u>Words From Our Sponsor(s)</u>
<u>Opening</u>

<u>Food for Thought</u>

1. <u>Speak On</u>: How do you believe lack of education affected your life?
2. <u>Speak On</u>: How did growing up poor affect your decision-making?
3. <u>Speak On</u>: How are you a product of your environment?

<u>Selected Reading</u>

- Business Course 1
- Teacher's Guide Study Guide 1

<u>Readers</u>

1.
2.

3.
4.

Facilitators should select persons to ask group members questions about that day's reading.

<u>Questions</u>

1.
2.
3.
4.
5.

<u>Closing</u>:

Week 2

<u>M.C.</u>
<u>T.R.Y. Factor</u>
<u>Words From Our Sponsor(s)</u>
<u>Opening</u>

<u>Food for Thought</u>

1. <u>Speak On</u>: My greatest gift is?
2. <u>Speak On</u>: The good I'd like to serve my community with?

<u>Group Activity</u>

Every group member is to be asked: What is your gift, skill or talent and how can you use it to make your life and community better?

<u>Selected Reading</u>

- Business Course 2
- Teacher's Guide Study Guide 2

<u>Readers</u>

1.   3.
2.   4.

<u>Note</u>: Considering how much time is left select people should be asked questions about that day's reading.

<u>Questions</u>

1.
2.
3.
4.
5.
6.

<u>Closing</u>:

<u>Week 3</u>

<u>M.C.</u>

<u>T.R.Y. Factor</u>

<u>Words From Our Sponsor(s)</u>

<u>Opening</u>

<u>Food for Thought</u>

1. Give your summary of Business Course 1
2. Give your summary of Business Course 2
3. Give your summary of Business Course 3
4. Give your summary of Business Course 4
5. Give your summary of Business Course 5

<u>Selected Reading</u>

- Business Course 3
- Teacher's Guide Study Guide 3

<u>Readers</u>

1.
2.
3.
4.

<u>Formulate Questions for Members</u>
<u>Questions</u>

1.
2.
3.
4.

<u>Closing</u>:

Week 4

M.C.

T.R.Y. Factor

Words From Our Sponsor(s)

Opening

Food for Thought

_________________ 1. Give your summary of Business Course 6
Name

_________________ 2. Give your summary of Business Course 7
Name

_________________ 3. Give your summary of Business Course 8
Name

Group Activity

A quick activity: Ask each person to name one good quality they have (such as respect, patience, listening skills, etc.)

Selected Reading

- Business Course 4
- Teacher's Guide, Study Guide 4

Readers

1.   3.

2.   4.

Formulate questions, if time.

Questions

1.

2.

3.

4.

5.

6.

7.

Closing:

Week 5

M.C.

T.R.Y. Factor

Words From Our Sponsor(s)

Opening

Food for Thought

__________ 1. Teach on T.R.Y.'s By-Laws in teacher's Guide
Name

__________ 2. What is the importance of leadership in building
Name   community?

Selected Reading

- Business Course 5
- Teacher's Guide, Study Guide 5

Readers

1.
2.
                                3.
                                4.

__Note__: These are the longest courses. Time must be created for
a few questions.

Questions

1.
2.
3.
4.
5.

Closing:

Week 6

<u>M.C.</u>
<u>T.R.Y. Factor</u>
<u>Words From Our Sponsor(s)</u>
<u>Opening</u>

Group Activity

Every member should be asked: As a leader I would like to solve this problem in the world (the members must mention their own problem to solve).

Selected Reading

- Business Course 6
- Teacher's Guide, Study Guide 6

Readers

1.
2.

3.
4.

Questions

1.
2.
3.
4.

<u>Closing</u>:

<u>Week 7</u>

<u>M.C.</u>
<u>T.R.Y. Factor</u>
<u>Words From Our Sponsor(s)</u>
<u>Opening</u>

<u>Note</u>: This section of line-ups is specifically for T.R.Y.'s Chrono
Format as listed in our T.R.Y. Reference Guide.

<u>Line Up</u>
1. Rights and duties of citizenship.

——————————
Name

2. Positive decision-making

——————————
Name

3. Violence, drugs and gang prevention.

——————————
Name

<u>Selected Reading</u>
- Business Course 7
- Teacher's Guide, Study Guide 7

<u>Readers</u>
1.
2.   3.
                                            4.

<u>Questions</u>
1.
2.
3.
4.

<u>Closing</u>:

Week 8

<u>M.C.</u>
<u>T.R.Y. Factor</u>
<u>Words From Our Sponsor(s)</u>
<u>Opening</u>

<u>Chrono Format Line Up</u>

1. Victims Awareness Insight

____
Name

2. Leadership Skills

____
Name

<u>Selected Reading</u>

- Business Course 8
- Teacher's Guide, Study Guide 8

<u>Readers</u>

1.   3.
2.   4.

<u>Questions</u>

1.
2.
3.
4.

<u>Closing:</u>

<u>Week 9</u>

<u>M.C.</u>
<u>T.R.Y. Factor</u>
<u>Words From Our Sponsor(s)</u>
<u>Opening</u>

<u>Chrono Format Line Up</u>
1. Inter-group Social Skills

<u>Name</u>
2. Legitimate Authority Insight

<u>Name</u>
<u>Selected Reading</u>
· Introduction to Advanced Curriculum
· Chapter 1 of Advanced Curriculum

<u>Readers</u>
1.
2.   3.
                                                             4.

<u>Questions</u>
1.
2.
3.
4.
5.
6.

<u>Closing</u>:

<u>Week 10</u>

<u>M.C.</u>
<u>T.R.Y. Factor</u>
<u>Words From Our Sponsor(s)</u>

<u>Chrono Format Line Up</u>

1. Communication Skills

____
Name

2. Cultural Diversity Tolerance

____
Name

<u>Selected Reading</u>

1. Chapter 2 of Advanced Curriculum

<u>Readers</u>

1.   3.
2.   4.

<u>Questions</u>

1.
2.
3.
4.

<u>Closing:</u>

<u>Week 11</u>

<u>M.C.</u>
<u>T.R.Y. Factor</u>
<u>Words From Our Sponsor(s)</u>
<u>Opening</u>

<u>Chrono Format Line Up</u>
1. Cognitive Behavior Insight

____
Name

2. Anger Management

____
Name

<u>Selected Reading</u>
· Chapter 3 of Advanced Curriculum

<u>Readers</u>
1.
2.   3.
                                            4.

<u>Questions</u>
1.
2.
3.
4.
5.
6.
7.

<u>Closing:</u>

<u>Week 12</u>

<u>M.C.</u>
<u>T.R.Y. Factor</u>
<u>Words From Our Sponsor(s)</u>
<u>Opening</u>

<u>Selected Reading</u>
• Chapter 4 of Advanced Curriculum

<u>Readers</u>

1.   3.

2.   4.

<u>Group Activity</u>
The last week of advance. Give every participant an opportunity to speak on what they got out of the class and what they feel they can offer their community.

<u>Closing</u>: To be conducted by the facilitator, thanking everyone
(including sponsor) for their participation.

<u>T. R. Y.'s Advanced Teaching Guide</u>
<u>for Mental and Social Transformation</u>

Building Leadership, Brotherhood and Community

<u>T. R. Y.'s Advanced Teaching Guide</u>
<u>for Mental and Social Transformation</u>

Building Leadership, Brotherhood and Community

"We change your outlook. You change your life."

<u>Summary of T. R. Y.'s 8-Week Curriculum</u>
<u>Business Class Meetings</u>
<u>Business Courses 1-8</u>

<u>First Week: Life as a Business</u>
Using traditional business concepts this lesson teaches our members
the necessity of planning, organizing, fulfilling and managing
their lives as business men.

<u>Second Week: Economics as a Lifestyle</u>
A lesson based on personal life management concepts and discovering one's
natural talents for earning a legitimate livelihood.

<u>Third Week: Work in Progress</u>
Teaching the science of work and the work ethic, this lesson emphasizes
the necessity of hard work and personal improvement as a means of progress, socially and personally.

<u>Fourth Week: The Noun Factor; Life as an Education</u>
Drawing from the rules of grammar in academics, this lesson exhorts one
to see everyday life, people and experiences we encounter as part of the
larger textbook of our education and learning.

<u>Fifth Week: A New Education</u>
This lesson delves into the etymology of education and uses the true
meaning behind education and intelligence to teach people about self-
empowerment and social and ethical responsibilities.

<u>Sixth Week: True Leaders are Problem-Solvers</u>
Leadership is defined in terms of solving problems and fulfilling primary needs of the individual self and society and seeking to eliminate
problems that hinder human progress and personal growth.

<u>Seventh Week: Methods for Solving Problems</u>
The traditional scientific method is used to teach people a systematic method for solving everyday problems they experience in life.

<u>Eighth Week: Brand New; Control Your Image</u>
Encourages the proper development of self-image and promotion of it
in the best way, by incorporating better habits and character into
people.

*<u>Advanced Program</u>: Will consist of 4 weeks of workshops, community
and leadership building. Those 4 additional weeks
are contained within this Advanced Course, bringing T. R. Y.'s weekly self-help group to a 12-phase
course. The four additional courses are:

<u>Ninth Week: A Good Citizen</u>
<u>Tenth Week: Freedom from Within</u>
<u>Eleventh Week: Living Freedom</u>
<u>Twelfth Week: Leading the Charge</u>

"Men are destroyed for lack of knowledge."
- Old Testament

INTRODUCTION

The oldest teaching adage known to mankind is captured in this simple phrase: "Man, know thyself." This phrase is written over pyramids and schools in Egypt, Greece, Peru and other ancient societies. The knowledge of self encompasses all of the human dimensions, drives & interests.

It is almost universally accepted that there is an instinctive & inherent knowledge that drives human life, an automatic self, that "knows without teaching," which has been called many things, listed but not limited to: conscience, collective unconscious, autonomic self, the subconscious, intuition, divine consciousness, etc.

Further, there is a part of all human beings (drives and needs) that we share in common with all other animals, such as the need for food, procreation, security and recreation. Whether it's a dog or human being the above mentioned drives and needs are held in common. Basically, needs are consistent and constant for all life, however much they vary in degree.

Needless to say, there is one critical dimension that separates humans from other lower animal species and that is our unique capacity to learn, reason and aspire beyond the lower nature we share in common with other species. It is a well known fact that nature has provided every animal a defense or means to secure its existence and it is our argument that man's greatest defense & means of survival is his mind: the store-house of knowledge and self-governance. Therefore, every human being comes equipped with natural-born gifts & talents which, if nurtured, are useful for securing one's livelihood. However, the usability of these innate "tools" require that human beings acquire expanded knowledge, usually from parents, teachers, textbooks, etc., to manifest that which lies within, making the disposition of innate learning almost valueless without the hard help of external education, teaching and training. The two knowledges operating as "hand-to-tool" to build upon one's future interest, needs and aspirations. There is a point where "the animal ends and the man begins" and that journey starts with the greatest of all teachings: "Man, know thyself"! The mind becomes the functioning bridge between the community, its resources and the constructs of larger society & government. This interaction necessitates that we become an informed citizenry, an educated class of men, to affect qualitative change within ourselves & our environment, while understanding & securing our legitimate interest now as well as for our eventual release into the larger society. We call this process & work societal transformation or "transition".

At T. R. Y. we believe that by changing minds, we affect a better citizenry and ultimately a better future for ourselves and for others, seeking to embody the "spirit of what lives on in the preamble of the U. S. Constitution, written over 200 years ago, which states:

> "We the people of the United States, in order to form a more perfect union, establish justice, ensure domestic tranquility, provide for the common defense, promote the general welfare, and secure the blessings of liberty to ourselves and our posterity, do obtain and establish this Constitution of the United States."

Governments, like leaders, solve problems and satisfy human needs and it is out of this framework that T. R. Y. seeks to <u>inform</u>, <u>inspire</u> & <u>motivate</u> its members to be better men & better citizens in their personal lives, their communities and also in the lives of others.

At T. R. Y. we teach that at least three consistent factors are at the base of our poor choices and criminal behavior, and they are:

1. Poor education
2. Poverty, and
3. Poor social conditioning

It is out of these relative constants in our native environments that we've decided to remedy our problems through the solutions of:

1. Seeking a new education and self-help knowledge
2. Study of economics, business and government
3. Study of social studies, psychology, sociology, etc., to raise our social awareness and behavior

Some form of all of these areas of knowledge will be met within this booklet.

T. R. Y. incorporates the idea of BROTHERHOOD and COMMUNITY as "microcosm government," providing the condition from which the modeled life of the businessman, reformed responsible leadership, can be forged.

A business has the same statistical chances of survival as a paroled inmate from prison, for the following similar factors:

1. Lack of capital (financial, material, informational & human resources)
2. Inadequate planning, and
3. Poor management

There are other factors shared by both businesses and recidivists (failed citizens) and they are:

1. Poor location. Many businesses, like parolees, exist in non-productive environments.
2. Lack of outside help. Many businesses, like parolees, lack good advisors.
3. Unqualified or trained workers. Like failed businesses, parolees lack proper job-skill training.
4. Poor customer service. Businesses, like parolees, lack the best suited social skills to handle people that they meet and interact with.

At T. R. Y. we believe one of the best models for Behavioral Reform (and America's oldest form of ethic), the business and work ethic, is a solid basis for a discussion and paradigm for change. One of the hallmarks of cognitive science and behavior modification is their interdisciplinary approach. These include philosophy, psychology, linguistics and neuro-science (and we'll add "business"!). Each field brings with it a unique set of tools & perspectives. The overriding belief is that when studying something as complex as the mind, no single perspective is adequate.*

"The sciences have developed in an order the reverse of what might have been expected. What was most remote from ourselves was first brought under the domain of the Law, and then, gradually, what was nearer: first the heavens, next the earth, then the animal and vegetable life, then the human body, and last of all (as yet very imperfectly) the human mind."

- Bertrand Russell, 1935

*Reference from: "Cognitive Science, An Introduction to the Study of Mind." By Jay Friedenberg & Gordon Silverman.

T. R. Y. CORE GROUP MEMBERS [2016]

"All wisdom lies in learning how to call things by their right names."
- Lao Tzu

Word Definitions

<u>Citizen</u> - 1. A person owing loyalty to and entitled by birth or naturalization to the protection of a state or nation. 2. A resident of a city or town. <conscientious citizens who regard voting as a duty as well as a right>

<u>Government</u> - 1. The act or process of governing, especially the administration of public policy. 2. The means by which a governing agent or agency uses authority. 3. A governing body or organization. 4. Political science.

<u>Business</u> - An organized effort of individuals to produce and sell for a profit, the goods and services that satisfy society's needs.

<u>Community</u>-1. A group of people living in the same location and under the same government. 2. A group of people having common interest. 3. Society as a whole.

<u>Brotherhood</u> - An association of men united for common purposes.

<u>Leader</u> - One who guides, conducts or directs.

<u>Lead</u> - To influence or induce; to tend toward a certain goal or result; to be at the head of.

<u>Need</u> - 1. A lack of something required or desirable. 2. Something required or wanted; requisite. 3. Necessity; obligation.

"Everything a man is, is the result of his mind."
                              - Buddha

CHAPTER 1

A Good Citizen

T. R. Y. sets a high and practical standard for its program and members by asserting at the outset of its curriculum that its mission is to "make better men and better citizens". This declaration of intent is interwoven in T. R. Y.'s pledge, (the "T. R. Y. Factor"), where the "T" stands for our program's goal of "Teaching ourselves a better way". Teaching, better yet, education, is the bridgeway between producing better men and better citizens as at T. R. Y. we teach also that "man means mind". Hence, the work of making future good citizens out of our group members rests upon the premise that each of our members are thoroughly informed as to the form of government they live under, their duties and rights as citizens within it and the historical social contract which enshrines the fiduciary duties of government to those of us who fulfill our roles as conscientious citizens.

The social contract is, like in business, a binding document and partnership between those men and women elected to government and their constituents, citizens, which means both parties must be enlightened as to their roles and commitments to each others interest. Therefore, at T. R. Y. we encourage our members to seek general academic and self-help education. "Self-improvement is the basis for social and community improvement." "Better mental makes better governmental." What we don't know, won't work.

The United States Form of Government

The system of government in the United States is known as representative democracy. In this form of government, citizens vote to elect representatives who make and execute laws.

The origins of democracy are ancient. The term 'democracy' is rooted in two words: 'demos' - meaning "people," and 'cracy' - meaning "rule". So a democracy is a government ruled by the people, the citizens, through representatives. In order to have elected officials represent us in government, it is important that each citizen is informed as to his or her interest and rights. Hence, democratic government presupposes that the citizens are enlightened & informed. So at T. R. Y. our emphasis is on gaining knowledge and being represented by informed & effective leadership in our community.

The Social Contract

The United States Constitution, with its first 10 amendments called the Bill of Rights, enshrines what the rights and duties of government and citizens are. The famous phrase: "All men are created equal and endowed by their creator with the inalienable rights of life, liberty and the pursuit of happiness" is a nutshell description of the goals of both government and its citizens or shareholders.

Citizens pay taxes to the government and with these monies the government organizes efforts and provides recourses for individuals through businesses to provide:

- Housing locations
- Clean water & electricity
- Schools & colleges
- Court systems & prisons
- Security forces, local and national
- Emergency response agencies
- Supermarkets & clothing stores
- Religious & social institutions, etc.

The social contract is rooted in the needs of human beings to have proper shelter, water, schools for education, food markets and security - local and national - by the government under which they live, pay taxes to and offer other duties and services, too. A good citizen goes to school, works, obeys the law and pays taxes as a requisite to receive in return the above mentioned amenities from the government. And at T. R. Y. we encourage our members to provide daily service in their community as social entrepreneurs for the ultimate rewards of peace and friendships in all walks of life.

Comparative System

At T. R. Y. we teach that each human life is its own government or business and therefore the same formula of "rights and duties" applies in the social nuclei called brotherhoods and communities. Governments and businesses are established to "satisfy human needs" as we are taught and so we encourage our members to accept a philosophy of leadership that works to function in 2 capacities and they are: 1. Work to solve human problems and 2. Work to solve one or more of the human needs. It is services, specifically to each individual, which provide the ultimate framework for anti-recidivism and pro-citizen behavior.

Without taking accountability & responsibility for our lives, like conscientious managers and leaders, staying free is a virtual impossibility. One of the cornerstone features of a democratic system of government is that each citizen shares within the decision making process of government and, by rule, is meant to self-govern. This keystone is one of the core teachings at T. R. Y. expressed in our curriculum as "Life as a Business" and our concept of "self-help through self-knowledge" and life management. We are all governments and "communities of self" with obligations to our "citizen-members" (our human bodies, our families, fellow citizens and colleagues).

"Every human need is a human right and every right is covered by those with the duties to fulfill them."

<u>Rights & Duties of Brotherhood & Communities</u>
<u>Needs</u>:

- Food & water
- Housing (affordable & safe)
- Education and work
- Safety & security
- Spiritual guidance

<u>Rights</u>:

- The right to have adequate food & water (supermarkets & running water)
- The right to proper housing
- The right to education & employment
- The right to be safe & secure in one's person & property
- The right to spiritual teachings or religious institutions

<u>Duty</u>:

Those duty-bound to protect & ensure human rights are the following leaders:

- Parents
- Governments
- Teachers (Career Coaches, educators, etc.)
- Social leaders
- Spiritual leaders

To benefit from the amenities of community, each member is required to respect the rights of all of its members and also fulfill their duties in return, which is a direct deposit into the "social capital" of society (e. g., schools, jobs, social, political & religious institutions, etc.). All life and relationships are built on the partnership model.

<u>Government Composition</u>

<u>Reps/Leaders</u>	<u>Laws</u>	<u>Citizens</u>	<u>Institutions</u>
Elected officials	Constitution	People of the	Water & Power
(Congress people)	Bill of Rights	nation or state	Electricity
Local representatives	State laws, etc.		Schools
			Businesses
			Emergency Services

<u>Community Composition</u>

<u>Homes</u>	<u>Businesses</u>	<u>Services</u>	<u>Institutions</u>
Families (parents,	Markets	Parks	Schools
children, etc.)	Clothing Stores	Emergency Services	Health agencies
	Maintenance Shops	Transportation	

<u>Business Composition</u>

<u>Owners</u>	<u>Services</u>	<u>Customers</u>
Sole owner	Goods or services	Clients or patrons
Managers	(product) based on	Other businesses
Partnership	human needs/wants	
Work force, etc.		

The comparative analysis between Government, Community and the interconnected service of business forms the basis for successful transition from prison release and success on parole. These systems are established to satisfy the needs of everyone.

"Help me, to help you, to help us."

There is Always Outside Help

1. The book, <u>Roadmap To Reentry</u>: <u>A California Legal Guide</u>, lists all of the government and social agencies which provide assistance to newly released prisoners.

2. Local resources exist in every community that are useful to parolees, including social and religious institutions.

3. There is always available work. Some businesses have a mission to hire disadvantaged people, including parolees. Some establishments receive extra government funding for hiring parolees and even tax benefi

Comfort arises when we understand that every institution, like the family, community, businesses and governments are established to fulfill human needs and the only thing that gives us direct access to these resources is knowledge, and informed mind, and the willingness to use every recourse at our disposal.

A Successful Transition Requires:

1. Access to capital - Through work, entrepreneurship, networking and knowledge.

2. A game plan - A step-by-step vision with goals as to how one intends to remain free (or do prison time successfully now).

3. Management and coping skills - The ability to survive crises and hard times.

4. Safe and peaceful location of residence - A positive and peaceful place to live.

5. The willingness to ask for help - Knowing how to seek quality advice when needed.

6. Qualified job-skill training - Vocational or academic assistanc

7. Excellent social skills - The proper way to live amongst and interact with people in society.

"If every American was given a dollar for what they don't know about economics they'd be rich."

- American Economist

CHAPTER 2

<u>Freedom from Within</u>

"The fact that a representation stands for something else means it is symbolic. We are all familiar with symbols. We know, for instance, that the symbol "$" is used to stand for money. The symbol itself is not the actual money, but instead is a surrogate that refers to its referent, which is actual money. In the case of mental representation, we say there is some symbolic entity "in the head" that stands for real money. Mental representation can stand for many different types of things and are by no means limited to simple conceptual ideas such as "money". Research suggests that there are more complex mental representations that can stand for rules, for example knowing how to drive a car, and analogies which may enable us to solve certain problems or notice similarities."

- Cognitive Science

The fact that we live in a very "money conscious" era might lead one to suspect that more people would be experiencing prosperity in their lives, however, that is simply not the case. It is a fact, however, that more money than ever passes through the hands of Americans (even the "symbolic money" of credit cards, etc.) than in any other time in our country's history, but financial transactions (income and spending) have not resulted in economic success for millions of people "who know the cost of everything, but the value of nothing" as it's been said.

There are recent books written and statistics which show how economically inept most people are. For instance, Nely Gelan wrote in her book <u>Self Made</u> that Latinos are the fastest growing market in America, but they don't even know it. In the book <u>Strangers in our</u>

<u>Own Land</u> it depicts a large population of poor Whites who feel worse than second-class citizens, disenfranchised by government, & economically ostracized. These people voted heavily in favor of Donald Trump for the Presidency and saw him as their political & economic "savior".

The economic plight of African-Americans is well known. Annually, Blacks' earnings are greater than Canada and Australia - $1 Trillion - but they have the highest unemployment rate. And it is a gross stereotype to believe that all Asians are "naturally smart," rich and great at mathematics. Financial illiteracy is pervasive.

The truth is that poverty knows no color-line, even though some ethnic groups may do better than others occasionally. The late Nelson Mandela once said that poverty and despair are not natural; actually, according to Mandela, poverty and despair are man-made and because they are, they can be un-made by man - the great flipside of the coin. "There are problems created by man," it's been said, "that only man can solve."

In order to solve our problems, especially the economic ones, we must first understand one of the least known facts about what economics is.

According to <u>The Complete Idiot's Guide to Economics</u>, written by Tom Gorman, economics is: one of the <u>social sciences</u>, as are psychology and anthropology.

Mr. Gorman goes on to explain that social sciences examine and explain human interaction and that as a "science" economics has most of the other characteristics of other sciences, which is why economists observe behavior and outcomes, systematically catalog those observations (by collecting data), and identify patterns & trends. Then they develop and test theories to explain the behavior, outcomes, patterns & trends they have seen. (See T. R. Y.'s curriculum, Business Course #7: "Methods for Solving Problems".)

This description of an economist is similar to what's described as a psychologist: one who understands, predicts and controls human behavior. But psychology, like economics, is the study of the human mind, human thinking, as it manifests itself into human behavior. Basically, it is about decision-making, choices, as supported by Karl E. Case and Ray C. Fair in their book <u>Principles of Macroeconomics</u>, where they write:

"Because of conditions imposed by nature and the choices previously made by society, resources are scarce. Economics studies how we <u>choose</u> to use these resources to best satisfy society's unlimited wants. In a sense, economics is the 'scientific study of choice'."

And:

"A study of economics helps one to learn a way of thinking, to understand society, to understand national and global affairs, and to be an informed voter. Essential to the economic way of thinking is the concept of 'opportunity cost' - choices involve foregoing some options."

The authors supply this learning tip: "Any time you make a choice where one alternative is chosen over others, remember that an opportunity cost is involved." Therefore, economics has less to do with money than it does with the choices we make after money passes through our hands. "Waste not, want not," as the old adage goes.

While in T. R. Y. we acknowledge academic, economic and social factors which are contributory to most of our poor choices & criminal behavior and our incarceration (see pg. 1, Introduction to T. R. Y.'s Basic curriculum), we also find it "therapeutic" not to cast blame on others for our continued failures to attain progress & success in life (see T. R. Y. curriculum pg. 6,"Work in Progress"). We, however, believe that: "Destiny is a matter of choice, not chance." Therefore, regardless of circumstances we all have a duty and a responsibility to find ways out of the undesirable conditions we find ourselves in. There is always a way out, a solution to every problem, a consistent theme throughout T. R. Y.'s message.

Our academic problems can be solved by making the choice to go to school, or to school ourselves. For our problems involving poverty, we can raise our work standards by participating in job-skill training (vocations, etc.) which increases our chances for employment in higher economic brackets. We can also learn how to save and invest our money wisely and avoid conspicuous consumption habits.

The same improvements can be made in our social sphere by finding alternative housing situations or better friends. However, in other more critical areas of our lives, such as mental and emotional health problems, we can do one or more of the following:

1. <u>Seek mental/emotional health services</u> inside or outside of prison.

2. <u>Pursue self-help cognitive therapy studies</u>. There are many books that teach people how to be their "own therapist" or their "own doctors" etc. Laughter or positive thinking can be a form of "medicine".

3. <u>Spiritual or mindfulness practices</u>. Buddha asserts that all human problems originate in the mind. The Bible says: "As a man thinketh, so is he." Rene Descartes wrote: "I think, therefore I am." Nathaniel Hawthorne stated: "A bodily disease, which we look upon as whole and entire within itself may, after all, be but a symptom of some ailment of the spiritual part." A similar point was made by Carl Jung, a well-known psychoanalyst, when he stated: "All human problems are essentially problems of the spirit." Further, it is written that: "Every disease is a musical problem, every cure, a musical solution." Meaning, as the Prophet of Islam wrote: "There is a solution to every problem."

These wise and true statements from the interdisciplinary field of religion, science, history and literature are expressed throughout T. R. Y.'s curriculum, especially in the following section (see Basic Introduction, pg. 1: "T. R. Y. is a pure self-help group that teaches its members the importance of the knowledge of self. The 'self' being one's gifts, talents and skills that can only be realized through self-examination, study and application.").

The 'self' has been defined in many ways throughout history, such as:

1. In Egypt the self, sakhu, is part of the nos or soul, the spiritual aspect of man.

2. The 'self', or lower-self, in Islam is referred to as

the Nafs, or lower soul. There are various levels of the soul or self, ranging from "bad-to-good".

3. In Christian beliefs the soul is partly the mind and the spirit.

So, as Socrates taught: "The unexamined life isn't worth living." We must delve into the core of who we are, and at T. R. Y. we teach self-examination as a means of self-discovery, purpose and healing.

In the book <u>Psychoanalysis and Religion</u>, by Erich Fromm, in speaking on the self as soul, he wrote:

"While in some cultures like that of Egypt the priests were the "physicians of the soul," in others such as Greece this function was at least partly assumed by philosophers.

"Socrates, Plato and Aristotle did not claim to speak in the name of any revelation, but with the authority of reason and of their concern with man's happiness and the unfolding of his soul."

Fromm further states:

"They were concerned with man as an end in himself as the most significant subject matter of inquiry. Their treatises on philosophy and ethics were at the same time works on psychology. This tradition of antiquity was continued in the Renaissance and it is very characteristic that the first book which uses the word "psychologia" in its title has the subtitle "Hoc es de perfectione Hominis" (This is the perfection of Man). It was during the Enlightenment that this tradition reached its highest point. Out of their belief in man's reason, philosophers of the Enlightenment, who were at the same time students of man's soul, affirmed man's independence from political shackles as well as from those of superstition and ignorance. They taught him to abolish those conditions of existence which required the maintenance of illusions. Their psychological inquiry was rooted in the attempt to discover the conditions for human happiness. Happiness, they said, can be achieved only when man has achieved inner freedom; only then can he be mentally healthy. But in the last ten generations the rationalism of the Enlightenment has undergone drastic change. Drunk with a few material prosperity and success in mastering nature, man no longer has considered himself the primary concern of life and theoretical inquiry. Reason as the means for discovering the truth and penetrating the surface to the essence of phenomena has been relinquished for intellect as a mere instrument to manipulate things and men.

"Man has ceased to believe that the power of reason can establish the validity of norms and ideas for human conduct."

Fromm goes on to connect the "soul" with other more common terms for it:

"Because the word soul has associations which include these higher human powers; I use it here and throughout these chapters rather than the words 'psyche' and 'mind'." (See T. R. Y.'s curriculum; The New Education, pg. 10.)

The word 'self' is also synonymous with the English letter 'I', which also is related to the word 'ego'. In the branch of psychology called "psychoanalysis" the ego is part of the person defined as:

1. The self, esp. as distinct from all others
2. In psychoanalysis, the part of the psyche that is conscious, controls thought & behavior, and is most in touch with external reality
3. An exaggerated sense of self-improvement; conceit

Since the ego, self, the 'I', can become self-centered, in psychoanalysis, it has to be 'checked' by another part of the psyche called the "super-ego" defined as: The part of the psyche formed through the internalization of moral standards of parents and society.

Basically, it is the part of us that is socialized, "the animal-self," per se, into being 'human'.

As discussed in the introduction, the human comes equipped with an animal nature, a nature that has similar inclinations & drives as all lower animals. However, the human being has the innate ability to rise above his base nature into higher realms of thinking lodged into the rational areas of the brain, the cerebral cortex, the 'human brain', as it's referred to.

So, the ego has to be taught that more people exist in the world than itself; basically, each person belongs to a larger group, with bigger interests than individual concerns, called 'community'. An un-checked ego is "self-will ran rampant" and it can be destructive to all good ends as it relates to the whole, and in many cases, the individual.

This is why at T. R. Y. we encourage our members to find total balance in their lives (mind, body and soul) which is commonly referred to as "hollistic health and healing". (See curriculum, Business Course 1, pg. 2 and T. R. Y.'s Teachers Guide, Study Guide #5.)

Prevalent ideas about health and healing have expanded beyond traditional concepts of medicine and treatment. Therefore, at T. R. Y. we consider our program & community method as a form of intervention between our members and the general uninformed prison population that resist help, change and a healthy life-style. Health is a daily life-style, not a momentary experience, so at T. R. Y. we use the phrase "Life-Style" after several of our courses, for instance: "Business as a Life-Style," "Economics as a Life-Style" and "Education as a Life-Style".

This method and practice comports with the healing concept of other self-help groups like AA/NA, which teaches that recovery is a lifetime process and that a recovering person should be aware that any momentary lapse in consciousness could have devastating results, so it's said: "You may have one more run, but that doesn't mean you'll have another recovery." T. R. Y. seeks to be a "daily force" in its members' lives, continuously teaching. And by teaching them that 'life is a business; manage it well,' they will keep their "governors" on and take care of business in every aspect of their lives: mind, body & soul. Not to mention, they will be duly aware of their "larger self," the community, in which the total of life's drama plays out. As it is said: "It takes an entire village to raise a single child." No business or individual can flourish against the general will and patronage of the community.

Health is a partnership between the community and its members and this is expressed in both Hebrew and Arabic where the words for 'woman', 'womb' & 'community' share common linguistic roots, making the community like a mother, an environment of nurturance, compassion and love. From the community, the "symbolic parent or mother," socialization & morality is inculcated in its community members or suppressed. Leadership and community growth is a partnership. This is one reason we list poor social conditions as one aspect of the factors which teach us poor habits. We are taught from the social curriculum of our environment and become products of what we are taught. That social input is what yields within us a "poor self-concept" (-image, -brand, -identity -personality) that T. R. Y. seeks to transform, as stated in its mission statement and Business Courses #5 & #8 of its curriculum. We believe that not all character defects (bad images) are chemical defects; but, partly just learned behavior that can be "unlearned" through a new education, re-socialization and identity and character building. "A bad act doesn't equate to a bad person." Everyone is re-teachable if they are reachable.

It is commonly known that even some mental health problems are "treated" with punishment through the criminal justice system, which is why some county jails and prisons are now being referred to as the "largest mental health institutions in the world". With the "treatment" approach movement being reinstituted, even for certain violent crimes, it is the perfect time to re-examine those non-traditional forms of holistic healing which arise from deep self-examination, self-inventory, community nurturance, meaningful work & positive association. At T. R. Y. we believe education, or "re-education," starts from within, as the word "talent" comes from a word meaning a unit or weight of currency (money). We are all born with some measure of worth but we must choose how we'll increase it & ultimately spend it (live life). "Life is like a coin," it's been said, "but no matter how much it's worth it can only be spent once." We have one life to live! How will we spend it?

Each of us have to make a deliberate choice to want change, to want healing, to want new growth. The choices we're making right now will dictate what kind of life we'll have in the future. "For weal or for woe," the choice is ours! Pursue happiness! Pursue freedom from within and all other areas of success will follow!

"If you don't know where you're going, any road will take you there."

CHAPTER 3

Living Freedom

The knowledge we gain in prison must be a bridge between our current situation and the society we wish to eventually re-enter. We call this societal transformation or transition at T. R. Y.

The Second Prison Project, a prisoners' advocacy group, asserts that there are thousands of laws & agencies across the United States which prohibit ex-cons from seeking employment or acceptance into certain job fields based upon past criminal convictions. These "bars" to progress are tantamount to what is considered a "second prison system" in the social domain and possibly one most inmates in the 'first prison' aren't prepared for.

Seeking to "bridge the gap," T. R. Y.'s program offers its participants the following instructions:

1. Gain knowledge. Seek education in all areas of life.
2. Understand life as a business and manage one's "assets" (gifts, talents, skills, time, relationships, etc.) as a company owner would. Have a strong work ethic.
3. Begin every day with an attitude of service & with a willingness to work on one's personal self and in the prison community.
4. Invest time in helping other inmates who have an interest in improving their lives or accomplishing a personal goal.
5. Prepare for societal re-entry be living every day on "real world" terms, setting realistic goals.

At T. R. Y. we teach that every man is "employed" and has the first and most important job of "doing for self". That is, the work of self-improvement and, secondly, community building.

We teach our members that we are all work-men and business men - leaders in our lives and our communities - and the success of both conditions rely upon our:

1. Quality of knowledge
2. Training & skill-set
3. Work ethic, and
4. Effective leadership

As a "business oriented" community we intend to inculcate those personal and communal traits which increase the probability that after "successful programming" in prison our members will be equally success- ful after leaving prison.

Part of our job-philosophy and profit-philosophy is to teach our members that:

1. They are social entrepreneurs, and
2. Their profit is peace and progress amongst men.
(See T. R. Y.'s introduction to the Basic curriculum, pg. ii.)

While most free-society businesses are S & P's (organized for Sales & Profit) we teach that by investing our time into increasing our self-worth and finding our true purpose we can return that good into positive services with the people we have relationships with, our friends, family and community, making our members true social- entrepreneurs. Our business is "personal & community service". T. R. Y. is not a 'meet-and-greet' program, but one that operates as a social work-service, daily building up people who have problems and disadvan- tages due to a myriad of reasons. We teach that true leaders are those who solve problems and work to fulfill legitimate human needs. (See curriculum, Business Course #6.)

Leaders, like businesses, are organized to:

1. Have an organized plan
2. Be productive
3. Serve with good, and
4. Satisfy the legitimate needs and interests of the community being served

That is why at T. R. Y. we teach, conceptually and practically, that there is no real "unemployment" because as long as there is work to do on ourselves and in our community we'll always have a job! Life is a business that serves both personal and community needs. Part of our management concept is that each individual must:

    1. Accept accountability and responsibility for his past criminal life and raise one's personal assets above liabilities

    2. Oversee the establishment and continuation of a positive & productive life, and

    3. Follow specific and logical steps towards accomplishing a progressive life-style

Below are some of the steps T. R. Y. promotes towards fulfilling a positive and productive life:

    1. Gather insight into one's purpose
    2. Develop a plan for that purpose
    3. Organize oneself around that purpose
    4. Use one.'s educed skills to evidence one's purpose, and
    5. Apply that purpose within the social & economic structure of society (See T. R. Y.'s curriculum, Business Course 1, Life as a Business.)

However, this vision and personal mission can not be undertaken without the willingness to work hard, pursue extended education and the development of effective leadership. Nothing is done, small or great, by lazy and unmotivated people.

A business man must have an idea and a business plan and realistic procedures for operation in order to accomplish his goals. That is why T. R. Y. acknowledges the 3 essentials to "goal achievement" as described in Jim Brown's self-help manual, _Amer-I-Can_, which lists 3 aspects of a goal:

    1. The goal must be realistic
    2. The goal must be attainable, and
    3. The goal must be worthwhile

At T. R. Y. we endorse these same tenets and attribute them to the notion of what makes a business (or a life) successful. (See 'Introduction' to T. R. Y. curriculum, pg. i.)

The notion of a successful business as taught in every standard & advanced economic business text is qualified in T. R. Y's Business Course #8 (see curriculum) where it states the following success formula for business:

1. Having a good location
2. Having a desired product, and
3. Having a sustained customer traffic

These notions are tantamount to successful transition from prison. As noted in Chapter 1, without a peaceful location to reside in, the ability to produce an income for a desired productive life, surrounded by a sustained and healthy support base, a successful transition from prison to society is virtually impossible.

So the business, work, leadership and community-based vision we teach at T. R. Y. is designed to give each person "on-the-job" training while in prison, in preparation for parole into the larger society.

Teaching business as a "success model" and necessary implementation for transition is even endorsed by California's New Start transition program (a CDCR endorsed transition program), the Federal Government's Office of Personnel Management (which has an outline about the application of KSA - Knowledge, Skill & Abilities) and the fact that more entrepreneurs exist in this century of America than in any other.

T. R. Y. is the right idea, at the right time and for the right people.

"Maturity will solve many of the problems we carry over from our childhood."

CHAPTER 4

Leading the Charge

"The history of psychiatry shows that many ideas and concepts that once had attained the status of incontrovertible facts were later discarded as nothing more than myths or superstition. We are forced to the realization that the study of the nature and treatment of the Neuroses - or emotional disorders - does not rest on any proven theorems or generally shared assumptions. In the absence of any general consensus regarding the value of theories and therapies, there are no bounds to the extent of disagreement among the competing schools of thought."

(From "Cognitive Therapy and Emotional Disorders,"
by Aaron T. Beck, M. D.)

T. R. Y.'s curriculum restates the age-old methods for solving problems in the area of mathematics and science, howbeit, as they are related to everyday personal, social & economical problems we face in our normal lives.

Since we face more than a single problem, and there's more than one way to solve our problems, then it becomes necessary to provide a multi-faceted approach to arriving at solutions. Below is what has been described as the "Leadership Method" and, upon close examination, has many similarities to the math and scientific methods referrenced in T. R. Y.'s Business Courses #5 and #7. Remember: T. R. Y. is a solution-oriented program!

Leadership Method

1. Observation. A leader must be conscientious of the people, talent and skills in his business, life, organization and community.

2. <u>Analyzation</u>. A leader must have the analytical skills allowing him to distinguish the variety of gifts, skills and talents available to him.

3. <u>Delegation</u>. A leader must be able to make appointments or assign tasks based upon each person's relevant & useful capabilities.

4. <u>Organization</u>. A leader must have the ability to organize the available skill-set of his organization, group, or community. And,

5. <u>Supervision</u>. A leader must be in a position to direct and inspect the work, actions or performance of those under his leadership.

In the collegiate textbook, "Business C100," a good manager is judged by his performance of four (4) functions:

1. The ability to plan; his planning skills
2. The ability to organize ideas & capabilities around objectives
3. The ability to motivate and lead over long-term processes and periods in the company's transition, and
4. Having the ability to control all operations under his supervision

A close examination of the leadership method and management functions will show the connections with how individual performances in prison and society can support and enhance progress. And these individual qualities are further enlisted in Business C100 as the skills which make a manager's performance successful:

1. <u>Interpersonal Skills</u> - Ability to effectively deal with employees, other managers, and people outside the business
2. <u>Analytical Skills</u> - Ability to identify problems correctly and find the best & most reasonable alternatives to solve problems
3. <u>Technical Skills</u> - Skills to accomplish a specific kind of work, especially training employees, and

4. <u>Conceptual Skills</u> - The ability to see the big picture.

The principle of leadership is firmly emphasized in T. R. Y. as evidenced by Business Courses 1, 3, 5 and 6. It is our belief that manhood, maturity and the business-man/leadership models are solution-oriented progressions and practices, which alleviate much of the contrived and extended problems we experience in adulthood.

The clear message that runs consistent through T. R. Y.'s curriculum and belief is that we teach manhood and leadership, period. As the saying goes: "If you wanna go, you gotta grow." And it's clear that no leader or man can rightfully fulfill that designation without:

1. Knowledge & experience
2. Planning & organizing, and
3. Skills

Everyday life must be about school and work - learning & living well is part of the solution! The application of leadership in government, community and one's personal life meets well with the leadership method aforementioned.

The leader must:

1. Be cognizant, aware, observant and know his rights and duties, and those of others
2. Make quality judgements and be progressively analytical
3. Know when to "wear his hats," or abilities, in different situations; be tactful, and know where, when and how to seek help and assistance
4. Be well planned and organized in his personal life and social endeavors, and
5. Be his own "boss," "doctor," and "teacher" in his life, family and community

The leader must also know how to work with people from all walks of life, cultures, religions and perspectives, especially in this diverse and multicultural world, as we teach in Business Course 4, "The Noun Factor: Education as a Lifestyle".

This is part of the interpersonal and conceptual skills of a good manager and having the ability to see the "bigger picture," something partly addressed in Business Courses 2 and 5. The leader is an educated man ("Leaders are Readers") and works well to draw out (educe) the greatness within himself and others and in doing so increases the "capital" of each man's life (i. e., business). In return, the well-being and worth of the entire community is raised.

What is Capital?

Capital is resources. The dictionary defines capital as: "Wealth in the form of money or property; the net-worth of a business."

At T. R. Y. we teach that one's life is his property & home, and that each of us are born with inner-wealth (talents, gifts) that only needs cultivation/manufacturing from raw (useless) material to useful (effective) application.

In Business C100, capital is defined as four kinds of resources:

1. Material resources
2. Human resources
3. Financial resources, and
4. Informational resources

These are all the "tools" which a leader (business) relies upon to build and maintain a positive & productive life. This is why at T. R. Y. we instruct our members to invest their time, while incarcerated, into the study of academics, economics and social awareness (social studies) to give them insight into being resourceful & industrious men and citizens.

The word "invest" gives great insight as to what benefits we gain by "spending" our time in prison wisely. The word invest is defined as: "To commit money or capital in order to gain a financial reward; To devote or spend time or effort for future benefit; To endow with authority or power; Property acquired for future income.

Let's examine, in line, the benefits of our "time-investment":

1. Financial rewards
2. Future benefits

3. Authority and power, and

4. Future property owners

So, at T. R. Y. when we recite our "T. R. Y. Factor," our pledge, and say: "The 'Y' stands for 'Yearning to become better men for the good of our future'," it gives us the results of our commitment towards:

1. Learning a better way of life (work, law-abiding citizens, etc.) and

2. Redefining ourselves through a new education (self-knowledge and empowerment)

This makes us "better men" and "better citizens" as revealed in Business Courses 3 & 5 of T. R. Y.'s curriculum.

Since the aforementioned definition of "invest" shows us the results of our investment, let us list the path to their accomplishment. We must commit our:

1. Lives

2. Time

3. Resources (Capital), and

4. Efforts - daily!

By doing so we gain power & authority over our lives, in our communities and over our possessions. These are the sacrifices & benefits of leadership as taught by T. R. Y. members and Career Coaches. The manhood (leadership) and business-model promoted and practiced by T. R. Y. is a perfect "fit" for every reformed prisoner's life after criminality, gangs, drug & alcohol addictions have been removed from their existence.

After we have gotten out of prison by going inside to discover our problems and solutions in this "House of Healing" (school of learning) we can utilize T. R. Y.'s practical teachings for living our lives positively and productively in free society as true business men, leaders!

The job is yours!

T. R. Y. CORE GROUP MEMBERS

G.A.M.E

THE
GAME
PLAN
SPORTS ACTIVITY
GROUP
GAMES, ATHLETICS, MAINTENANCE & EXERCISE

<u>The Five Elements of Every Game:</u>

       1. Knowledge

       2. Skill

       3. Rules

       4. Time

       5. Purpose

" Fitness is a life style. "
Kevin Hart

<u>Overview of Program</u>

This is an 8 week course. It is purely voluntary. We welcome every one who has signed up for this fitness program with a desire to learn some information to better your outlook on life, on health and best practice methods for staying in shape. These will be short lessons on basic insight and we encourage everyone to follow up on what they learn in this class and become your own best expert; however, with your judgements rooted in sound expert knowledge about health and fitness.

Since we only meet once a week - and only for a short period of time - we request that participants show up on time, cooperate with the instructor for the day, and don't delay the set program of the day.

This program will consist on many aspects so at the end of each session the following weeks program will be provided. Here is a short list of things that will take place in the class:

1. Video exercise program
2. Physical fitness exercise
3. Agility & warm-up stretching
4. Nutrition lessons
5. Organized sports activities (basketball, volleyball, relay-races, strength test, etc)
6. Meditation
7. Short group discussions or lectures from those informed in health (e.g: coach facilitator, etc)

So, during each weeks session some combination of the above listed features will be performed during class. The goal is to raise awareness about health, create exercise and nutrition as a life-style and find time to enjoy this experience with others seeking an improved state of existence. Advice and methods will vary. Most of the information gathered for this program is derived from different sources. Take what works for you.

G.A.M.E.

WARM UP ADVICE

Many people are alive inside of their bodies and rarely take notice of it (the body) until an injury befalls it or we experience hunger pains. The body is alive, every inch of it. The skin is actually the largest organ.

Today we will take notice of our physical being by taking a few minutes to:

1. Stretch out and
2. Perform a few warm up exercises

1. Warmup

Move through each of these steps, working to be as smooth and controlled as possible. Hold each position long enough to inhale and exhale once. Repeat the entire sequence as many times as you can in 4 minutes, being careful not to rush through any motion.

Bear Hold Mobility Flow

A Start on all fours, hands directly below your shoulders, knees below your hips. Your knees should be off the ground, shins parallel to the ground, feet about a foot apart. Tighten your core.

B Raise your butt high in the air, straightening your knees. Work to get your torso in line with your arms; you should look like an upside-down V. If you need to, walk your hands a few inches forward. Try not to let your lower back round as you do this.

C Shift your torso forward into pushup position, then move your left foot alongside your left hand, bending your left knee. Keep your right leg straight while you do this; you should feel a stretch in your hips and groin.

D Keeping your hands in pushup position and keeping your core tight, shift your left foot back alongside your right foot, returning to pushup position. Then repeat part C, this time with your right foot alongside your right hand and your left leg staying straight

In a month let's build our strength & stamina up to perform the full work out on pages 2-3

The Bodyweight Burner

The anytime, anywhere workout for staying on track during the least predictable month.
TRAINER: BEN BOUDRO, C.S.C.S.

YOU'RE AT THE AIRPORT. You're shopping for gifts. You're shopping for gifts at the airport. We know you don't have as much time to hit the gym this month. Instead, you're doing a 25-minute, no-equipment-needed burner from Ben Boudro, C.S.C.S., of Xceleration Fitness in Detroit, who's trained several NFL players and specializes in crushing you with body-weight workouts. Do it any place, whenever you can (heck, even twice a day if your flight's delayed long enough), to hit every muscle in your body, rev up your metabolism, and improve balance and coordination.

DIRECTIONS: Do this workout at least three days a week; for optimal results, try to do it six days a week. (Remember: It takes only 25 minutes!) Aim to go for a 10- or 15-minute run on days when you can't find time for this workout.

THE WARMUP

Before you start training, loosen up your hamstrings and hips and relax your back with 2 minutes of quick drills.

1. Pushup to Downward Dog
Start in pushup position, hands directly below your shoulders, core tight, then do a pushup. Return to the start, then raise your hips high, bending at the waist. (Shift your feet forward if you need to.) Keep your legs straight as you do this, stretching your hamstrings, and try to form a straight line with your arms and torso. Return to pushup position. That's 1 rep. Do reps for 1 minute.

HE SAYS
"Don't focus on the number of reps. Fewer is better in the warmup; do each one slowly. Feel the stretch."

2. Spider-Man Lunge with Overhead Reach
Start in pushup position, hands directly below your shoulders. Keeping your left leg straight, bring your right foot forward so that it's just outside your right hand. Pause, then lift your right hand from the floor and raise it toward the ceiling, reaching as high as you can. Reverse the movements. That's 1 rep. Alternate sides for 30 seconds.

THE WORKOUT

Do 2 rounds of this circuit. In the first, do each exercise for 40 seconds, rest 20, then do 40 more seconds. Rest 90 seconds. The next round, do each move for 30 seconds, rest 15, then do 30 more seconds.

1. Around-the-World Pushup
Set up in pushup position, core tight. Do 1 pushup rep. Then, keeping your core tight, lift your right arm from the floor, rotating your torso as you reach your arm toward the ceiling. Continue rotating your torso so that your chest faces the ceiling (you can shift your feet as you do) and then place your right hand on the floor. Try to form a straight line from shoulders to ankles. Reverse the moves to return to pushup position. That's 1 rep. Alternate directions with each rep.

HE SAYS
"When your chest is facing the ceiling, squeeze your glutes to straighten out your body."

2. Superman Hold
Lie facedown on the floor, arms and legs extended. Tighten your glutes, raising your feet and thighs a few inches in the air. As you do this, squeeze your back muscles, lifting your arms and chest off the floor. Hold for 2 seconds, then lower back to the floor. That's 1 rep.

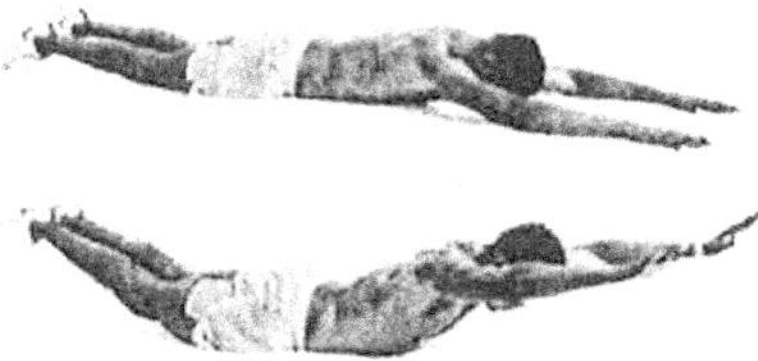

HE SAYS
"If you have time for just one exercise every single day, make it this one. It'll fire up your mid-back muscles—a key to helping improve your posture."

3. Lateral Bound to Pushup

Start in an athletic stance, feet shoulder-width apart, knees bent slightly, then leap to your left as far as you can, landing on your left foot. Gather yourself as quickly as possible, then leap back to the right, landing on your right foot. Complete 5 total jumps back and forth, then immediately do 5 pushups. Stand back up and repeat the pattern until time is up.

4. High-Knee Run

Start standing, knees bent slightly, feet shoulder-width apart, arms relaxed, then begin running in place, concentrating on driving your knees up as high as you can. Aim to get your thigh higher than parallel to the floor on each stride.

HE SAYS

"Don't let this only be a lower-body movement. Make sure you're pumping your arms as if you're really running; that'll help you drive your knees higher, too."

5. Knee Tuck

Lie on your back, then press your lower back into the floor. Raise your shoulders off the floor slightly, supporting yourself with your hands. Keeping your legs straight, raise your thighs a few inches. This is the start. Now pull your thighs toward your chest, bending your knees as you do; squeeze your abs. Return to the start. That's 1 rep.

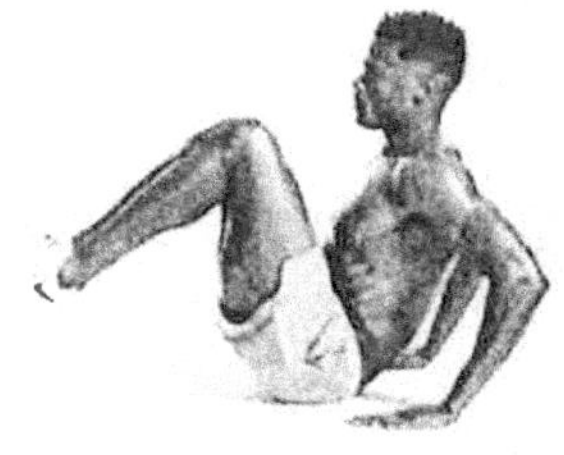

6. Burpee Broad Jump

Start standing, feet shoulder-width apart. Squat down and put your hands on the floor. Kick your feet backward into plank position, then lower your chest to the floor, as if doing a pushup. Reverse the movements to stand back up, then leap forward. Backpedal to your starting position. That's 1 rep.

Illustration by Kyle Hilton

THE FINISHER

Set a timer for 3 minutes. Do 1 pushup, then 1 Russian twist, Then do 2 pushups and 2 Russian twists. Keep laddering up until time expires; rest as needed.

1. Pushup

Get in pushup position. Bend at the elbows, lowering your torso until you're an inch from the floor. Pause, then straighten your arms and return to the start. Focus on keeping your core tight and keeping your elbows close to your torso on each rep.

HE SAYS

"It's easy to get lazy with pushup form, so here's a way to avoid that: Count your reps out loud."

2. Russian Twist

Lie on your back, knees bent, feet a few inches off the floor. Tighten your abs, raising your torso so it's a foot above the floor. Clasp your hands together just above your chest. This is the start. Keeping your legs as steady as possible, twist your torso to the right and touch your hands to the floor on the right side. Then twist to the left and touch the floor on the left. That's 1 rep.

CLOTHING:
Nike

Warm Up's

1. 50 Jumping Jacks
2. 25 Squats
3. 50 Knees to Chest
4. 2 Laps

Todays Exercise Regiment Will Consist of:

1. _______________________

2. _______________________

3. _______________________

Sleep

As long as I'm getting eight hours of sleep, does it matter what time I go to bed? —DOUG, Lima, OH

Not if you're consistent. If you always turn in at 2:00 A.M. and rise at 10:00 A.M., you're good. Or 8:00 P.M. to 4:00 A.M., also good. But if your bedtimes and wake-up times vary wildly, you may be setting yourself up for sleep problems, says Rodney Radtke, M.D., a neurologist specializing in sleep medicine at Duke Health. That's because irregular sleep patterns can mess with your body clock over time, making it harder to fall asleep, stay asleep, and wake up when you want to. Late night? Be sure to get up at your usual time, says Dr. Radtke: "That sets your clock."

Do you ever feel like there's not enough time to do every thing you wish to do in a day? Lets read the following article and discuss it.

*Does that headline stress you out as much as it does us? There's a word for that. (A German word, of course.) And **JEFF CSATARI** has a way to fix it.*

SOMEWHERE between anxiety and dread is that feeling that creeps in on a Sunday evening. You still haven't finished the spreadsheet that was due Friday EOD. Or cleaned up after the party on Saturday. Or bathed the bulldog. Or yourself. Oh, and it's five minutes to midnight.

The Germans, who have an uncanny ability to capture in one word a feeling that would take a full sentence in English to explain, call this dread *Torschlusspanik.* Literally "gate-shut panic." It's the medieval fear of not making it safely behind the castle gate before nightfall. In modern usage, it describes the fear of running out of time...to act, to accomplish, to meet deadlines real or perceived.

Torschlusspanik can be triggered by trivial stuff like an overly ambitious weekend chore list or, say, a surprise visit from the boss, who plants himself in your office to chat when you have less than an hour to prep for a critical meeting. Often, all it takes to get that feeling started is procrastination and the guilt that stems from that inaction. ("You shouldn't have left such a complicated project for the last minute!") Or, on a grander scale, upward comparison, the dangerous practice of holding yourself up to someone you think is almost at the top of the mountain while you're still trying to figure out which ropes to use.

Whether your fear of time running out is short-term or more epic, there are ways to make it...*kaput:*

There are 24 hours in a day - that is the obvious. This space of time is usually divided into "3 parts of 8" and used as a measure for atleast 4 areas of human endeavors.

1. Eight hours of sleep
2. Eight hours of work/education
3. Eight hours of repose/recreation

How do you use your 24 hours?

<u>Exercise</u>

<u>Let's Do the Eisenhower Box</u>

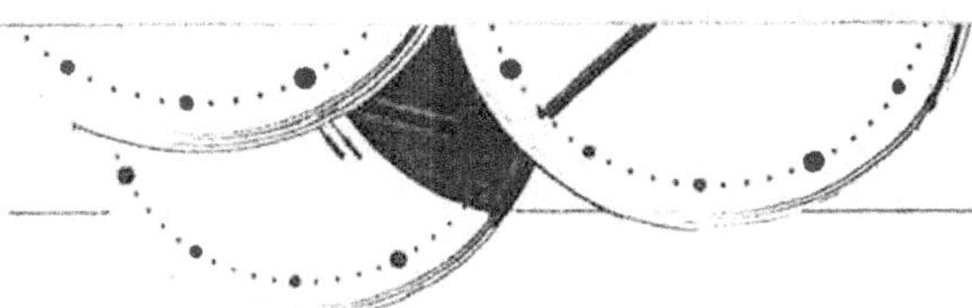
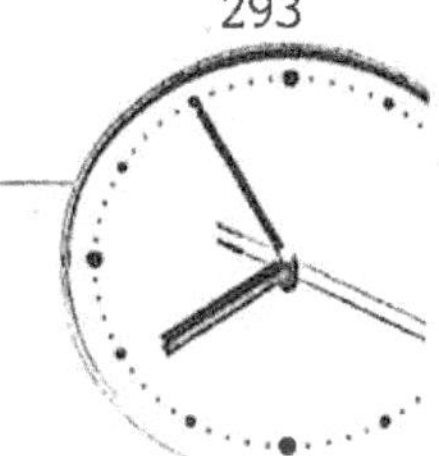

WHEN TIME IS RUNNING OUT...

THIS HOUR

If you're faced with 60 minutes to finish a report, answer "urgent" emails, and fill out this week's fantasy-baseball-team roster, tackling three tasks at once may seem wise. But studies prove the opposite: Multitasking lowers attention span, increases stress, and makes each task take longer. So keep it simple, says Jordan Etkin, Ph.D., a professor at Duke University's Fuqua School of Business who's researched multitasking. When you have deadlines of 60 minutes or less:

1 | TRUNCATE YOUR TO-DO LIST.

High achievers are ruthless about prioritizing, she says: "Take a step back, figure out what's most important, and work on that thing."

2 | REFRAME THAT HOUR.

Duke researchers discovered that when students cramming for an exam thought of one hour as 60 minutes, the hour seemed longer, they felt more productive, and they found the subject matter more interesting.

3 | TAKE TEN SLOW BREATHS.

We know everyone and their six-year-old has told you to "belly breathe" when you feel stressed. It's not BS: Dozens of studies have shown how deep breathing activates the part of the nervous system that works like a brake on the stress train, helping you focus enough to get stuff done. In other words, when you're under the gun, these breaths help you be filled with fewer "I can't pull this off" worries and have more success at just pulling things off.

TODAY

Now you have 24 hours to play with. The trick to feeling like there's still sand in the top of the hourglass is to stop glorifying being busy. Our culture values action, so working through lunch makes us feel more productive and less guilty... while in fact ceaseless work makes us *less* efficient. Instead:

1 | DO 90-MINUTE INTERVALS.

"Humans weren't made to work in a linear way," says Andrew Deutscher, managing director of the Energy Project, a performance consulting firm. "We're built to pulse like waves." So step away from work every 90 minutes; people who do so have a 28 percent higher level of focus than people who take one or no breaks.

2 | LET NATURE HELP.

Hunt for a natural scene. When a group of students viewed a rooftop meadow for 40 seconds, they had greater concentration and made fewer errors on an attention test than those who looked at an empty concrete rooftop.

3 | KNOW WHAT TO IGNORE.

President Dwight D. Eisenhower used what became known as "the Eisenhower Box" to get things covered before nightfall. Try it: Draw four boxes, two stacked over two. In each, write one of these things: urgent and important daily tasks; important but not urgent work; urgent but not important tasks; work that's neither urgent nor important. Use it to determine what to ignore, leave for later, delegate, or do immediately—you know, like launch the D-Day invasion of Normandy.

THIS YEAR / THIS LIFE

Perhaps your head has run these lines: How is it March? How did I get to be this age without starting a family/hot VC firm/counterculture revolution (hell, I haven't even broken 10,000 Twitter followers yet)? This is a deeper level of fear than the temporary panic of having too much to do. It's the anxiety of falling short of your own expectations coupled with the feeling that you don't have enough time left to meet them. When it hits, breathe and:

1 | ASK BIGGER QUESTIONS.

The larger question you should ask isn't how to cram it all in. It's why you think you have to do all those things you set out for yourself, says Raj Raghunathan, Ph.D., of the University of Texas, Austin. Instead of tallying up a life by job titles and degrees earned, he says, rethink what a meaningful life is. It might not be what's on your LinkedIn page.

2 | GO OUT MORE.

People who meet with friends more than once a week are 27 percent more likely to be satisfied with life than those with no friends or who get together only a few times a year.

3 | DON'T OVERTHINK IT.

Regrets over things we *could* have done can instigate Torschlusspanik too. These tend to haunt us much longer than regrets over things we *should* have done (like go to your friend's son's wedding), says Cornell psychologist Tom Gilovich, Ph.D. So stop wasting additional time fretting over the "what if"s and "wish I had"s, and just plunge in. After all, the gate is closing. But there's time to make it in.

First let's recognize our physical body's and stretch out.

<u>Warm Up</u>

50 Jumping Jacks

25 Squats

50 Knees to Chest

2 Laps

<u>Regiment</u>

____

____

____

1 Find a balance between courage and humility.

You want to work hard, but work smart, too. Doing supersets (back-to-back exercises) isn't your license to rush. Move quickly, but form is foremost. "You know you're on it if your last rep looks pretty close to your first," says Jack.

2 Don't push through pain.

A midworkout burn and postworkout soreness are good signs. But pain from an everyday activity is different—like that shoulder twinge while you're reaching into a cabinet, or an aching knee on the stairs. If it's in a joint, that's pain. Don't push through: "It's our brains telling us something isn't right."

3 Use the cooldown as time to reflect.

Don't think it's "just a stretch" or "what we're supposed to do." Feel your heart rate recover. Reflect on your workout. The cooldown is your transition "back into the speed and pace of the world. That's what fitness is about—helping you to manage that world well."

4 Look at the directions.

Men tend to dive into things, ignoring instructions. "We end up with five extra screws and the thing half-put-together," Jack says. Same with fitness: Go over the directions, take your time, and the results will accelerate. "It will pay dividends for the rest of your life."

Here's Why You Can't Stop Being Hungry

Are you frequently covered in pretzel dust?
Do you partake, like a hobbit, in "second breakfast"?
ABBY LANGER, R.D., *helps you stop all that.*

REASON #1:
YOU'RE NOT REALLY EATING
▼

Maybe you've never liked breakfast. Or your work schedule pushes meetings through lunch. Or you just "forget" to eat. It's time to prioritize consistent mealtimes. People who don't eat regular meals have poorer diet quality, and skipping breakfast is associated with a higher intake of added sugars, according to a 2017 study published in *Circulation*. The same research found that eating breakfast also reduces impulsive snacking. **THE FIX:** Don't skip meals—intentionally or unintentionally. When you're awake, your stomach takes about four hours to empty after a meal. If you're hungry before then, you didn't eat well at the preceding meal (more on that soon). If you frequently forget to eat, set a phone alarm or calendar alert.

REASON #2:
YOU'RE NOT EATING ENOUGH PROTEIN OR FIBER
▼

Pick up a breakfast wrap or two from the drive-thru and you'll stay full till lunch, right? Nope. Though they have some protein, most fast-food breakfast wraps are empty carbs. This is also why you can slam an entire order of pad thai at lunchtime and still be hungry two hours later. **THE FIX:** At every meal, aim to eat about 30 grams of protein—a quantity that will increase satiety (your body's feeling of fullness postmeal), found Purdue University researchers in 2015. As for fiber, shoot for at least 10 grams per meal. "That amount of fiber will slow emptying from the stomach and contribute to satiety," says gastroenterologist Scott D. Levenson, M.D., director of the Digestive Care Medical Center in San Carlos, California.

REASON #3:
YOU'RE DRINKING YOUR MEALS
▼

Most packaged "meal replacement" shakes or fruit smoothies won't keep you satiated for long. First, liquids empty out of your stomach in less than an hour, says Dr. Levenson. By comparison, solid foods take two to four hours. Second, blending foods pulverizes their fibers, so your body breaks them down faster, reducing satiety. **THE FIX:** Listen to Mom and chew your food. A 2015 review of studies found that higher levels of "oral processing" (otherwise known as chews per bite) at a meal affect the gut hormones linked to reduced hunger and increased feelings of fullness. Try nuts in your morning Greek yogurt, jerky with your afternoon cheese snack, and al dente vegetables as a dinner side.

REASON #4:
YOU'RE HAVING PROBLEMS IN BED
▼

Lack of sleep may disrupt the appetite-regulating hormones, according to a 2016 report by the American Heart Association. Ghrelin, the hormone that stimulates hunger, can rise when you're sleep-deprived. Leptin, the hormone that signals satiety, can decrease. In addition, the more hours you spend awake, the more likely you are to go and nibble something from the refrigerator. **THE FIX:** Try for seven to eight hours of sleep per night. Set a regular bedtime, and remember that blue light from your devices can negatively affect sleep. Make a rule: Screens in bed, like breakfast in bed, should be a special occasion.

REASON #5:
YOU'RE NOT ACTUALLY HUNGRY
▼

False hunger is a real thing. Next time you think you're hungry, run through a quick checklist: Are you bored? Tired? Thirsty? Ingesting too much social media? A 2016 study review in *Brain and Cognition* found that looking at food images can increase your desire to eat, triggering physiological changes that occur in anticipation of food. **THE FIX:** Do your snack binges correspond to social-media binges? If so, false hunger may be at work. The next time you reach for your phone, instead take a short walk or tackle a small project with your hands. If you're still hungry afterward, then consider a protein-rich snack.

Stretch!

After we stretch lets try some new exercises!

Warm Ups

* 50 Jumping Jacks

* 50 Mountain Climbers

* 50 Toe Touches

* 3 Laps

Regiment

THE NUTRIENT YOU NEED NOW///

Vitamin D "When you are in your 20s, your body can still lay down the materials needed for strong bones that will sustain you through life," says Mike Roussell, Ph.D., a *Men's Health* nutrition advisor. "Vitamin D plays a key role in bone health." Aim for 600 IU of D daily. (Three ounces of cooked sockeye salmon has 570.)

Eat more: Sockeye salmon, canned tuna, sardines, egg yolks, milk, Swiss cheese

FACE YOUR FEARS

FIRST, I RULE out any medical causes of anxiety, then we focus on symptoms. The goal of treatment isn't to turn off a patient's radar but rather to tune it. Anxiety tends to get stuffed down instead of surfaced and understood. So honor your anxiety as a signal to look deeper. Usually this feeling has a pattern to it, and my patients use this pattern to help crack the code of their anxiety. The feeling often relates to our perceived notion of control (which is why the fear of flying is so common) and our unconscious fears of our own fragility and mortality.

Tim and I did a deep dive into his worries. When did his anxiety start? Does it "live" in a certain part of his body? What are the triggers? What makes it better or worse? Did he worry as a kid? Are other members of his family anxious? Family dynamics, especially conflicts with parents, spouses, and children, are common triggers. I asked Tim to be Sherlock Holmes, as the details of a person's anxiety lie in the cognitive distortions and psychology that drive it.

Clinically, some worries have a clear, conscious explanation, like a meeting with the boss, and they become amplified in a patient with anxiety. Other times, they're part of a syndrome such as generalized anxiety disorder or panic disorder (which was part of the case with Tim). Anxiety also runs in families; having a family member with an anxiety disorder greatly increases the odds of your having one as well.

But sometimes the cause isn't clear. Tim would describe a feeling of tightness in his throat some days, even when relaxing at home. This was a major hint. What emerged was that Tim had serious relaxation issues. As his career took off, family time became an afterthought.

He wasn't worried about his in-box; he was worried that he was an absent, overworked, and irritable father. It wasn't rocket science, but it was an idea that he hadn't ever aired out as meaningful. Today, Tim knows his tingly fingers and chest pain are symptoms of his panic disorder. He now sees the choking feeling as a sign that he's not present with his wife and kids in some way. Then he follows the essential next steps to support his recovery.

GRAB YOUR TOOLS

THESE STRATEGIES are like having a mental-health Leatherman in your pocket.

RECRUIT YOUR BREATH: Breathing is your number-one anxiety fighter because it soothes your nervous system. We reframed Tim's tingly fingers as a signal to focus on his breath. Many breathing techniques work; start as simply as inhaling through your nose for four counts and out through your mouth for six.

BURN AND NURTURE: Panic attacks and other anxiety symptoms don't feel like superpowers. But having the skills to know your body's cues and to stay nourished and rested to prevent the panic? That makes you unstoppable.

I recommend discharging anxiety through intense physical exercise. For Tim, that meant CrossFit three times a week. And since you're more susceptible to bouts of anxiety after a few nights of poor sleep or during times of low blood sugar, it's important to create a structure of healthy eating and self-care.

Are you guys ready to try meditating? Meditation has remarkable results and should be a part of our daily lifes' regiment. The breath of life, like our bodys, are the most obvious signs of human life.

REBOOT YOUR MIND: Cognitive behavioral therapy helps people better understand, express, and reframe their internal emotional experience. CBT is based on the premise that much of our distress is caused by faulty thinking patterns. You learn to recognize "cognitive distortions," such as all-or-nothing thinking, catastrophizing, and scolding yourself.

3. TEST YOURSELF, OVER AND OVER

WHILE THE psychological causes of anxiety are complex, the approach that works is rather simple: Understand and confront your fears through exposure. Exposure should be gradual, intense, and frequent. For some forms of anxiety, how to confront your fears is obvious. Worried about public speaking? Join Toastmasters and make speeches. Terrified of dating? Time for Tinder! You get the drift. Other times, as with Tim, it takes a minute. Tim wasn't scared of email; after all, his email game was tight. He was worried that valuing his family put him in conflict with his boss, who didn't have kids, and with his professional goals.

Tim's entire world had become his in-box. It struck me one day how much he valued his family time but how the fear of looming emails dominated his weekends. My long-term plan for him was ambitious: a vacation with his phone off. We started with no phone for a few hours on Saturday morning. Just 45 minutes in, his mind was racing, his fingers were tingling, and he was so distracted he burned the French toast he was making for his kids. The road to recovery is like this at first. Naming anxiety doesn't tame it.

For Tim, the Lexapro helped him tolerate more exposure and also improved his mood a bit. Instead of having him go on vacation with his phone off, we replaced that challenge with a daily one: He now has a "phone jail" that stores his device during dinner and for much of the weekend.

4. PLAN AND MONITOR

FINALLY, being vigilant about triggers can really help you use your anxiety in a positive way, because it's all about listening to your alert system. For instance, Tim's anxiety worsens during the first week in December—that's when his father passed away, and it's the same week his annual reports are due. Rather than dreading the season, he now spends time listening to his dad's favorite music. He also doubles down on exercise and sends voice memos to his assistant about his early annual-report concerns.

I saw Tim several weeks ago for a check-in; he shook his head in disbelief about his anxious state when we first met. He continues his high-stress job, but he has tapered off the Lexapro and works an impressive self-care plan, including daily breathing and relaxation, exercising with friends, eating a healthy diet, and drinking alcohol much more sparingly. His anxiety still exists ("I'm a worrier!"), but he sees it as a way to sense the sticky conflicts that are central to his work before others do. He's aware of his tendency to catastrophize. Of course, with more focus on his family, he worries, like all fathers, about his kids and his wife . . . and that strikes me as just about right. Severe anxiety brought Tim to my office for all the right reasons. He dialed into it and now knows how to use it to maintain the life of connection that he truly desired.

Stretch!

After we stretch lets' sit and meditate!
Just for a few minutes! Quiet our minds and focus on
the breath of life.

Warm Ups

50 Jumping Jacks

50 Wind Mills

25 Lunges

3 Laps

Regiment

____

____

____

SCORE **CORE** STABILITY

All movement starts with your core. Use these exercises from Alex Guerrero to improve your overall athleticism and reduce back pain. The resistance of the band should be high enough that you must brace your core to prevent the band from pulling you. Do 3 rounds.

1 BANDED PALLOF PRESS SQUAT

Anchor a band at shoulder height and hold it directly in front of you. Pull to your chest, then press out and squat down until your thighs are parallel to the floor. Rise and repeat 10 times per side.

2 LATERAL-RESISTED BIRD DOG

On all fours, place a band around your hips and anchor on your left side. Brace your core and raise your right arm and left leg. Alternate sides and repeat 10 times. Switch the anchor to your right and repeat.

3 RESISTED LATERAL WALKING PLANK

Get in a high plank, hands under your shoulders, with a band around your hips anchored on your left side. "Walk" away from the anchor by jacking your feet and hands. Go out 5 steps and then back.

4 FOUR-WAY BAND RUNNING IN PLACE

Stand with an anchored band around your hips and run in place, facing away from the anchor for 20 seconds; repeat in 3 other directions (facing the anchor, to the left, and to the right).

YOUR TIME, YOUR WORKOUT

SPEND 1 MINUTE ··· OR 15 ··· STAYING LIMBER AND PAIN-FREE AT HOME.
By Ebenezer Samuel, C.S.C.S.

1. Kneeling Hip-Flexor Stretch
For tight hips, hold for 30 seconds, then switch sides.

1 min

2. Child's Pose
To loosen your lower back, hold for 30 seconds, rest for 30 seconds. Do 3 reps.

4 min

3. Glute Bridge Do 3 sets of 10 to hone your posture.

8 min

4. Side-Lying Clam
To avoid knee pain, do 2 sets of 30 per side.

11 min

5. Lying Windmill Stretch
To avoid upper-back pain, do 2 sets of 10 per side.

15 min

PETER SUCHESKI (illustrations)

<u>Read and Discuss</u>

Did you know about this critical tissue that pervades our muscles, nerves, and organs?

Fascia the Truth!

*The secret to building a leaner, stronger body (and moving pain-free, too!) lies not **in** your muscles but in all the stuff **around** them.*
BY MARISSA GAINSBURG

FOR YEARS, scientists researching pain, movement, and recovery had no interest in the weblike tissue known as fascia, which coats your muscles, nerves, and organs.

But things have changed. Researchers—and savvy trainers—now view fascia as your secret weapon both in and out of the gym. If you take care of it, your body will perform better while you're working out and you'll experience less pain overall. "Fascia is one of the most important and pervasive systems, because it connects every system together," says Rebecca Pratt, Ph.D., a professor of anatomy at Oakland University.

To understand how this critical tissue works, imagine an orange. The peel is your skin. Directly beneath that peel is a white, gauzelike substance that surrounds each orange wedge and ensures that the orange maintains its spherical structure. That gauzelike substance is your fascia, a connective wrap made of gelatinesque glycoproteins that soak up water, collagen, and various other cells. Its main job: to hold your muscles, joints, tendons, and bones in place.

Fascia covers every muscle in your body, and when it tightens in the wrong places, it causes pain. You've felt this pain before, all those times you wrapped up a serious muscle sesh and could barely walk upstairs.

Much like a sport coat, the tissue surrounding your muscles can bunch, wrinkle, and stretch. And when it gets injured, it rebuilds as scar tissue, with fibers in a crisscrossing pattern. Fibers on healthy muscles and fascia all run in the same direction; when they crisscross, they bunch up even more and can pull and tug at joints.

There's a good chance you've experienced this before, too, and you may have solved it with the most common method of realigning these fibers: foam-rolling. Doing so properly helps loosen damaged areas, relaxing and smoothing them. Take your fascial care to the next level with these strategies.

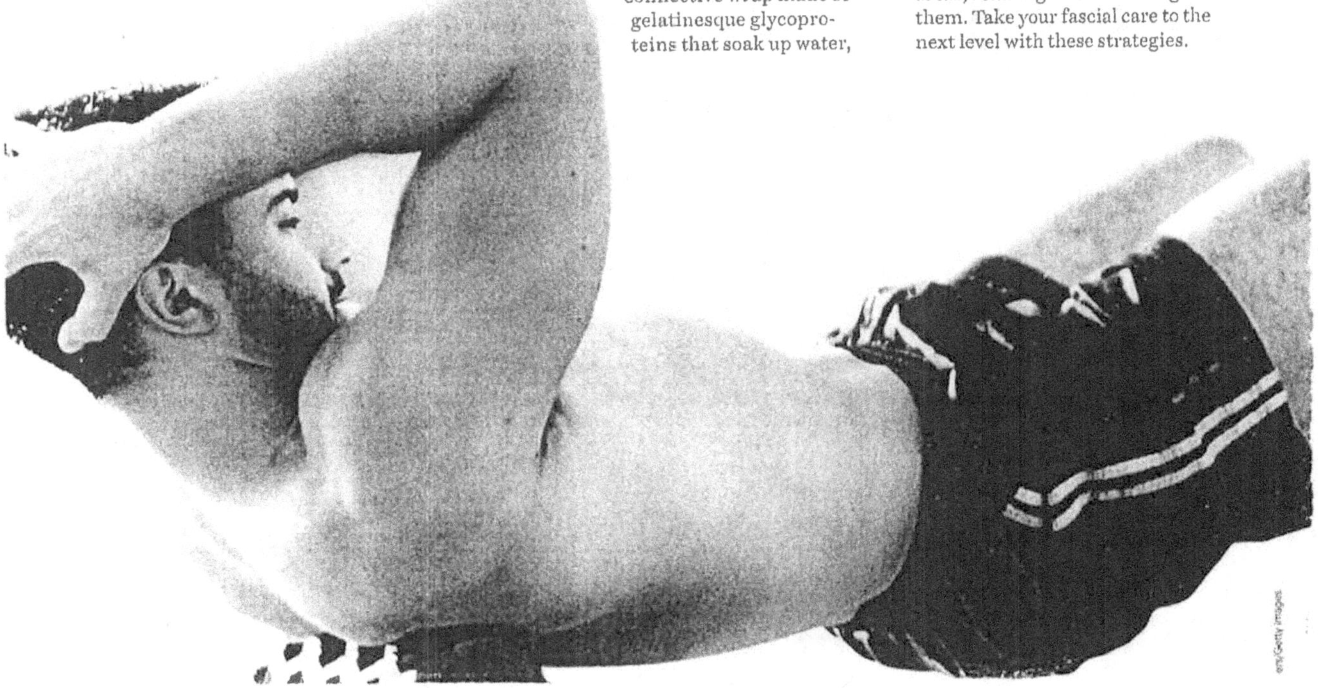

Six Problems, One Fix

Fascia can be the cause of—or solution to—any muscle issue that saps energy or mobility. Here are six common problems—and how you can control them.

Headaches

Blame your desk job: That stabbing pain at your temples is often related to cranky neck fascia. When your head and shoulders shift forward instead of staying aligned with your spine, the muscles (and the fascia around them) at the base of your head tighten, while the ones that control your shoulders grow weak. Your pectoral fibers also tighten, pulling your shoulders further forward. The combo in this sensitive area leads to tension headaches. **YOUR MOVE:** Strengthen your shoulder and back muscles and open your chest all at once with seated rows. Aim to do 3 sets of 12 at least 3 times a week.

Limited Movement After Injury

After surgery or a severe injury, your body forms collagen-based scar tissue that can replace healthy fascia. The problem: Normal tissue fibers line up parallel to one another. Scar tissue develops in a haphazard way, limiting your muscles' ability to lengthen and contract. **YOUR MOVE:** Once the damaged area has healed, begin gentle massage techniques, like gliding the skin forward and back, then side to side, for several minutes a few times a day, realigning fascial fibers.

A Lack of Athleticism

Researchers recently discovered that fascial tissue stores more kinetic energy than any other type of tissue. In fact, the springiness of fascia (not powerfully muscled calves) is the driving force that allows kangaroos to make 30-foot leaps. Because of this relationship, experts think plyometrics training makes your fascia more durable and resilient by increasing its density. **YOUR MOVE:** Forget fixing your fascia and actually strengthen it. Three times a week, spend up to 5 minutes doing agility ladder drills. Don't have a ladder? Do 3 sets of 10 to 20 jump squats.

Sticky Joints

Tightness in muscles and surrounding fascia can cause joints to stiffen, making your body move in ways that can create long-term issues. An example: Tight calves reduce your toes' ability to flex toward your shin, changing your gait. **YOUR MOVE:** Foam-roll or stretch any tense area right after each workout, since your muscles respond best when warm. Try to do three 30-second standing calf stretches (legs straight, heels down) daily.

Back Pain

Where your thoracic (middle) and lumbar (lower) spine meet is a nightmare zone. Restricted fascia anywhere—particularly in your hamstrings or quads—can pull on the fascia here. If you work a desk job, it likely means trouble in your psoas, a muscle in your hip flexors that lets you lift your knee and is vital to core strength. **YOUR MOVE:** Because it's located so deep in your pelvic region, releasing the psoas is challenging. Stretch your hip flexors (try pigeon pose), and foam-roll your hamstrings at least twice a week.

Unhappy Feet

Plantar fasciitis, or heel pain due to inflamed fascia in the sole of your foot, strikes 2 million people each year, especially runners. It's often due to calf tightness—or flat feet. **YOUR MOVE:** Roll your feet over a lacrosse ball for a minute each, ideally every day. In addition to that, foam-roll your calves for up to 5 minutes each.

<u>Stretch!</u>

Let's repeat our meditation again!
Everything gets better with practice!

<u>Warm Up's</u>

* 50 Jumping Jacks
* Run 3 Laps

<u>Regiment</u>

Today we will do the body weight burner on page 2! Our time has come.
We've worked ourselves up for this work out.

Don't dig your grave with your own teeth! The word die is in the word diet! Learn to eat 2 live!

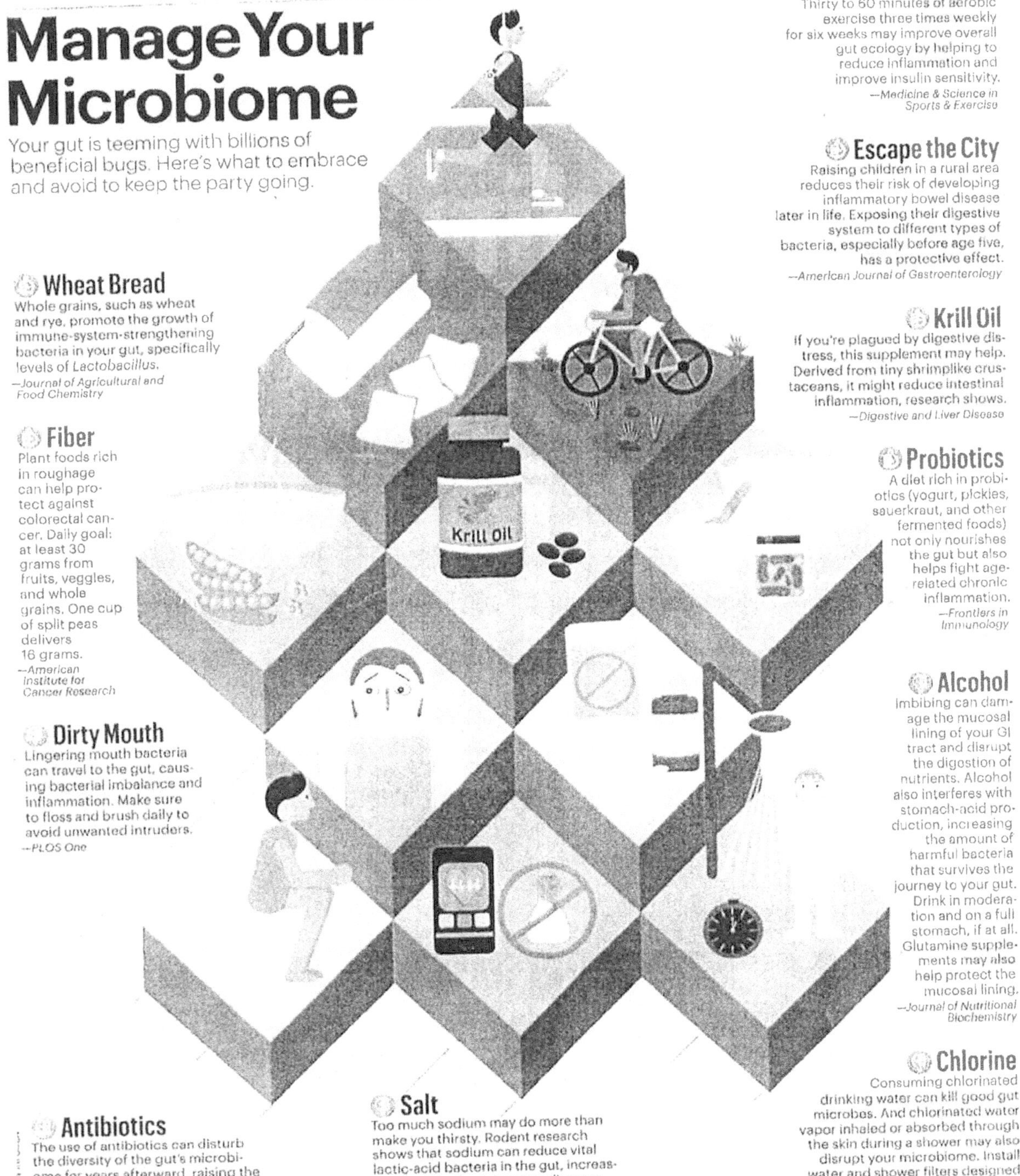

Manage Your Microbiome

Your gut is teeming with billions of beneficial bugs. Here's what to embrace and avoid to keep the party going.

Wheat Bread

Whole grains, such as wheat and rye, promote the growth of immune-system-strengthening bacteria in your gut, specifically levels of *Lactobacillus*.
—*Journal of Agricultural and Food Chemistry*

Fiber

Plant foods rich in roughage can help protect against colorectal cancer. Daily goal: at least 30 grams from fruits, veggies, and whole grains. One cup of split peas delivers 16 grams.
—*American Institute for Cancer Research*

Dirty Mouth

Lingering mouth bacteria can travel to the gut, causing bacterial imbalance and inflammation. Make sure to floss and brush daily to avoid unwanted intruders.
—*PLOS One*

Antibiotics

The use of antibiotics can disturb the diversity of the gut's microbiome for years afterward, raising the risk of intestinal infections. Don't use these drugs indiscriminately.
—*Frontiers in Microbiology*

Salt

Too much sodium may do more than make you thirsty. Rodent research shows that sodium can reduce vital lactic-acid bacteria in the gut, increasing the risk of autoimmune diseases such as MS. Eat plenty of potassium to balance out the sodium.   —*Nature*

Cardio

Thirty to 60 minutes of aerobic exercise three times weekly for six weeks may improve overall gut ecology by helping to reduce inflammation and improve insulin sensitivity.
—*Medicine & Science in Sports & Exercise*

Escape the City

Raising children in a rural area reduces their risk of developing inflammatory bowel disease later in life. Exposing their digestive system to different types of bacteria, especially before age five, has a protective effect.
—*American Journal of Gastroenterology*

Krill Oil

If you're plagued by digestive distress, this supplement may help. Derived from tiny shrimplike crustaceans, it might reduce intestinal inflammation, research shows.
—*Digestive and Liver Disease*

Probiotics

A diet rich in probiotics (yogurt, pickles, sauerkraut, and other fermented foods) not only nourishes the gut but also helps fight age-related chronic inflammation.
—*Frontiers in Immunology*

Alcohol

Imbibing can damage the mucosal lining of your GI tract and disrupt the digestion of nutrients. Alcohol also interferes with stomach-acid production, increasing the amount of harmful bacteria that survives the journey to your gut. Drink in moderation and on a full stomach, if at all. Glutamine supplements may also help protect the mucosal lining.
—*Journal of Nutritional Biochemistry*

Chlorine

Consuming chlorinated drinking water can kill good gut microbes. And chlorinated water vapor inhaled or absorbed through the skin during a shower may also disrupt your microbiome. Install water and shower filters designed to remove the chlorine.
—*PLOS One*

YOU CANE DO IT!*

TAKE THIS QUIZ AND SEE HOW MUCH YOU KNOW ABOUT THE EFFECTS OF SUGAR ON YOUR HEALTH.

*The Men's Health *staffer who wrote this punny headline has been told to lay off the Skittles.*

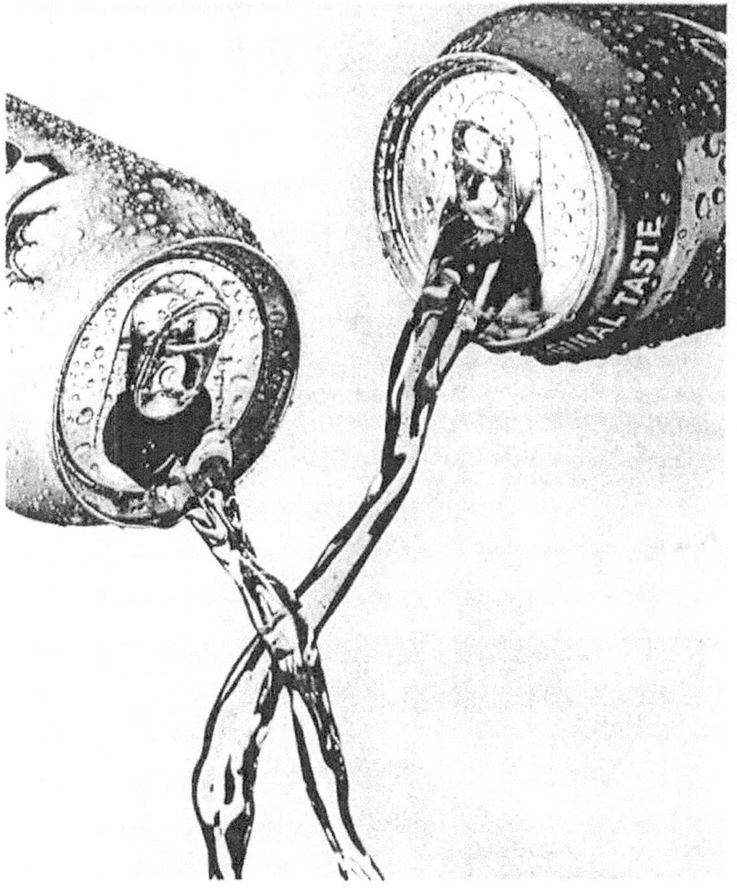

1. Let's get the most important sugar delivery out of the way. Chocolate: Good or bad?

(A) Bad

(B) Bad(ish)

(C) Good(ish)!

Depends. If you choose highly processed and sugary milk chocolates, you're missing out on flavonois, beneficial plant compounds found in higher levels in dark chocolate. These may help enhance the function of blood vessels, decrease blood pressure, and improve cholesterol levels. Unless you eat too much, and then there's the bad-for-your-heart obesity thing. *Answer: C*

2. Kill a sugar craving by playing:

(A) Khalid

(B) Volleyball

(C) Video games

Stay in your seat: A University of Plymouth study found that three minutes of Tetris can weaken cravings for food. *Answer: C*

3. You're most likely to want sweets when:

(A) Tired

(B) Angry

(C) Tangry!

Anger makes you do lots of things you regret, but inhaling sweets isn't usually one of them. Late nights give sugar cravings the upper hand; Sleep loss blunts activity in brain regions needed for decision-making, according to UC Berkeley research; fatigue also amplifies activity in parts of the brain that control desire, making it hard to keep "gotta have it" urges in check. *Answer: A*

4. Research shows that sugary drinks speed up cell aging by how many years?

1.5   **4.6**   **7.3**

A mere 1.5 years is wishful thinking: People who drink 20 ounces of soda or the like per day have DNA changes typical of cells a little bit older.
Answer: B

5. You've hit the 3:00 P.M. slump. Instead of a Snickers from the vending machine, go for:

(A) A Twix, a Milky Way, M&M's…

(B) A walk around the building

(C) A look at Instagram

Research from Germany suggests that all that #foodporn on Instagram may actually induce spikes of ghrelin, a hormone responsible for stimulating appetite. A brisk 15-minute walk, on the other hand, can chase away sugar cravings, different research found.
Answer: B

6. Adding sugar to your coffee can f___ your memory.

(A) -ocus

(B) -orestall

(C) -uck with

A UK review found that combining your daily caffeine fix with sugar helps with cognitive performance. But over time, a sugary diet disrupts brain-cell communication and can hinder learning and memory, UCLA researchers say.
Answer: A and C

7. Honey is better for you than sugar.

(A) True

(B) False

Molasses, corn syrup, brown sugar, cane sugar, fructose—and honey: They're all still sugar.
Answer: B

8. The best way to get some energy before training is to reach for:

(A) A sports drink

(B) A banana

(C) That vending-machine Snickers you declined earlier in the day

Heavy weights and sugary foods make for bad training partners. A 75-gram hit of added sugar causes a 25 percent drop in testosterone levels, according to *Clinical Endocrinology*. Peel a banana instead.
Answer: B

9. Sugar does the following to your sperm:

(A) Makes it swim faster

(B) Tanks its quality

If you won't cut back on soda for yourself, do it for your grandchildren. High intake of sugar-sweetened beverages is linked to poor sperm motility.
Answer: B

10. Which of these can make dessert sweeter without extra calories?

(A) Your silverware   (B) The lighting   (C) Your companion

Oxford researchers found that heavier spoons trick us into finding food sweeter. Company also helps us better enjoy food.
Answer: A and C

0 to 4 Sugar Oblivious
What you don't know about sugar could be keeping you in the cycle of reaching for it.

5 to 7 In the Sweet Spot
You know when sugar cravings hit and how to counteract them the right way.

8 to 10 A Sugar Savant
The facts shouldn't keep you away from all sweet stuff all the time. A little is really okay.

<u>Stretch!</u>

<u>Warm Ups</u>

* 5 Laps

<u>Regiment</u>

Organized Sports Activity

* Basketball
* Volleyball

Why You Don't Finish The...

There's a phase in the middle of every project that threatens to tank it. **GINNY GRAVES** *helps you find your way through.*

MAYBE IT'S the garage clean-out. Maybe it's your side-hustle documentary. Maybe you're... writing a piece for *Men's Health*. Regardless of the project, the story arc is usually the same: You embark on the journey feeling exhilarated and capable. Fast-forward a few days, a week, maybe even a month. Now there are half-empty boxes all over the driveway, reference materials burying the dining-room table, tools in the hall. And what are you doing instead of finishing your project? (Is that Fortnite? Are those *Cheetos*?)

There's a reason many of us have something like a half-painted kitchen weighing on our conscience, according to Harvard Business School professor Rosabeth Moss Kanter, Ph.D., author of *Confidence: How Winning Streaks and Losing Streaks Begin and End*. In between the thrill of starting a project and the joy of completing it lies the interminable middle, where enthusiasm sputters and your effort takes on the grim patina of failure. "The middle is where the project gets hard and you have to face reality," says Kanter. It's taking longer, costing more, other people are saying WTF. Getting stuck in the middle is so cartoonishly predictable, Kanter says, that you can plan for it and possibly even prevent it. Your best moves:

FIRST:

ESTIMATE THE AMOUNT OF TIME AND EFFORT IT WILL TAKE—THEN DOUBLE IT.

Why? Because when you're in the throes of your initial enthusiasm, you're overly optimistic, and as a result, you underestimate how hard the project is actually going to be. When Canadian researchers asked undergraduate psychology students how long they thought it would take to complete their theses if "everything went as *poorly* as it possibly could," their average answer was 48.6 days. If things went smoothly, they predicted it would take roughly 27.4 days. Wrong, and superwrong. The average time it took was 55.5 days.

You can't blame youth for the misjudgment. Building the Sydney Opera House took a decade longer and cost 14.5 times as much as the architects initially projected. **It's called the planning fallacy,** says Jon Acuff, author of *Finish: Give Yourself the Gift of Done*, and failing to account for it is one of the most common reasons people abandon projects midway through. If doubling the time you allot sounds daunting, Acuff suggests downsizing your projects instead. Aim to clean off half your workbench or write three blog posts a week rather than seven. "'Shoot for the moon' is a recipe for failure," he says.

THEN,

BE CAREFUL WHAT YOU TELL PEOPLE UP FRONT.

Conventional wisdom holds that you should state your intentions openly, the theory being that **when other people know what you're up to, you'll be forced to finish**—or be forced to publicly own up to the fact that you didn't. But sharing has a serious downside, says Acuff. Say you tell your friends you're going to landscape the backyard. What do they do? They slap you on the back and say, "Good for you!" They *congratulate* you. You get the high of finishing before you start, and that can undermine your enthusiasm once you're immersed in the hard work. Why eat your vegetables if you've already had dessert? If you do tell someone, ask them to be your ally and check in with you once a week and ask you what you've accomplished.

 BREAK

IT DOWN INTO SERIAL STEPS.

Obvious, right? Well, yes and no. **We often get bogged down in the middle because we're overwhelmed** by a project's scope. So instead of thinking about everything you need to do, define the next small task and focus on that. Say you want to build a tree house for your kid. The first step could be as simple as calling a neighbor with a cool tree house and picking his brain, says Frank Buck, Ed.D., an organization and time-management coach near Birmingham, Alabama. Buck suggests writing down each step like this: Call Jim Smith xx Finished Tree House. "The 'xx' serves as a separator between your current action step and the goal line," he says. "Seeing both together is a reminder that every small task is bringing you closer to your ultimate goal."

AND FINALLY,
UNDERSTAND THE COSTS OF NOT FINISHING.

"Unfinished projects don't go away. **They become ghosts that haunt you,**" warns Acuff. If you repeatedly give up, the person you're betraying is *you*. Finishing, on the other hand, shields you from the specter of projects past, helps you trust yourself, and gets the boxes out of the driveway.

FRONT-LOAD
AS MUCH WORK AS YOU CAN.

In 2011, when he was 23, Scott Young, a writer in Vancouver, decided to try to complete an informal version of MIT's computer-science curriculum in one year—33 classes, including physics, chemistry, and economics. (MIT puts some classes and exams online.) "It wasn't the exact MIT curriculum, but it was a pretty good approximation," he says. By then, **he knew himself well enough to recognize that he would burn out as time went on.** So he structured the MIT Challenge, as he called it, to account for project fatigue. "I finished the first ten classes in three months, which gave me momentum and made the last half easier than the first." It worked. He didn't get credit, but he completed all 33 classes in just under a year.

NAME
YOUR OWN RULES.

Acuff once set out to read 100 books in a year—and began posting about it on social media. "People would say, 'That book doesn't count because it's a graphic novel or it's an audiobook.' At first it made me question the whole project. Then I thought, *Who gets to judge?* And I realized I do. **My project, my rules.**"

Stretch!

Warm Up's

Integrated Style Exercise

- Toe Touchers
- Kness to Chest
- Squats
- Jumping Jacks

Regiment

____

____

____

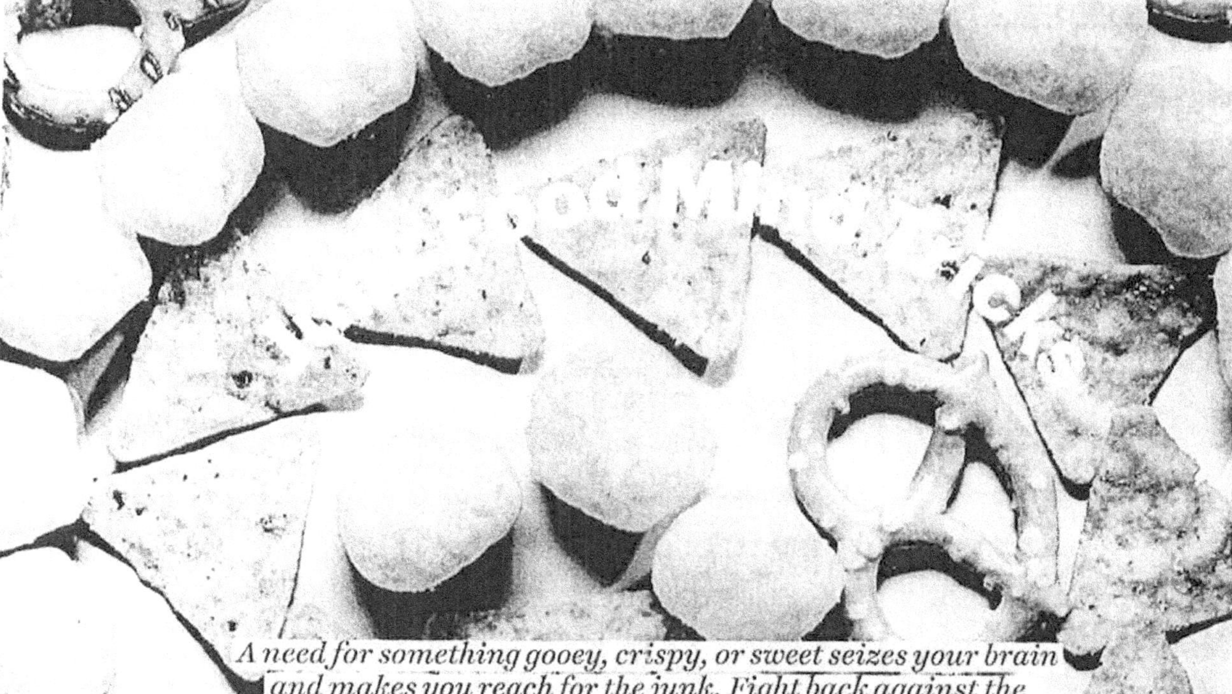

A need for something gooey, crispy, or sweet seizes your brain and makes you reach for the junk. Fight back against the four stages of craving with these neuroscientist-approved moves.

BY CINDY KUZMA

① TRIGGER:
An urge arises

The smell of french fries drifts through the food court; pepperoni sizzles in a pizza commercial. Your senses lead to your brain retrieving memories from your hippocampus and moving them into your working memory. Feel-good neurochemicals dopamine and opioids start to trickle into your reward-focused areas.

HOWTOFIGHTIT:
If you intervene right now, you're more likely to resist the temptation. So try to distract yourself by taking a brisk stroll or playing a visual game that commandeers your working memory, like Tetris.

② DRIVE:
Desire swells

Your orbitofrontal cortex hops into the game. This region evaluates memory, senses, and current experiences to determine how good the decision is to ingest chocolate or Cheetos. The drive to repeat a past pleasant experience grows stronger and turns physical, firing up your autonomic nervous system.

HOWTOFIGHTIT:
Escape further cues by placing physical barriers between you and temptation. Stash the ice cream way back in the freezer. Choose a route home from work that won't take you past the yellow arches.

③ DECISION:
Self-control checks you—or doesn't

Your dorsolateral prefrontal cortex, situated toward the front of your head, factors in any long-term consequences of your actions, social norms, and other motives for restraint. And fair warning: If you're hungry, sleep-deprived, or stressed, you're far more likely to cave in to your junk-food craving.

HOWTOFIGHTIT:
Focus on the downsides or imagine that doughnut fell on a filthy floor. A brain-imaging study showed that these thought exercises immediately increased activation of the dorsolateral prefrontal cortex.

④ CONCESSION:
Doomed at first bite

One nibble engages nearly all your senses, delivering a payload of sensory data to your gustatory cortex. Flavor-seeking cells throughout your digestive system send signals of pleasure back to your brain. Dopamine and opioids flow freely, and it's hard to stop eating before the whole bag, bar, or box is kaput.

HOWTOFIGHTIT:
Regular exercise strengthens your dorsolateral prefrontal cortex, perhaps by sparking the flow of blood rich in oxygen, hormones, and stored glycogen. The more often you sweat, the stronger your discipline may be.

Sources: Peter Hall, Ph.D., of the University of Waterloo, and Nicole Avena, Ph.D., of Mount Sinai Health System.

BUILD MUSCLE
TO FIGHT FAT

"Muscle is the opposite of fat," says Mayo Clinic cardiologist Francisco Lopez-Jimenez, M.D. All over your body, muscle is metabolically active in ways that counteract visceral fat—extracting glucose from your blood, helping your liver process fatty acids, and reducing inflammation. Dr. Lopez-Jimenez and his colleagues have found that people with big guts often lack lower-body muscle mass, and the correlation is stronger as people age. It stands to reason: Strong muscles add bulk to your legs and butt—your biggest muscle groups—providing a better balance of muscle to fat in your body and powering a healthier metabolism.

▶ How to Burn More Fat
If you have to choose one type of exercise, strength training may be best for specifically trimming your gut. In a Harvard study, men who did 20 minutes of daily weight training had less of an increase in age-related abdominal fat than men who spent the same amount of time doing aerobic activities. Emphasize exercises that challenge your whole body: squats, deadlifts, pullups. However, the same study found cardio had a greater impact on overall weight. Dr. Lopez-Jimenez suggests a mix of both, but combine them the right way by alternating cardio and weight training on different days. Men who do that may burn more visceral fat than they would by stacking workouts on top of each other in the same session.

How much do you really
know about yourself?

OUTSMART
YOUR BRAIN

Belly flab may be due as much to what happens in your head as in your gut. Losing visceral fat is difficult because your body defends fat like a castle on a very round hill, through the processing of hormones in brain circuits that control appetite. That's because in evolutionary/survival terms, fat is good. It seems to be your body's inherent system for stockpiling food, and it served mankind well when actual, edible stores were meager. Your ancestors who could sock away the most fat from the least food and release its energy in the most frugal, thrifty way possible had a genetic advantage. Your prepare-for-the-worst body isn't in sync with the indulge-every-whim bounty of food markets and restaurants—or the lack of exertion that comes from neither hunting nor gathering.

Over the years, your body matches energy intake and output with about 99 percent accuracy, says Michael Schwartz, M.D., codirector of the Diabetes Institute at the University of Washington. But even a finely tuned system can't compensate for gradual gains from endless calorie bombardment. As a rough estimate, "most obese people don't gain more than five pounds of fat a year, but that adds up over ten years," says Dr. Schwartz.

▶ Hack Your Metabolism
Evidence suggests that keeping calorie consumption confined to an earlier window means less weight gain than eating more later in the day. One new study tested the 16:8 diet—16 hours of fasting and 8 of eating. Researchers instructed 23 obese participants to eat any food in any amount between 10:00 A.M. and 6:00 P.M., but stick to water and calorie-free drinks at other times. After 12 weeks, volunteers ate about 300 fewer calories a day than a control group and lost about 3 percent of their body weight—enough to cause a discernible drop in visceral fat compared with the control. No participants leaving the study complained about the diet, so it's likely that volunteers found it fairly easy to stick with. Researchers say that's critical for improving metabolic health in a sustainable way.

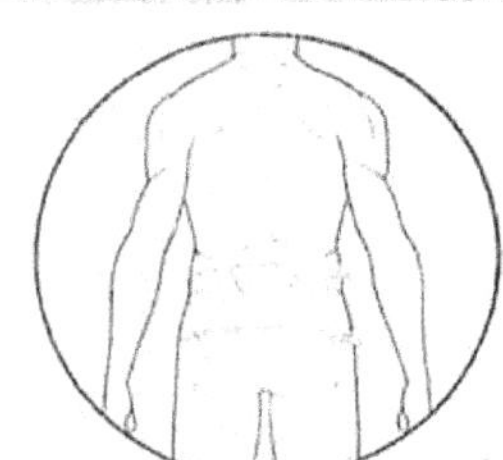

IS YOUR BELLY A HEART THREAT?
For an accurate determination of heart-attack risk caused by abdominal fat, calculate your waist-hip ratio, Mayo Clinic cardiologist Francisco Lopez-Jimenez, M.D., advises. Here's how:

1. While standing, wrap a tape measure around your waist about midway between your lowest rib and the top of the bony part of your hips. Write down the number.

2. Then measure your hips around the widest part of your buttocks.
3. Divide waist by hips. If the number is 0.9 or higher, you have central obesity and your metabolic risks are substantially higher.
4. For a more accurate assessment of fat, ask your doc for a dual X-ray absorptiometry scan.

NURTURE YOUR
INNER RAIN FOREST

One of the most important parts of your metabolism is your microbiome—the ecosystem of gut bacteria that break down food and produce chemicals that may prevent obesity, likely by reducing inflammation. A healthy microbiome should be like a rain forest. A big-belly microbiome is kind of barren. The key difference is biodiversity. "Obese people have fewer species of microbes in their gut," says Dan Knights, Ph.D., an associate professor at the University of Minnesota's Biotechnology Institute. "These microbes are like a factory producing thousands of compounds, good and bad. You want to provide food for the microbes making good compounds."

⊳ How to Eat Wilder
To restore your inner Amazon, eat food closer to nature. "Most Americans are living in a fiber desert," Knights says. "Every plant has its own set of fibers, with different chemical structures and different microbes that break them down." Aim for about 30 grams per day. Fiber-rich foods like fruits, vegetables, legumes, and whole grains are linked to a rise in short-chain fatty acids, which may reduce your risk of inflammation and metabolic problems. In one study, each ten-gram increase in daily fiber intake was associated with a 3.7 percent drop in visceral fat. Supplementing can help: Add two table-spoons of psyllium husks to your cereal or salad. Knights snacks on Nu'Go dLish bars, which deliver 12 grams of fiber from diverse sources.

What Your Poop Says about You: Microbiome

Stool that has surface cracks and looks like a sausage, or is smooth and like a snake (scoring 3 or 4 on the Bristol Stool Scale—yes, that's a thing), may be associated with greater bacterial diversity. Hard, lumpy stools had fewer bacterial species in a recent study.

CHANGE
THE NATURE
OF YOUR FAT

Not all body fat is harmful. Visceral fat is white fat—a type associated with an unhealthy metabolism. But another kind—brown fat—burns calories and helps the body generate heat. We don't have a lot of brown fat and lose it as we get older, says Dr. Cohen. Preliminary research also suggests that as you gain girth, you may actively switch healthy brown fat to unhealthy white fat.

⊳ Turn the Color Wheel
If brown fat can turn white, can white fat turn brown? It's a hot area of research. Investigators have found a third type of fat called beige fat that can be activated so it has fat-burning power. "Beige fat tends to be embed-ded in subcutaneous fat, which may be why subcutaneous fat is relatively benign and may even be protective," Dr. Cohen says. "Our dream is to find a pharmacological target—five to ten years away—that would turn unhealthy white fat to healthy brown fat." You may already have a natural way to make beige fat brown. New research suggests you can turn on the beige-fat furnace by notching your home's thermostat down to 66 or below for ten hours a day. Cold temps activate beige fat to keep you warm.

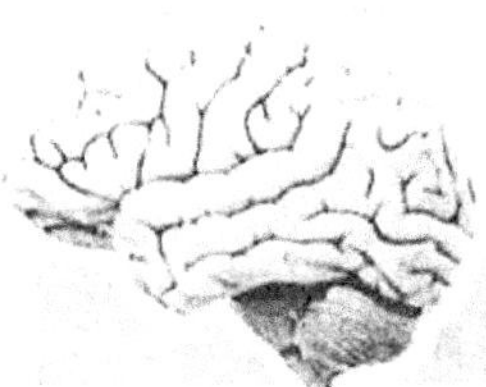

WAYS TO NATURALLY BOOST BRAIN POWER

Focus better with meditation!

A 2018 study from the University of Miami found that of the people who attended a three-month-long meditation retreat, those who continued the practice regularly and intensively did not show age-related decline in sustained attention seven years later.

Get more done with chocolate!

The active ingredient in dark chocolate, cocoa flavanols, may immediately improve visual information processing and working memory performance. Have a square or two and stick with natural cocoa: "Dutch processing" reduces flavanol content.

Augment your memory with games!

A 30-minute brain-training session based on the "n-back test," requiring participants to recall squares and letters they'd seen previously, improved their working memory (compared with those who didn't train). Try it yourself at cognitivefun.net/test/4.

Cultivate your creativity with tea!

In a new study, people who drank a cup of hot black tea were better at spatial creativity and language innovation than those who drank hot water. One explanation: People believe that tea drinkers are smart and innovative, so they act the part when served a cup.

Hike your happiness with exercise!

As little as ten minutes of exercise per week may elevate mood. More research is needed to determine which forms of exercise produce the most pronounced effects, but preliminary findings show that aerobic and stretching/balancing activities (yoga, tai chi) have benefits.

Tips on Getting Ripped

Abs at 40+!

"Keep your abs tight on every single exercise you do in the gym," says Ron Mathews, Joe Manganiello's trainer for the past ten years. "We treat ab training much like Franco Columbu [the 1970s bodybuilding legend]. Every exercise we do is also training the abs!" That's not all, though. Every other day, Manganiello hammers his abs with 10 to 15 minutes of dedicated core work, too. Here's his routine.

1 GHD Situp

▸ Set up with your legs in a glute-ham developer, chest pointed toward the ceiling. Lower your torso as far as is comfortable, then tighten your abs until your torso sits up. Aim to touch your toes. That's 1 rep; do 4 sets of 15.

2 Hanging Leg Raise

▸ Hang from a pullup bar, arms straight, feet together, maintaining light tension in your back. Keeping your legs straight, contract your abs, raising your legs until they're parallel with the floor. Slowly lower. That's 1 rep; do 4 sets of 15.

3 Bicycle Crunch

▸ Lie on your back, hands on your head and legs raised 1 inch off the floor, feet together. Pull your left leg in toward your torso and touch your right elbow to your left knee. Return to the start and switch sides. That's 1 rep; do 4 sets of 20.

4 Hollow Rock

▸ Lie on your back with your legs straight and your arms extended past your head. Contract your abs to lift your shoulders and arms a few inches off the floor. Lift your legs a few inches off the floor and rock forward. Do 3 sets of 10.

Checking Your Results!

ARE YOU CUT, RIPPED, JACKED, OR SWOLE?

Over at MensHealth.com, Associate Fitness Editor Brett Williams finally, definitively lays down the terms of fitness. Lest you call a cut guy jacked, go to menshealth.com/cut-ripped-jacked-swole.

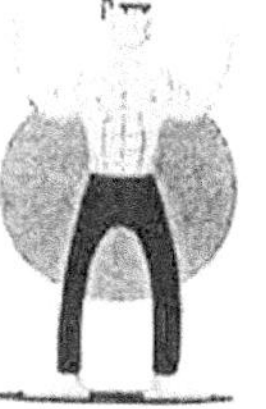

Less about size than definition—lean muscle and defined abs.

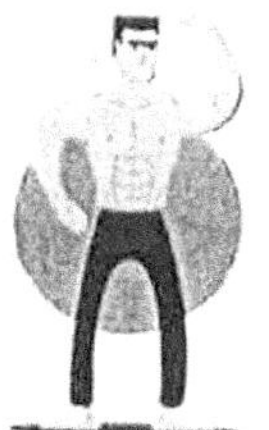

Where mass built on arms and shoulders eclipses the abs.

Pecs, arms, neck, and shoulders are all big. Protein is life.

The biggest of the big, where every muscle is huge. See also *yoked*.

Works Cited

Boudro, Ben "Mens Health: The Bodyweight Burner." Hearst Magazine, Inc. 2017 Print

Csatari, Jeff "Mens Health: Not Enough Time." Hearst Magazine, Inc. 2017: 14 Print

Gainsburg, Marissa "Mens Health: Fascia the Truth." Hearst Magaine, Inc. Print

Graves, Ginny "Mens Health: Score Core Stability." Hearst Magazine, Inc. Print

Guerrero, Alex "Mens Health: When You Don't Finish the..." Hearst Magazine, Inc. Print

Kuzma, Cindy "Mens Health: Junk Food Mind Tricks." Heasrt Magazine, Inc. Print

Langer, Abby "Mens Health: Heres Why You Can't Stop Being Hungry." Hearst Magazine, Inc. Print

Lima, Doug "Mens Health: Sleep." Hearst Magazine, Inc. Print

Samuel, Ebenezer "Mens Health: Your Time, Your Minute." Hearst Magazine, Inc. Print

Williams, Brett "Mens Health: Are You Cut, Ripped, Jacked, or Swole." Hearst Magazine, Inc. Print

"Mens Health: Manage Your Microbiome." Hearst Magazines, Inc. Print

"Mens Health: You Cane Do It." Hearts Magazine, Inc. Print

"Mens Health: 5 Ways to Naturally Boost Brain Power." Hearst Magazine, Inc. Print

"Mens Health: The Nutrient You Need Now." Hearst Magazine, Inc. Print

All works cited are from Mens Health magazines printed between 2016 and 2018.

WRITE OUR WRONGS

WRITE OUR WRONGS

PRISONERS INITIATIVE TO
COMPENSATE VICTIMS
& TO SUPPORT CHARITIES

LETTERS TO VICTIMS, POEMS AND SHORT STORIES

Writing project for inmates at High Desert State Prison

Write Our Wrongs Introduction

This writing project is a prisoner's initiative whose primary purpose is to demonstrate rehabilitation through remorse and restitution for victims of crime.

Write Our Wrongs borrows much of its title from the book, "Writing my Wrongs", by Shaka Senghor, a former prisoner, who changed his life while incarcerated and now spends his time speaking on victims impact related issues and also criminal justice reforms. Throughout this four month course each participant is required to commit to the following:

1. Writing a <u>poem</u> with a theme of remorse to victims,
2. Writing a <u>letter</u> to victims of ones crime and,
3. Writing a <u>short story (or lesson)</u> about the impact of crime on the lives of individuals and communities.

Moreover, the combined work will then be compiled and proposed for publishing. All proceeds from the book will go towards victims restitution and charity funds to assist children and poor families. **No participant will** benefit financially **from this project.**

Participation Requirement

Each participant must have the ability and be willing to do, in short, the following:

1. Qualified writing abilities. This is not an academic course, so our aim is not "teaching" others to write but, drawing upon those who've honed the skill already.
2. Demonstrable rehabilitative behavior. This course targets those inmates who are making strides to change their lives and renounce criminal activity and violent conduct.
3. Provide your own stationary and allocate personal time for each writing project.
4. Be willing to participate in victims impact group discussions throughout this course. (There is no requirement to speak about particular charges or names of victims, unless one volunteers this information).

Although this is a "writers project", we would be remissed in our duties if we didn't allocate time to discuss issues related to victims impact. So, some courses are designated specifically for this most important study and discussion.

5. Read copywright and publishing material provided to meet requirements for this goal during ones own time and in group setting to understand the publishing process.

6. Provide a single book of stamps (20 stamps) by the 5th week of the course. The stamps are to be used to pay for copyright expenses.

7. As initial admittance, provide the poem one desires to be part of his final work (letter, short story, etc.). The poem is an "initiative and entry fee."

8. Be willing to meet at least once a week for reviews, evaluations, and discussions per availability of sponsor or time allocation.

9. A victims pledge will be recited prior to every weekly meeting.

Further Insight

1. Each participants poem will be titled: <u>The Next Time.</u> The words for the poem are to be drawn from each persons own heart.

2. The title of each short story will be: <u>In Retrospect.</u> (The essential message is: "If I knew then what I know now.")

3. Finally, the victims impact letter will be titled: <u>A letter to my victims</u> and governed by the following principles:

   A. <u>Remorse</u>

   B. <u>Accountability</u>

   C. <u>Responsibility</u> and

   D. <u>Amends</u>

Each inmate participant will have a section (or chapter) which includes their written work-product bearing their names and CDCR numbers. **No Nicknames allowed.** Additional insight for this writing project will be provided during weekly meeting sessions (courses designated as "project overviews.")

We would like to thank everyone in advance for their participation in this project to giveback to individuals and communities that have suffered from our actions.

We can try to make things right by our efforts to write our wrongs.

                                                    —Core Group Members

<u>Write Our Wrongs writing, review and discussion sessions</u>

<u>Project Overview</u>
<u>Week 1</u>

1. Pledge recited.
2. Participant introduction.
3. Initial Poem Submittal.
4. Copyright information passed out and read in group (Form TX, etc.)

<u>Project Overview</u>
<u>Week 2</u>

1. Pledge Recited.
2. Review and recital of poems by authors in group setting.
3. Discuss details of next writing project (victims impact letter).
4. Set time-table for final submission of letter.
5. Discuss actual book format and singnificance of entrys and their respective order.

<u>Project Overview</u>
<u>Week 3</u>

1. Pledge recited.
2. Victims impact study session.
3. Group discussion about letter to victims and their significance.

<u>Project Overview</u>
<u>Week 4</u>

1. Pledge recited.
2. Discuss 3rd writing project (In Retrospect) and the elements it will contain:
   -Back story of writer (minus details of particular crime and victims names).
   -No glorifying past or self gratification.
   -No rationalizing criminal behavior, excuse making, or blaming others, including society.
   -However, events and experiences that steered you the wrong way are permissible
   -Further, talk about what events/experiences put you on the path to change your life and how you plan to remain crime free and live a victimless life, both while in prison and when/if paroled. Remember: The esence of the message is "If I knew then what I know now" things would have been different, my actions would have been ndifferent.
   -Writing is to be 3-5 pages long and legible.

<u>Project Overview</u>
<u>Week 5</u>

1. Pledge recited.
2. Book of stamps required from each participant.
3. Review of copyright and publishing material.

<u>Project Overview</u>
<u>Week 6</u>

1. Pledge recited.
2. Submission of victims impact letter for review and discussion.

<u>Project Overview</u>
<u>Week 7</u>

1. Pledge recited.
2. Review and evaluate progress on "In Retrospect" writing.

<u>Project Overview</u>
<u>Week 8</u>

1. Pledge recited
2. Victims impact discussion

Note:

The remaining classes will be for proof reading, editing, and preparing work product for publishing.

FREEDOM COMMITTEE

THE FREEDOM COMMITTEE PROJECT

"TRANSFORMING THE CRIMINAL MIND INTO CITIZENSHIP."
PREPARING INMATES FOR PAROLE SUITABILITY AND A CIVIC LIFE-STYLE

SUPPORT PRISON REFORM AND REHABILITATION

FREEDOM COMMITTEE

Member's Resume
And
Contact Information

JOIN THE MOVEMENT AND SUPPORT THE CAUSE...

"Prison became my monastary"

-Mahatma Ghandi

Introduction

We are members of the Freedom Committee. Our primary goal is to prepare ourselves and other inmates for positive programming while incarcerated and citizenship upon release from prison.

The greater part of our day is spent mentoring inmates individually and facilitating self-help groups, five of which we cofounded and/or participate in weekly. A list and overview of these groups will soon follow.

During our incarceration we have successfully completed most of the available self-help programs in our facility. Therefore, we remain students, open to continuous learning.

We believe that freedom is not free. So we spend every opportunity on earning our space on this earth and helping others find their way as well. Our check list for existence (besides Gods Grace) and release are:

1. Punishment. We accept guilt for the crimes we committed and the judgement of the courts.

2. Rehabilitation. We accept that our crimes, while horrible, will not define us. Therefore, we are motivated to transform our lives, in order to do so, we avail ourselves of every self-help group we can.

3. Restitution. While we seek forgiveness from our victims and society and have repented for our criminal behavior; we believe that the final act must be atonement and restitution is just one part of that process.

So, we have either paid off our court imposed victims impact funds or causes. That will be discussed shortly.

"Prison is second to college"

-Malcom X

Brief Bio-Sketches

Donel Poston
(AT-2512)

I am a 45 year old male serving a life sentence for second-degree murder. Since my incarceration I have:

1. Obtained three Associate degrees, several educational certificates, and currently finishing my last semester before earning my Bachelors degree.

2. Co-authored several self-help groups (Life Choices, New H.E.A.R.T.S, Write Our Wrongs project, Reaching Out From Within, G.A.M.E, Inter-Faith Dialogue, and The Freedom Committee)

3. Been elected spiritual leader for my religious community

4. Served on the Inmate Advisory Counsel (I.A.C)

5. Written and Published three books

6. Completed several self-help groups, including: Criminal and Gangsters Anonymous, Victims Impact, Houses of Healing, Positive Parenting Workshop, Alternatives to Violence Facilitator, Fatherhood Focus, Path 2 Restoration, and many more.

7. Completed The Peer Literacy Mentor Training Program and The Juvenile Diversion Mentoring Program.

8. Received laudatory Chronos from C.D.C.R employees for behavior that deserves extraordinary merit.

James Wilson
(AU-5200)

I am a 46 year old male long-term offender, incarcerated for manslaughter and carjacking. Since being incarcerated I have:

1. Paid my victims restitution

2. Completed my G.E.D

3. Written several unpublished books with the intent of keeping kids out of prison.

4. Co-authored and published Write Our Wrongs with Poston, a Victims Impact

Iniative. Funds from this project will go to victims of crimes and charities.

5. Co-authored several self-help groups: Truly Redefine Yourself (T.R.Y), New H.E.A.R.T.S, Reaching Out From Within, The Self Improvement Class, Write Our Project, Inter-Faith Dialogue, The Freedom Committee, and G.A.M.E

6. Completed several self-help groups: Lifers support group, Criminal and Gang- sters Anonymous, GOGI, Alcohol Anonymous, Narcotics Anonymous, Alternatives to Violence (AVP), Peer Health Education, Cancer Awareness, and Many More.

7. Received laudatory chronos from C.D.C.R employees for positive programing and assisting other inmates as a mentor.

8. Authored several books: Writing Our Wrongs, Freedom by Degrees, Evidence of long, lost letters, Profiles in Rehabilitation

"I went from excon to icon"
-Danny Trejo

Self-Help Group Authorship

<u>T.R.Y</u>: is a group that uses business as a model for living ones life. It teaches one to manage (be accountable) for every aspect of ones life: Human, Information, Material and Financial resources and turn these benefits into assets to help society.

<u>New H.E.A.R.T.S</u>: Hearts is an acronym for: Helping Everyone Articulate Rehabilitation through Story-telling. Essentially, it is a writing class which helps incarcerated men and women express moving from their past into their future and gaining a new (positive) heart.

<u>Reaching Out From Within</u>: Aims to assist incarcerated men and women with identifying painful experiences in their lives and transforming them into personal power.

<u>Self-Improvement Class</u>: Covers historical, spiritual, and social sciences. The guiding philosophy of this class is: self-improvement is the basis for community development.

<u>Write Our Wrongs</u>: is a victims impact iniative where up to 10 incarcerated men (every four months) engage in an effort to write a book together, with the intent to publish and donate all profits to victims impact groups or charities.

<u>Inter-Faith Class</u>: Seeks to educate inmates as to other religions besides their own.

<u>Life Choices</u>: is an insight group that seeks to explore ones past in order to discover the root of their anger, fear, and criminal thinking. This course forces the incarcerated individual to inventory his/her past through a comprehensive time line that will be whittled down to a concise story.

<u>G.A.M.E</u>: is a sports, athletic, and health class that motivates sedentary incarcerated individuals to get outside and get active.

The curriculums for these programs are available on: prisonsfoundation.com

Authors: Poston and Wilson
Title: Reaching Out From Within

The Freedom Committee Project

"TRANSFORMING THE CRIMINAL MIND INTO CITIZENSHIP."
PREPARING INMATES FOR PAROLE SUITABILITY AND A CIVIC LIFE-STYLE

SUPPORT PRISON REFORM AND REHABILITATION

To: Community Resource Manager's Office
Date: August, 2019
From: D. Poston #AT2512 and
      J. Wilson #AU5200
Re: Proposal to Institute Freedom Committee

The Freedom Committee

Overview

The Freedom Committee is a panel of inmates on Facility-A who desire
to make the rehabilitation, religious, and educational facilities the main
focus of our prison community. It is not uncommon for an inmate to ask: "What
kind of programs are available here? How do I sign up for religious services?"
Or, "How do I get into voluntary G.E.D.?

With all that Facility-A has to offer in regards to the above common
inquiries, there is still a disconnect between actual program availability,
their promotion, and inmate access to these services. We've discovered that
simply posting information in the dayroom does not suffice. The Freedom Committee
wants to change this condition by making rehabilitation, religious service,
and academic pursuits more attractive and accessible for interested and willing
inmates on Facility-A without coercion, proselytizing, or prompting inmates
decision-making toward any specific self-help group. We want to collect the
dots and connect them.

Function of Committee: Membership and Think-Tank

In order to accomplish our goal we intend to enpanel a diverse group
of 14 inmates to meet twice a month to operate as a think-tank body, and
will be composed of:

- 4 inmates from building's 1-4, and
- 2 inmates from building 5.

However, the panel is not to exceed 20 inmates at one time. These select
inmates will be either:

- Chairmen or self-help facilitators
- Religious clerks or representatives
- Hub mentors
- School clerks
- Lifers or long-term offenders

The Freedom Committee will operate primarily on three fronts:

(1) As a think-tank to brainstorm on new methods to promote positive programming;

(2) As an outreach group; and,

(3) Community building platform.

Some of the Goal of the Freedom Committee: Outreach

Listed below are some outreach aims set to be achieved by the Freedom Committee:

- To publish a 1 page news letter (typed or handwritten) at least every 30 days and circulate it to:

    1. Hub Mentors
    2. School Clerks
    3. Religious Clerks and Reps
    4. Self-Help Facilitators; and,
    5. A select group of inmates in each building.

This short news letter will cover important issues related to:

- Self-help groups
- Rac-Credit and Milestone info
- List of building (Rac-Credit and Milestone) facilitators
- New Laws
- Uplifting quotes from religious and historical figures
- Relevant and factual info related to Facility-A program; including sports tournaments, events, outside visitors, etc.

Our goal is to ensure that important information is making it to people (mentors, facilitators, etc.) who are in a position to share it with other inmates in their classes, groups, work areas, or housing units. We want to build a cohesive and comprehensive community.

Further Operations of Committee: Community Building

The Freedom Committee will also oversee:

1. The write our wrongs book project. We will select ten new inmates every 120 days to participate in this publishing process.
2. Assist inmates (via the lifer support group, etc.) with preparing for parole, pardons, or commutations.
3. Hosting special community events like: facilitator symposiums, Pledge

For Peace, interfaith religious dialogues, tournaments, talent shows, etc.;
and,
4. Informing inmates of the availability of religious, educational, and
rehabilitation options on Facility-A; and,
5. Teaching and inviting inmates to their civic duty to support their own
community's health and progress.

There are various information sources inmates are unaware of, for instance:
San Quentin News, Lifer's Alliance, Initiate Justice, and a standard local
newspaper. Freedom of the Press does not mean full access to the press. We
recognize that some inmates do not have T.V.s, lack family support, function
in uninformed "circles", and even lack quality reading skills.

The Freedom Committee wants to bridge these gaps and use information
and leadership as the instrument to make our community integral, informed,
and prepared for any possible release or long-term prison stay.

The Freedom Committee will operate by the following by-laws:

1. Invite and enpanel a diverse committee of 14-20 inmates.
2. Meet at least twice a month. Anyone can sponsor or oversee our 2 hour
meeting (a c/o, a chaplain, a self-help sponsor, etc.) in the gym, yard,
chapel, etc.
3. Present a written itinerary for participants and the C.R.M.'s for
each meeting detailing our aims, discussions, and findings.
4. Publish a newsletter once a month for circulation of relevant programming
and parole information.
5. Oversee the Write Our Wrongs publishing project.
6. Operate with non-bias toawards and religious or self-help group.
No member will coerce or proselytize.
7. Function with complete transparency and integrity, and set no agenda
outside of what is set forth in our overview, goals, and by-laws.
8. Work toward ensuring that form 2016's are available for sign-ups
for self-help groups.

9. Assist inmates of any religious faith with making contact with a
representative of their choice.
10. Seek to hold some form of community event at least every 120 days
to bring a diverse segment of the community together for creative enterprise
or educational exposure.

Freedom Committee's

Ultimate Aim

This committee's ultimate goal is to prepare inmates for their eventual release back into society. In order to achieve this goal we intend to engage in:

-Self-Help Groups

-Community Events

-Board Preparation and

-Job Readiness.

We will seek the fullest range of exposure from available resources to provide inmates with valueable information in order to give them their best opportunity inside and outside of prison.

Example of the Itinerary Report:

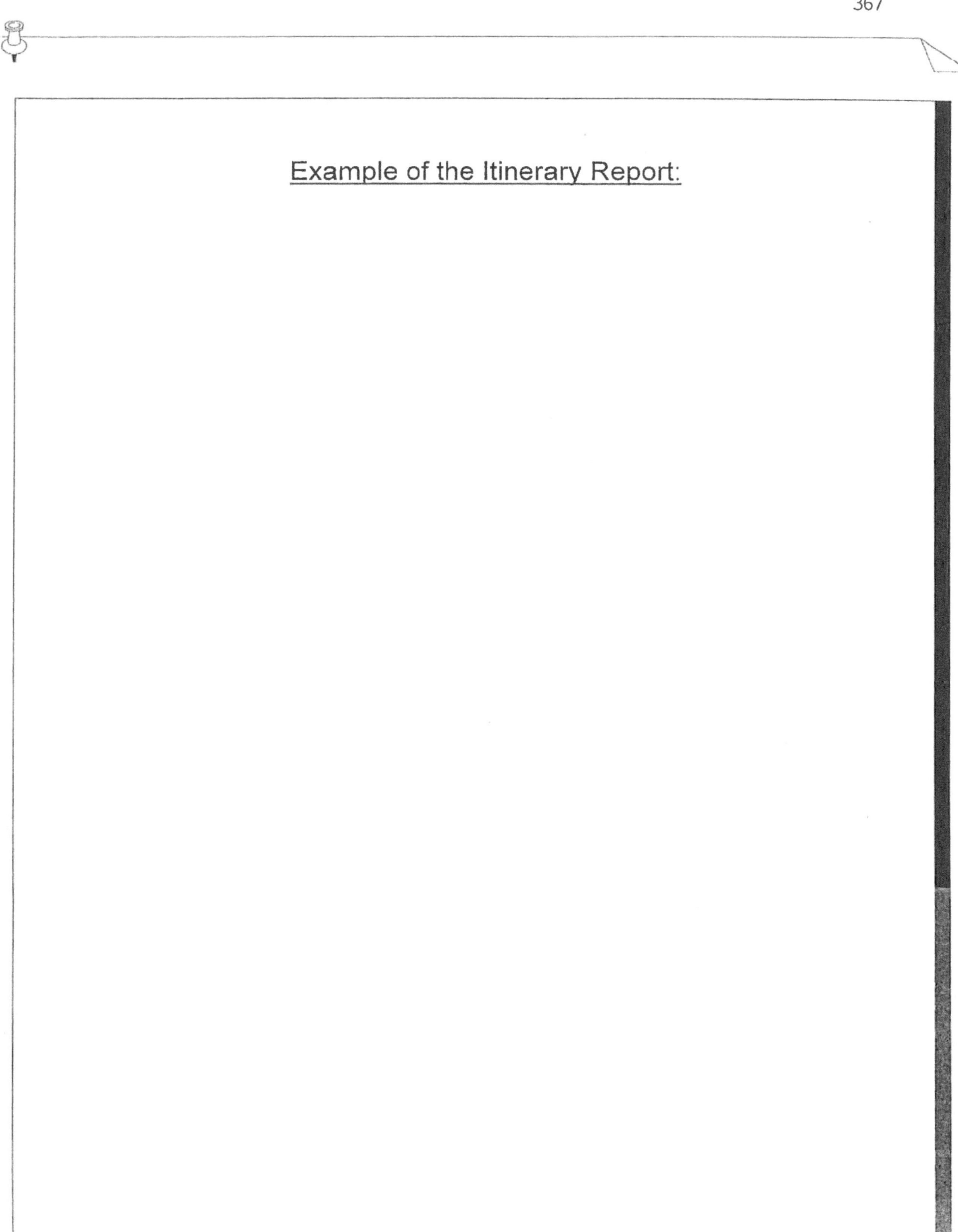

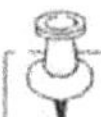

Freedom Committee
Monthly Itinerary Report

Month:_______________   Year:_______________

Panel members present:___

Tabled for Discussion

-
-
-
-
-
-
-

Monthly Goals

-
-
-
-
-
-

Request, Updates, and Reports to CRM's Office

LEADERSHIP COURSE

THE ISLAMIC COMMUNITY, SCHOOL OF P.E.A.C.E. AND SELF-IMPROVEMENT CLASS

Presents

THE LEADERS OF THE FUTURE WORKSHOP

A BRIEF GUIDE FOR LEADERSHIP DISCUSSIONS...

"The spirit of the Lord is upon me.. to free the prisoners."—Prophet Jesus

By: James Wilson, Donel Poston, & Michael Adams

"If you want to know what a nation is like,
Visit it's prisons"-Nelson Mandela
(Former South African Prisoner)

"Regimes may come and go, but Prison's go on forever, although change occurs within its walls. When a revolution succeeds, the gates of the prison are opened and the prisoners, victims of the regime that has just fallen, go free, literally on their heels, the gates close on new prisoners, victims of the new regime that has just been set up.

Humanity is still waiting for the revolution that will not exchange prisoners but will do away

with prisons."-Menachen Begin
(Former Prisoner in Russia)

"I went from ex-con to icon"-Danny Trejo
INTRODUCTION

This is a basic curriculum. It is not designed to cover every aspect of what a Leader is. The purpose of this information is to provoke thought and also stimulate dialogue about the noble principle of guidance that we call Leadership. This brief material will cover three (3) topics:

1. What Leaders do
2. What leaders shouldn't do
3. What kind of leaders are you?

You will not be criticized for your answer. But prepare to elaborate on any of your input if called upon.

LEADERSHIP METHOD

1. <u>A Leader is observant.</u> -He observes talent, skills, and circumstances too.
2. <u>A Leader analyzes</u> -Where others talents and skills (and circumstances) can be used to overcome a problem or reach a goal.
3. <u>A Leader deputizes</u> -He knows how to delegate based on his observations.
4. <u>A Leader organizes</u> - After he selects positions based on skillset, he organizes people, resources and plans to fulfill a goal.
5. <u>A Leader supervises</u> –He evaluates his decisions as they relate to people, positions, and outcomes.

WHAT IS YOUR SKILLS OR TALENTS?

1.

2.

3.

4.

"Leaders solve problems and satisfy human needs."

PROBLEM-SOLVING METHODS
SCIENTIFIC METHOD

- Observe the problem
- State the problem
- Analyze the problem
- Develop a hypothesis (or educated guess as to why the problem exist)
- Test the hypothesis (to see if it matches your Observations)
- Produce your result (true or false)

COMPLETE EXERCISE BELOW
OBSERVING PROBLEMS

UNFULFILLED NEEDS	CREATE PROBLEMS	THAT LEADERS SOLVE
1. Lack of Education		
2. Poverty (insufficient basic needs: Food, clothing, healthcare, etc.		
3. Poor social conditions (negative living conditions: Ghetto, Barrio, Trailer Park, etc.		

"True Leaders are problem-solvers."

LIST SOME OF THE PROBLEMS THAT EXIST IN OUR COMMUNITIES THAT NEED TO BE SOLVED, IN PRISON OR THE FREE WORLD.

(Stating Problems)

1.

2.

3.

4.

5.

6.

7.

"Prison was my Monastery"-Mahatma Ghandi

Topic 1: What Leaders Do?

Leaders Create Opportunities

Opportunity is defined as: Favorable circumstances or outcomes; a good chance for advancement or progress.

Analyzing Solutions to Problems

What are some opportunities a Leader should create? (And do they solve some of the problems listed on the previous page?)

A.

B.

C.

D.

What type of character should a leader of opportunity possess? List some of the qualities below:

A.

B.

C.

D.

E.

F.

Note: Remember the following quote, *"Good conduct opens doors that knowledge can't"*.

There are a few ways Leaders of opportunity are described. Below are a few ways Leaders exercise or put their knowledge to the test:

1) Leaders open doors.
2) Leaders build bridges.
3) Leaders create institutions.
4) Leaders stand up for what's right and against what's wrong.
5) Leaders are problem-solvers.

QUESTIONS

What is a "door" to you?

1.

2.

3.

4.

5.

6.

What does "building bridges" mean to you?

-
-
-

What institutions are our communities most in need of and why?

-
-
-
-

What problem(s) are you working to solve in your community?

1.   3.

2.   4.

Name one Leader you believe stood up for what was right. What did he challenge (past or present)?

Examine Some Results

Do you know of any Leaders that built institutions that serve people's needs today? Who is he or she? What did they build?

❖

❖

❖

"False ideas are the worst kind of oppression"-
Muhammad, (The Prophet of Islam)

Topic 2: What shouldn't a Leader do?

Character is defined as: one of the attributes or features that describe an individual.

Here are some of the examples of good qualities, just a few;

➢ A Leader is a protector.

➢ A Leader is firm.

➢ A Leader is a provider.

➢ A Leader is honest.

➢ A Leader can be trusted.

➢ A Leader is courageous.

➢ A Leader is compassionate.

Now that we know what a quality is, tell us some qualities a Leader shouldn't display or possess.

"A man can walk out of prison to be a King"-King Solomon

A Leader shouldn't be:

-
-
-
-
-
-

Do you know of a person called a Leader that has these negative qualities above? Who is that person?

"In a country that imprisons man falsely, the place for a righteous man is then in prison"-**Henry David Thoreau**

<u>Backstory</u>

There is an old saying; "Do not look for Africa's Leaders in school. But look for them from in prison".

This quote had its origin in a time when African countries had been invaded by foreigners' and all of the men were being arrested and imprisoned.

But this is not unique to just Africa, you will find that that large scale men, were imprisoned in parts of Asia, Europe, Latin America, and now the crisis of mass incarceration in north America. So many men have been locked up that it is predictable that, "the Leaders of the future will come out of prison".

"I put prison second to college as the best place for a man to get an education" **Malcolm X**

<u>Topic 3: What kind of Leader are you?</u>

Use the information provided and developed in topics 1 and 2.

<u>What are you doing for the people?</u>

❖ Are you opening doors? If so, which ones?

❖ Are you building bridges? If so, which ones?

❖ Are you creating Institutions (or opportunities)? If so, how?

<u>How would you describe your character? What are your strong points?</u>

1.

2.

3.

4.

5.

<u>What are things you need to work on?</u>

<u>1.</u>

<u>2.</u>

<u>3.</u>

<u>4.</u>

<u>5.</u>

"Our job is to transform the criminal mind into a revolutionary mind."-George Jackson

List some men and women who went to prison and came out and were successful-What did they do?

1.

2.

3.

4.

5.

6.

7.

8.

9.

"Not a prison of brick and bars, but one of laws and policies."

Breaking the Law

The second prison project is a prison reform group. They report that there are thousands of laws across the United States which affects a parolee's chance at employment, education, loans, and housing.

How do we overcome (or break) these laws?

1.

2.

3.

4.

5.

6.

7.

8.

9.

10.

BIO

BIO
BUILDING INDIVIDUAL OWNERSHIP

Nathan Ramazzini - Ray Anthony Bracamonte Sr.

Table of Contents

Dedication

First and foremost the workshops, literature and autobiographies of (BIO) Building Individual Ownership is dedicated to the victims of our lives:

Daniel Edward Cox and Erik Ingebretsen.

We also dedicate this work to the family and friends of our victims, our own families, and to the community impacted by our crimes and society as a whole. Including, but not limited to:

The responding police officers, initial crime scene investigators, paramedics, corners, and medical examiners. The detectives who were looking for us while we were on the run as fugitives, arresting officers, district attorneys, attorney generals, public defenders, paid attorneys and our preliminary trial and sentencing judges.

The tax payers for our court fees and yearly incarceration. Both members of BIO, the Founder Ray Anthony Bracamonte Sr. and Co. Founder Nathan Ramazzini; acknowledge and understand the pain we have inflicted on those we harmed, this includes psychological, emotional, spiritual and financial effects, as well as the breakdown of the family and social stability.

We also dedicate our service of work to the state senators and assembly members who believed in a second chance for youth offenders, passing AB1308 (STONE) and SB394 (Lara and Mitchell) the vision of your heart's are not in vain.

BIO would like to be the first towards demonstrating rehabilitation for youth offenders.

Finally we dedicate our life's work to every citizen who voted to pass these laws, wrote letters of support and campaigned to change the laws. We are eternally grateful for you. Each and every one of you played a major role in helping those whom we wanted to reach while creating the material for our self-help group.

Special Thanks: I would like to extend a special thanks to my dear sister Roberta Bracamonte for taking the time to edit, type and format the BIO literature, all while serving the community in great capacity working in the medical field during the Covid-19 Pandemic. Through this process we have both found the closure and healing needed for a healthy lasting reconciliation. I love you, and we will change the world together.

Ray & Roberta Bracamonte

Introduction

The biographies (we) Ray A. Bracamonte Sr. and Nathan Ramazzini put together are about making the connections from our past in order to understand who we are today. Growing up we never understood why we felt the way we did or why we made the decisions we did. We felt alone in the world and felt like nobody could ever understand what we were feeling or what we were going through.

It took a long time to realize that all of the negative, hurtful and painful events in our lives had caused us to feel all of these negative things, which we held deep inside of us. We built up an identity based on all of those negative feelings. We then acted out on all of those negative feelings by transferring the hurt and pain (we) felt inside on to others in ugly, destructive and violent ways. It felt good, even powerful, getting these things out. The more we acted in this manner, this type of behavior made more sense and soon seemed normal to us. We even felt protected and safe by this. It led us to do terrible things including murdering another human being.

We wrote these workshops based on our life events. As changed men, we now look back with deep sorrow and regret for the destructive and violent ways we lived our lives and for the people we have hurt along the way. Being able to open up and speak about our life events was a major step towards our self-healing. It is our hope that whomever reads our literature will connect to the life events we have shared and also connect with some of the emotions we have felt. (Just know that you are not alone.)

We have opened our lives to you to show that it is normal to feel the things you feel, and have the thoughts you do. The big difference is what you do with those feelings and thoughts. The decisions you make, your actions; those are the things that will live on in ways which you no longer have control over.

We have been in your shoes, locked up as teenagers and young adults. The truth is that we are still living with the consequences of our feelings and thoughts that lead us to those acts of violence. Often we get asked- if we could go back to the beginning, "what is the one thing you would do differently?" Answer: Be brave enough to ask for help and talk about whatever we were going through.

We are here for you:

Ray Anthony Bracamonte Sr. CDC# K-85547

Nathan Ramazzini CDC# P-04587

Becoming A Part of BIO

PHASE ONE

In a group setting format:

Phase One consist of 13 topics that are broken up into 36 weeks of:

- Intense Self –Examining

- Exploring Causative Factors

- Emotional Stability

- Destructive Behavior

All of which encompasses both Negative and Positive Life Span Development.

Emotional Neglect/ Passive Abuse

We deal with many forms of neglect on a daily basis. We witness these things at home, media, school, work, in public and every social setting imaginable. However, when it comes to children; Emotional Neglect/Passive Abuse from parents or care givers take place for many different reasons. On many levels, in every age group and in every walk of life. It usually takes the form of withholding love, affection, support, guidance, correction or through rejection, abandonment, and threats, constant criticism, isolation, corruption and exploitation. This demonstrates a pattern of negative behaviors that interferes with and influences the emotional development of a child's well-being, self-worth and the ability to interpret and process life events properly.

1. Household:

Situation / Problem – Ray: Growing up there was a lot of partying, drinking, drugs, overdoses, arrests, yelling, cussing and fighting at all hours. When parties were at my house, my uncles and step dad would get drunk and make my cousins and I fight for money. I was forced to go to school tired or some days I was given the opportunity to stay home from elementary school. When I needed help with homework I'd be told "figure it out" or "you see what happens when you don't go to school stupid" or "hold on, I'll be right there" but "right there" never came. My step dad and older sister would tell me to cheat and copy the answers from someone in class. That is exactly what I did for most of elementary school.

Situation / Problem – Nathan: As an only child, I grew up with both parents in the home. However, both my parents were emotionally distant. They both worked full time jobs, and rarely interacted with me. Shortly after giving birth to me, my mom went back to work. Throughout my childhood I was cared for by different women in their homes. Each of them had their own unique ways of raising me. At home all of my tangible needs were met (food, clothing, hygiene, etc.) but conversations, life lessons, affirmations and quality time was non-existent. I was given a toy(s) to play with alone. During weeknights and weekends we all spent time in different parts of the home. We never ate meals together as a family, nor did my father spend any time playing with me, helping with school work, or teaching me anything. I became emotionally disturbed, when my disabled grandpa suddenly died. No explanation was given to me.

Internal: We felt lost, confused, unimportant, unwanted, hurt, lonely, inadequate, unsure and angry. This lead to the beginning of our low self-esteem.

External: We began to act out for attention; talking back, not doing homework, refusing to do chores, lying and ignoring our superiors when they tried talking to us.

Consequences: We began to hold everything in. We were unable to relate to others who seemed to be engaging with their parents, relatives or siblings. We became jealous of their relationships. We lost respect towards authority figures. We felt worthless and were labeled as troublemakers and gave our households a bad name.

<u>Solutions / Coping Skills:</u> Today, we are able to identify people, places and things that trigger us and bring up the emotions we once ran from. We understand emotions are a gift from God, they help guide and protect us. We have experienced the power of self-forgiveness and have forgiven others. Today we are in control of ourselves and no longer blame others for how we feel.

Questions for the Class:

1. Were you able to speak truthfully about your feelings to your parents or caregiver?

2. How did you cope with loneliness or rejection?

3. What extremes did you go to, to get your parents or caregivers attention?

4. How do you act today when your needs are not being met?

5. Do you use emotional neglect and abuse to punish others?

Emotional Neglect/ Passive Abuse

2. Outside of Household:

Situation / Problem – Ray: Expressing myself in disruptive, needy, challenging, angry and defiant manners outside of the home was easy and a new freedom. However, it brought negative attention to me. In elementary school the teacher would make me stand in the corner and face the wall while the other children were told to laugh at me. This was my punishment for being the class clown. As a kid I stuttered; to belittle me the teacher would make me do the reading, knowing the class was going to laugh and make fun of me for not being able to pronounce the words. During my first time at juvenile hall I was placed in a cell alone. I began to kick the door because I did not want to be there. The staff came to the cell door and told me "if you don't stop kicking the door, you will have something special coming to you." At the time I did not know what that meant, so I continued to kick the door. About 10 minutes later the door opened and 2 kids came into the cell and beat me up. There were times I'd go to the store with my cousins, sister, mom or other family members and roam around only to get stopped and accused of stealing something.

Situation / Problem – Nathan: Outside of home I expressed my pent up and confused emotional states in a loud, disruptive and angry way. I was free to challenge anyone over any situation. This lead to conflicts with my peers, teachers and other authority figures. At school I was told to sit outside the classroom because I could not "act normal." I was sent to the principal's office and was constantly asked what was wrong with me? I was sent home and told they did not want me at school. On the playground at recess, the catholic priest would grab me and force me to sit next to him. He would shake me and hiss that I was "bad" and "no good." I was often called names and told to shut up by teachers and other adults. I was forced to isolate myself because I couldn't "play nice" with others and not be "disruptive."

Internal: We felt isolated, hated, angry, resentful, embarrassed, confused, scared, alone, humiliated, betrayed, not accepted and abandoned.

External: We became aggressive, prejudice, closed off and standoffish. We wore a mask to cover up the pain and hurt, acting as if everything was okay. We eventually stopped trusting people.

Consequences: We began to question everything and everyone. We could not be ourselves around people. Our parents, family, teachers, and friends did not want to be around us or want us around certain kids; in fear that we would corrupt them. We were not to be trusted, we were also accused of things we did not do.

Solutions / Coping Skills: Today, we are comfortable with who we are, we no longer seek attention through negative behaviors. We enjoy our solitude, we are able to trust others without judging them. Treating others the way we would like to be treated. We follow and respect the rules and laws. Respecting those we work for and work with.

Questions for the Class:

1. Have you ever been accused of something you did not do? How did that make you feel and act?

2. Does your behavior still get you in trouble? If so, how?

3. How do you view authority figures today? Do you treat them all the same?

4. Do you make fun of those who are being picked on? Or those who are not as smart as you?

5. What have you learned about yourself?

Emotional Neglect/ Passive Abuse

3. Inconsistent Affection/Mixed Messages:

Situation / Problem – Ray: Growing up, my step dad and uncles would take me and my cousins to be lookouts when they broke into garages and empty apartments. My older sister would take me to the store to be her lookout while she stole make-up and hairspray. When I got caught stealing marbles and Big League chewing gum; I was hit and grounded. I did not understand. I asked my stepdad, uncles and sister "why am I being punished?" They would all laugh and say "you are not supposed to get caught!" I was the only boy in my family and when my sisters were gone I would try to help around the house by washing dishes or vacuuming. When my stepdad would see me doing this, he would say "are you gay?" or "Cleaning the house is for women!"

Situation / Problem – Nathan: As a child, I was put into sports and Boy Scouts and over time I became good at it. I hoped my dad would be proud of me but he rarely made it to my games or events. When he did come to watch he never told me I played good or that he was proud of me. I would ask him to practice with me, but he was always too tired. At times he would get involved but it never lasted long. I found it difficult to work up the courage to ask him for help in the future. I felt he was telling me I was not good enough. I was an only child born to parents who had already been married for 15 years. They showed me little attention in teaching me life lessons or helping me build my self-esteem. They would interact with me when they were relaxed and in a good mood from drinking alcohol; but mostly I was ignored.

Internal: We felt confused, lost, belittled, not appreciated, forgotten, hurt, irritated, frustrated, rejected, angry, and not needed. We formed low self-esteem.

External: Our facial expressions looked sad and angry. Our body language became sluggish and aggressive. We began to throw personal issues in our families faces and blame others when things did not go our way.

Consequences: We overreacted to situations and began to personalize everything. We did not know how to control our actions. We reacted in extreme ways to emotions we did not understand.

Solutions / Coping Skills: Today, when someone lies to us or we receive mixed messages; we ask for clarification without taking things personal. We understand that everyone has bad days and past issues they may be dealing with, not everyone has found the closure they need to move on. We no longer feel that we are solely responsible for other people's feelings or actions. We have now set healthy boundaries in our lives and no longer allow negative influences to control our emotions, thoughts, speech conduct and actions. We use our healthy coping skills to process our feelings.

<u>Questions for the Class:</u>

1. When people say "do as I say, not as I do" how does that make you feel? How do you act upon those feelings?

2. How do you feel when family or friends push you to pursue a sport or education, give you help, and then put you down? How do you act upon those feelings?

3. When trying to help out, only to be looked down on, mocked and told "I don't need you" How does that make you feel? And how do you act upon those feelings?

4. When someone you love asks you to do something wrong, is it hard to say No, Why?

5. After accomplishing a task, someone says "you could have done more" how does that make you feel, how do you act upon those feelings?

Summary: By understanding how the lack of emotional support played a role in us creating a warped belief system, developing low self- esteem and loss of identity. We are now more responsible for our feelings, thoughts and actions. Today we are able to treat one another including ourselves with the respect we all need and deserve to be productive in our communities and social relationships.

Molestation/ Child Sexual Abuse

Child Sexual Abuse always involves a child's inability to comprehend, process and respond correctly. From experience and knowledge, to the manipulation, coercion, bribery and deceptive persuasion of someone in a position of influence and power; such as: parents, step parents, siblings, uncles, aunts, grandparents, neighbors, baby sitters, teachers, coaches, doctors, clergy and friends. A key factor for an abuser is to take advantage of a child's trust through betrayal.

There are two types of Childhood Sexual Abuse:

A. **Physical Contact:** Which involves sexual intercourse; anal or vaginal penetration, oral sex, masturbation and fondling.
B. **Non-Physical Contact:** Which involves indecent exposure, forced to watch pornographic movies or magazines, seductive facial expressions, sounds or suggestions.

1. Sexual Emotional Trauma:

Situation / Problem – Ray: In my adolescent years (age 10) I had no preconceived notion, desire or craving of anything sexual. My sister's dad took advantage of my innocence through bribery and catering to the things he knew I enjoyed, sports, skateboards, bikes, cartoons, movies, having fun and laughing. The first encounter began with him saying "you look bored, do you want to watch a grown- up movie?" Naturally I responded enthusiastically and said "Yes" hoping to watch something action packed like Rocky, Rambo, or something scary. He put on the movie; we sat down on the couch and not soon after he said, "this is where it gets exciting." I remember the grin on his face. To my amazement the woman in the movie began to flirt and act very seductively with a man, licking her lips, rubbing on his thigh and private parts. Which led them to having sex. My sisters' dad told me "boys, men and woman love to act like this because it brings them closer together."

Situation / Problem – Nathan: At the age of 9 years old, I had no sexual desires or any understanding of how sexuality played into relationships with others. At that age, an older neighborhood boy; who was my friend, began to molest me. The first encounters began with non-physical contact in the form of exposing private parts. This led to physical contact in the form of touching and sexual acts. Over the next year; these sexual acts took place in many different locations. (Anytime we were alone) He told me "this is what friends do to show they care for one another." I was confused as to what was going on, but began to see these acts as gestures of friendship.

Internal: We did not know how to feel or how to act. We were in shock, confused, nervous, excited, feeling accepted, cared for, special and important because we had our own secret. Their actions told us that we were trusted and able to handle what boys, men and women do.

External: We became more energetic and adventurous. We were able to keep the secret and act as if nothing happened. We drew closer to them and always wanted to be around them.

Consequences: We became co/dependent to them and sought their approval. We became bored when that person was not around. We lost interest in school and sports. In some ways we even thought we were better than other kids our age.

Solutions / Coping Skills: Today, we are aware of what we are feeling and when triggered we are able to remain in the present. We understand healthy acceptance is being liked and appreciated for who we are with no strings attached. Today we are comfortable relying on our past experiences, knowledge and wisdom in situations that are unforeseeable (or) unpredictable.

Questions for the Class:

1. Have you ever been unable to interpret someone's affection for you? How do you feel when this happens?

2. Have you ever become co/dependent because someone pays attention to you? How do you act when this happens?

3. Have you ever, or do you still use manipulation tactics to get your way? If so, how?

4. How do you feel when you read, hear, or watch someone on TV being molested by a person they should be able to trust?

5. Do you still seek acceptance even though you know you are losing a part of yourself?

Molestation/ Child Sexual Abuse

2. Betrayal:

Situation / Problem – Ray: The molestation began to intensify as I grew emotionally attached to my step dad. All the one on one attention and affection I would get from my stepdad, along with the gifts and privileges I would receive in front of my mom and sisters kept me completely dependent on him for happiness, direction and acceptance. In a short amount of time I began to realize I had been tricked, manipulated, lied too and deceived about the sexual morality of what we were doing. What added to the realization of betrayal was each time he did not get his way, I would be ignored. Given no affection or support from him. He would refuse to attend any of my soccer or baseball games.

Situation / Problem – Nathan: As the molestation continued, I became more attached to my friend because the sexual contact was a new intimate foundation that our friendship was built upon. At the time these acts were forms of attention, affection and affirmation that I was not receiving from any other person in my life. However over time I began to notice the dynamic of these acts; they only took place when we were alone or hidden away. When we were around others he would act differently, as if we were not close friends. He would tell me it was our secret and not to tell anyone. I soon began to realize that what was happening was not normal. I felt like I was doing something wrong; something I was tricked into doing.

Internal: We felt rejected, devalued, abandoned, alone, confused, unwanted, forgotten, afraid, angry, betrayed, resentment, hurt, depressed and anxiety.

External: Without any good reasons, we made strong efforts to avoid our parents and family members. At times we ran away from home. We did not want to change our clothes in front of others. (Especially older males.) Sometimes we wet the bed and had no appetite most days.

Consequences: We began to lack trust in ourselves as well as others. We played mind games with people to see if they would pay attention to us. If they did, we believed they loved us. If not, we pushed them away by treated them rude and unfair. We developed emotional and mental health issues. We felt too damaged to love or to be loved. Finally we lacked the ability to sustain healthy relationships.

Solutions / Coping Skills: Today, we are able to regulate our emotions properly. We set boundaries with people who are unfair, one sided or hostile towards us. We are able to address how we feel by communicating in healthy and effective ways. Today we can identify when our time, love and friendship is being abused. We know it is ok to say "No" in any situation when it is not in our best interest. We also understand that terminating a relationship is a part of life. It keeps us safe in our recovery.

Questions for the Class:

1. When you are lied to and betrayed by someone you love and respect, how do you feel and how do you act?

2. How does it make you feel when you get all of someone's attention but it stops because you refuse to be manipulated, How does that effect you mentally and emotionally?

3. When did you begin to manipulate family, friends and boys/girls, and in what ways?

4. What consequences do you still experience because of someone you looked up to and trusted abused you in some form or fashion?

5. When you have done nothing wrong, how do you handle being ignored?

Molestation/ Child Sexual Abuse

3. Powerlessness:

Situation / Problem – Ray: Growing up without a voice in the home had already made a negative impact on my life. I was taught not to call the cops because they would only break up our home and place us children in foster care away from everyone we loved. Having that belief system already established; I did not know what to do or how to make it stop. I tried to tell my stepdad "No, please stop", "I don't want to do this anymore, its wrong" but he would say "shut up," and against my will he would continue to invade my body space. I felt trapped and did not understand how I got into this situation. I was unable to express myself correctly. He would often make me believe it was my fault and that I deserved it by saying things like "you had a smile on your face" "you said you enjoyed making me happy" and "You did not say no when I gave you money or bought you gifts." He always used my words against me.

Situation / Problem – Nathan: Growing up as an only child in an emotionally distant home, I never felt like I could go to my parents for help. I already viewed authority figures as a source of ridicule and pain. (Not to be trusted) I never had any contact with the police. I felt trapped and insecure about how to stop the molestation. I avoided my friend but when he isolated me and began to molest me; I could not get any words out and simply went along with it. One day my dad walked into my room while the molestation was taking place. To this day, I do not know exactly what he witnessed. I felt powerless to say anything. After that day, the molestation stopped. Neither my dad nor I ever spoke about this.

Internal: We felt guilt and shame, self-directed anger and blame. We felt empty, hopeless, frightened, fearful of our future and alone. We developed low self-esteem, anxiety, depression and believed we were worthless.

External: We became protective of others (especially of my sisters) we felt safe by distancing ourselves from others. We were hyperactive and vigilant. (Which got us into trouble) We were passive and then very aggressive. We began to cuss people out.

Consequences: We gravitated towards people who were broken, delinquents, thieves, daredevils and had no respect for authority. We had compassion for others our age but not for ourselves.

Solutions / Coping Skills: Today, when someone tries to assert power over us, we understand we have a voice and a choice to say "NO!" We have learned to address our past causative factors and acknowledge the consequences of not being able to regulate our emotions or by ignoring them and holding them in. Today we have taken our lives back by establishing a new belief system built upon healthy and positive morals. Principals and ethics that have sustained us in both good and bad times. We have self-worth and confidence in our ability to make choices based on positive values.

<u>Questions for the Class:</u>

1. When someone invades your privacy after you told them "No" how do you feel? How do you respond with your actions?

2. When you experienced peer pressure as a child or teenager, how did it affect your choices and shape your belief system?

3. How does it make you feel, when someone uses something personal against you to get their way?

4. What does being trapped mean to you?

5. Do you know why you assert your power over another person when they are weaker then you?

Molestation/ Child Sexual Abuse

4. Stigmatization:

Situation / Problem – Ray: Having a gay cousin named Dominique, and seeing him be mistreated by his parents only caused me to keep the molestation a secret. My grandma was very religious and she would tell my cousin "God does not love you," "God did not make you that way." My uncles had been to prison and were gang members. So, whenever a homosexual would be on TV or a child molester on the news: they would say "They need to die!" and by my stepdad telling me "this is our secret! Nobody can find out because we will get in trouble." I understood what he meant.

Situation / Problem – Nathan: After being pressured into sexual acts by my friend, I became more aware of my society's views on sexuality. Hearing the words "fagot, homo & queer" and playing the tackle game "smear the queer" with other boys I began to understand that my small religious community was not accepting of homosexual behavior. At that time there was no openly gay people in my community. I realized that homosexuals were hated and viewed as less than. After my dad walked in on me being molested, he became even more of a distant figure in my life. I was confused and afraid of ever speaking about this secret because of how people would react, and view the behavior I had been involved in.

Internal: We felt trapped, lost, confused, mentally, emotionally and physically drained, depressed, and full of anger. Resentful, misunderstood, and helpless, without an identity.

External: We continued to act like everything was okay when it wasn't. Out of nowhere we would get an attitude, even when people were nice to us. Other times we would be nice to everyone around the house to get attention. We began to lie and manipulate in order to get our way. We started to act tough and mistreat people. I (Ray) would play rough with my sisters because I was angry they had a dad.

Consequences: When we became angry we were unable to stop ourselves from mistreating people. We continued to hold things in and keep secrets. We began to play mind games with people to see if they really cared about us. We began to hate child molesters and homosexuals.

Solutions / Coping Skills: Today, we live by spiritual principles found in the Serenity Prayer - God, Grant me the *Serenity* to accept the things I cannot change, the *Courage* to change the things I can, and the *Wisdom* to know the difference. Today we can no longer blame people for our actions. We know we have the power of choice in any situation. We accept people for who they are. We live with compassion and empathy for those who still struggle, and for those who have experienced childhood molestation or any other form of sexual abuse.

Questions for the Class:

1. Do what others think about you matter? Does it change how you think, speak, treat yourself or others?

2. Does it still bother you when people do not accept you because someone has labeled you a murderer, child molester, liar, violent predator, homosexual, different, quitter or untrustworthy? If so, Why?

3. Do you blame God for what happened to you?

4. Have you forgiven yourself for the abuse that took place, the abuse was not your fault you did not ask for it?

5. Do you or have you put labels on someone else to keep the heat off of yourself?

Summary: There is hope of recovery for all who have been molested. The first step is to report it to someone; a teacher, counselor, police officer, school principal, family member, or a friend who is not associated with the abuser. This will allow the door of communication to release you from what has kept you in bondage. You will find the proper support you need to bring healing, closure, forgiveness and a new beginning as a survivor. You are not alone and you deserve to feel safe, respected and valued.

Domestic Violence/Child Abuse

Domestic Violence does not discriminate. The perpetrator exists within heterosexual and same-sex relationships. It does not matter your age, race, background or economic status. The perpetrator exercises domestic control over the victim's free will to choose. They strip away their identity and ability to think, feel and act for themselves. This is done by using the victim's failures, weakness, insecurities, regrets and losses to create the guilt and shame needed to keep the victim isolated from family and friends, as well as being dependent on the abuser. There are three key phases of Domestic Violence: 1. Intimidation (tension building) 2. Violent 3. Honeymoon.

1. Intimidation Phase:

Situation / Problem – Ray: Growing up in my household was like walking on eggshells. Anything would set off my stepdad. Especially when he was drinking or strung out on drugs. Over time I began to spot when things were wrong and tension was beginning to build. There would be silence in the house. My sisters and I were not allowed to play. Every sound got on my stepdads nerves, causing my mom to become stressed and pace the house making sure no lights were on, windows opened, or appliances left on. (If they were not currently being used.) If they were on he would cuss my mom out, slam the door, and throw things against the wall breaking the dishes. He would make threats and not answer her, or us kids if we asked any questions. He would give this angry look that said "Say one more word and you know what to expect!" When the tension was really high, my mom would take it out on my sisters & I. We could be eating or doing our homework in the room and my mom would find something to blame us for. She would criticize us for no reason; just like my stepdad did to her.

Situation / Problem – Nathan: My house hold was either strangely quiet or explosively loud. The mood of the house mostly centered on my behaviors. It was a source of dispute between my parents. They would argue with tense words, rush off into their bedroom and slam the door. When they had disagreements; my mom would yell my dad's name in high pitch tones. They would go behind closed doors to settle their issues. After wards they would go their separate ways drinking and smoking in the backyard or washroom. Things in the house would be slammed around, meanwhile I was ignored or getting the death stare if I tried to talk with them. Often, out of nowhere I would be cornered and getting yelled at, called names or pointed at aggressively and told to get out of there sight. I began to notice the ritual of this behavior and would leave the house or stay at a friend's house for as long as possible.

Internal: We felt scared, worthless, powerless, not appreciated. Confused, lost, worried, anxious and depressed.

External: We were often tense and tired. When we were out in public and saw people arguing we would panic and want to be as far away from them as possible. We would clean around the house so my stepdad/parents would have nothing to complain about.

Consequences: We lost the joys of being children. We misunderstood situations by reading too much into things that were said or by not understanding people's body language. I (Ray) began to mistreat my sisters. We began to mistreat people that got in our way. We started to lose empathy and compassion for other people.

Solutions / Coping Skills: Today, we are responsible for our words and actions. We no longer mimic what was exposed to us as children in order to get what we want. We understand people have problems and the only way they feel control is by bullying others to get what they want. Today we no longer have to stay in a toxic work place, home environment, prison cell or friendship. We can choose to exercise our freedom and do something healthy by removing ourselves from a violent situation.

Questions for the Class:

1. How did it feel to be picked on or criticized when you were not doing anything wrong? What went through your mind?

2. What habits did you pick up from your childhood (experiencing the intimidation phase) and use to get your way later on?

3. What did you want to do when you saw your mom/dad living in fear and unable to be yourself?

4. When you look back at your childhood, what options did you really have to get help when violence was in the home?

5. Do you or have you lived with someone at home or in a cell where you had to walk on egg shells because there was always tension? How did you handle the situation?

Domestic Violence/Child Abuse

2. Violent Phase:

Situation / Problem – Ray: The violence would occur because keeping my mom scared was not good enough for my stepdad. He acted like he couldn't stop himself from slapping, punching, or pulling her hair, throwing her down to the floor and kicking her. When we were in public and he got mad, (causing people to stare) he would tell my mom "when we get home I'm going to beat your ass!" I did not understand why he treated her like that, because she always did everything he wanted. Cooking, cleaning, laundry and gave him all of her welfare check. She would lied to the cops and his parole officer to keep him out of jail. There were days I would see my mom being slapped multiple times. The worst thing I experienced as a teen was being asleep and my girlfriend waking me up saying "your mom is screaming for you!" I instantly knew something was wrong. The tone in her voice was full of fear and panic. I grabbed my bat and ran down the hallway to their room and kicked the door open. I saw my mother naked and crying, trying to cover up her breast, she was bleeding from her mouth. My stepdad had his grape knife in his hand. He has just rapped my mother.

Situation / Problem – Nathan: When things turned physical, I would be snatched by the arm; yanked into the room, thrown down then spanked. I remember my mom saying to me "You made me do this to you!" My parents played their roles in this dynamic. She was the judge and jury and my dad was the executioner. Over time these "punishments" became humiliating and I was forced to remove my clothes before being hit. I felt helpless and trapped. I did not understand why I needed to be "punished" like this. As I got older I was shoved and hit with all types of different objects. One time when my dad got drunk; the violence turned dangerous as he attacked me. I tried to get away from him, but my mom had to step in between us holding a knife to stop the attack. She then ordered me to leave the house.

Internal: We felt scared, unprotected, out of place. Confused, powerless, traumatized, unloved, unneeded, shame and guilt for not being able to help my mother. I (Ray) had severe resentments and anger because she let my stepdad back into the home.

External: When we were angry we began to rebel. We became submissive when we could not defend ourselves or when there was too much fear in us. We began to cuss people out and make a scene.

Consequences: I (Ray) began to look down on my mom for not standing up to my stepdad. We thought women were weaker than men. We thought all a man had to do was yell, humiliate a woman or use violence to get what we wanted. We began to exert power and control in our relationships.

Solutions / Coping Skills: Today, we have compassion and empathy for all life. We understand there is no such thing as a victimless crime. We respect the boundaries of others, both their person & property. We have embraced the power of forgiveness. Today the freedom we get from sharing our stories; has put us in a position to help others, giving them hope and helping them find peace and closure in their lives. We have found purpose in being our true selves.

Questions for the Class:

1. When you see a woman being beaten up and yelling for help, with no one helping her, how does that make you feel? What do you do afterwards?

2. Do you look down on women who do not standup for themselves?

3. Are you able to sense when a woman is about to get hit? What emotions arise in you at that moment?

4. If a woman provokes a man by testing him after he told her to "stop or else she is going to get slapped" is he justified by his actions?

5. Do you think you have the responsibility to stop someone who is beating a defenseless woman?

Domestic Violence/Child Abuse

3. Honeymoon Phase:

Situation / Problem – Ray: After my mom would get hit and the yelling stopped, I would notice a pattern in the relationship. My mom would be crying, cleaning up blood or something broken, that was when my sister's dad would begin to talk sweet to her. He would always catch her in a vulnerable state. He would say things like "baby, why do you make me do things like that to you?" "Do you know I cannot live without you?" "Didn't I ask you not to do that? You said you would not do that again, but you continued to do it." "We are both at fault don't you think so?" "The kids heard everything we were first fighting about" "baby there is no reason to go to your mom's or sister's house" "baby if you leave that is only going to teach the kids to give up on their family!" When she would open up and begin to communicate with him; they would go into their bedroom for a long time and come back all happy, like nothing ever happened. He would shower her with gifts.

Situation / Problem – Nathan: After all of the madness calmed down, my parents would be full of smiles. Nice to me and more outgoing. We would order take-out or go out and do something fun. I think it was their way of saying "sorry" without having to actually say it. I used this time to get what I wanted out of them. My parents would make a point of telling me that we did not need to go through all of this, if I would just "act right." Life would get better for a little while, then the whole cycle would start all over again.

Internal: We were very confused on how our moms would forgive them so fast. We did not understand what they would do in the bedroom until we got a little older. They were having sex. I (Ray) wondered what was going through my mom's mind when she saw her bruises or when she saw how the violence scared us kids.

External: When I (Ray) would act out or do something wrong and my mom would get upset with me, I'd throw in her face "why am I getting hit, yelled at, or punished, I don't hit you like my sisters dad!" we lost respect for our parents and any person who tried to tell us "do as I say", but their actions revealed them to be hypocrites.

Consequences: We began to think we could talk our way out of things. We started to lie to women to get our way. We would make promises to women & others only to fulfill half-truths so they wouldn't get upset and leave us. We had no sense of reality and thought all women were the same. We could not deal with rejection from women.

Solutions / Coping Skills: Today, we no longer prey on peoples weaknesses. We own up to our mistakes and take responsibility for our own actions. We try to help people who are lost, confused or do not have any support in their lives. We sign people up for groups; mentor them and become sponsors or accountability partners.

<u>Questions for the Class:</u>

1. How do you feel when the women in your life; sister, niece, daughter, wife, mom, aunt or grandma is being manipulated with lies?

2. Was it easy to manipulate and hurt someone you love? Why or why not?

3. What tactics did you use on women to get them to forgive you?

4. How long did it take you to repeat the domestic violence cycle?

5. How did you know when you began to lose your influence and power on a woman?

Summary: There is help for those who have witnessed domestic violence as children. There is also help for both the victim and the abuser. If you have not experienced domestic violence but think someone you know is being abused in a relationship; pay attention to the warning signs and get them help. The warning signs are: hiding bruises, wearing sunglasses all the time, wearing long sleeve clothing in hot weather, missing social events, family gatherings. Missing school or work often. Isolating themselves, never having any money when they work, not wanting to be seen in public with their partners. Frequent injuries, having unexplained anxiety, fear, mood swings, low self-esteem and depression. Ask them if they need any help. If they make a ridiculous excuse that does not seem to make sense; they may be suffering abuse.

Self-Esteem/Self-Worth

When it comes to Self-Esteem it can be expressed with several descriptions such as:

Self-worth, self-concept, self-image, or self-perception. All of these terms refer to the way we think, feel, view and place value on ourselves. Each person's self-esteem is derived from the child's own subjective evaluation of their upbringing. Whether their belief system is developed negatively or positively, this establishes how they view themselves in the world, and their place in it.

1. Warped Beliefs = Low Self-Esteem:

Situation / Problem – Ray: Growing up in a dysfunctional household where negative messages and put downs were constant, I slowly began to form a warped belief about myself that mirrored what was being told to me. I was told "shut up stupid", "figure it out dummy" and "you are just like your dad; good for nothing and a quitter." I finally met my dad when I was in the 4th grade. I was so excited when my aunt Delia came to pick me up to meet him. I kept asking her "when is my dad coming home?" I ended up falling asleep and was woken up hours later, when I heard keys trying to open the front door. I jumped up, opened the front door and said "Dad!" he took a few steps, and looked down at me and fell down, passing out on top of me; knocking me to the ground. This was my first encounter with my dad. There would be times when it was cold, foggy or raining; my sister's dad would tell us "I'll be there to pick you up from school, so be ready!" But he would never show up.

Situation / Problem – Nathan: Growing up in an emotional distant home was lonely. Not being taught any life lessons by my parents left me feeling unsure about who I was. The negative messages I received from adults; being told "what's wrong with you?" "Why can't you act right?" and "don't be stupid!" it left me with no confidence in myself. Being labeled as "bad" or "no good" and "trouble maker" caused me to have a negative attitude towards myself and others. I began to see myself as the person people told me I was. That I was undesirable. I looked for and found all the negative examples I needed to reinforce these new beliefs. Things like; no one believing me, accusing me of things I did not do, or something being blown out of proportion in embarrassing ways. These beliefs were built upon all of the hurtful, negative, disappointing, and shameful things that had taken place in my life.

Internal: We began to believe we were unlovable, unwanted, unappreciated. Forgotten, unimportant, like a mistake, not needed, not good enough, inferior to people, not able to fit in, unattractive and useless.

External: We stared to lie to get attention. Gravitating towards kids who were older than us and were trouble makers. We wore a mask every day and acted like we were ok. Often the pain was too strong and we could not maintain the mask, we suffered from emotional outbursts.

Consequences: We saw ourselves through the eyes of other people and began to over compensate seeking acceptance and acknowledgement in any way we could find it. We formed a negative warped belief system about ourselves that became unhealthy, unrealistic, and extremely detrimental to our development as people. We strengthened false facts about ourselves as truths, resulting in self-hatred and loss of identity.

Solutions / Coping Skills: Today, we know that we are unique and that there is only one Ray Anthony Bracamonte Sr. and Nathan Ramazzini in the world. We no longer have to over compensate in our lives. We know our self-worth and place value on who we are and all of our positive accomplishments. We have cultivated our talents and recognize the need to share these positive attributes with others.

Questions for the Class:

1. In what areas of your life do you let people still define you?

2. What has over compensating in your life cost you?

3. Do you know what your triggers and warning signs are for low self-esteem?

4. What are some untruths about yourself that you believed as facts?

5. Who have you hurt because of your own self-hatred?

Self-Esteem/Self-Worth

2. Low Self-Esteem & It's Impact:

Situation / Problem – Ray: I was unable to receive compliments from my mom, stepdad, sisters, relatives or friends without second guessing them or myself. I thought they were just trying to appease me and felt sorry for me for some reason. However, compliments from people I didn't know were much easier to receive and believe. I would give gifts to my stepdad, mom, sisters, relatives and friends. I would constantly ask them if they really liked my gift. I had no belief in myself and I second guesses everything I did. I would not ask for help because I thought I knew how that person was going to respond. In relationships, I was unable to speak up for myself. I could not express what my needs were. I constantly compared myself to others and would give up easily if I felt I did not measure up. I did not want to be around social settings in fear that I would be judged. Some days I did not care what I looked like. Other days I wanted to dress better then everyone and needed to look absolutely perfect.

Situation / Problem – Nathan: I became suspicious of everything people said or did as it directly related to me. I had no belief in myself. I began to identify and believe in things I saw on TV, in movies, or heard through music – none of it was age appropriate or based on reality. I feared being judged so I would not take any initiative in public. But when alone or around friends, I was a risk taker. I only did enough school work to get decent grades so I wouldn't be bother by the teachers or the school. I still played sports but never gave my full effort. I stayed up late watching mindless TV. I'd leave home in the middle of the night and walk around town. In my heart I was a coward, but I became a confident jerk to authority figures to gain popularity. I worked hard to cover up my fear of rejection and hide my low self-esteem.

Internal: We constantly felt pity for ourselves. We felt lonely, and insecure, believing we couldn't do anything right. We felt no one would really accept us if they knew how broken we were. We always felt guilt and shame, but didn't know why.

External: We closed ourselves off from others. We acted brave when things were clearly wrong, or when people were around who knew more than us. We forced ourselves to be risk takers.

Consequences: We could not sleep at night because we replayed things in our heads that we wanted to do differently but were too scared to. We did not live in reality, instead we ran from ourselves and situations. We did not stand up for ourselves when we needed to. We could not maintain healthy relationships. We created problems to get attention; developing self- defeating behaviors. We could not appreciate people because we believed they did not appreciate us. We became class clowns in school to avoid being put on the spot.

<u>Solutions / Coping Skills:</u> Today, we like the person we have become. We are honest with ourselves and with others. When we struggle with things; we are able to ask for help. We are friendly with everyone we encounter. We no longer allow what people think about us define who we are. We no longer personalize things, nor are we afraid to face our emotions or our past when triggered. We have reinvented ourselves by embracing who we were meant to be.

<u>Questions for the Class:</u>

1. Can people make you feel what you don't want to feel? Yes/No, Explain why?

2. How has low self-esteem influenced your life?

3. Do you accept what people do to you, just so they will remain in your life? Why or Why not?

4. How have you overcome low self-esteem and gained self-worth? How did you do it?

5. Are you satisfied with just being mediocre and barely getting by? Please explain why or why not?

<u>**Summary:**</u> When your self-esteem lines up with your self-worth, your past no longer defines you or keeps you trapped and chained to the external things done to you. The negative self-evaluations you had of yourself and others is replaced with self-respect, self-awareness, self-care, and healthy self-esteem. You now have the power to find solutions to any internal or external problems that may arise in your life. Self-esteem and self-worth allows you to live in a holistic life style because your values are now based on truthful facts. This change in your life becomes a gateway for your true self to walk through and be free.

The Cycle of Anger

Anger is a secondary emotion aroused by a perceived hurt, pain or an injustice done to us. Whether or not that anger is based on a false belief, uncontrolled anger is always a lack of emotional responsibility to an external event we have personalized. Once a person is in this state of mind, internally they will justify a reason to seek revenge by placing value and satisfaction in aggressive behavior.

1. External Events/Influences = Causative Factors:

<u>Situation / Problem – Ray:</u> Growing up I had a really poor relationship with anger. It was due to emotional neglect and passive abuse. I suffered from the molestation I experienced and being a witness to the domestic violence and rape of my mother. I had very low self-esteem and no self-worth. Never feeling like I had a voice in any situation left me angry, even if I tried to speak or just stood there crying. I had no healthy life experiences which allowed me to draw solutions from. Everything was done in the form of anger and aggression in order to bring resolve. I mimicked the anger my stepdad and mom expressed to get my point across.

<u>Situation / Problem – Nathan:</u> Growing up I had no understanding of the negative and destructive role anger could play in my life. I was left unprepared for how the hardships of life would cause anger within me. The emotional distance of my parents, the lack of closure of my grandpa's death, my dad not doing anything about the molestation, abusive punishments I received in the home. These were all emotional events which caused me to stuff my anger. My self-concept left me unable to speak about these events or know how to ask for help. With no coping skills or safe spaces to resolve things, I released my internal anger through external destructive acts.

<u>Internal:</u> We had resentment, were unforgiving and built up unresolved pain which was the driving force for our justification of anger. There were times we did not even understand why we were angry, and to make it worst after we calmed down we felt guilt and shame. However, we still blamed others for being the source of our anger.

<u>External:</u> Our posture and the tone in our voice was aggressive. We gave attitude and were rude for no reason. We developed self-destructive behaviors.

<u>Consequences:</u> Family and friends did not want to be around us because they said we acted "bipolar." When lost in anger we would lose focus of things. We used our anger to get our way. We personalized everything, believing people were trying to provoke, frustrate or irritate us. Our anger drove us to seek control over everything around us. We constantly denied that our anger was harmful to ourselves and others.

<u>Solutions / Coping Skills:</u> Today, we no longer try to control the things around us that we are not responsible for. We understand our life experiences (causative factors) and the role they played in causing anger during our upbringing. We also understand they no longer have control over our thoughts, speech, beliefs, or actions. Today we are confident with our place in the world, because we understand our power comes from having choices. Today, we live within our means, exercising patience, forgiveness and extend mercy to others.

<u>Questions for the Class:</u>

1. What external life events and influential people caused you to act out in anger?

2. Does your resentment anchor you to the past, preventing you from finding closure?

3. How does your anger negatively affect your life?

4. What gets you angry that people do around you?

5. What happens when you personalize things when angry?

The Cycle of Anger

2. What We Feel & Think = Internal Triggers:

Situation / Problem – Ray: As a kid, seeing my stepdad begin to drink made me angry. I would get angry even before he started breathing hard, cussing everyone out, or becoming aggressive. Even when things did not turn out ugly, I knew the next time they would. At night my mind would replay all the awful things that had been done to me. These memories and images would get me furious, mad upset, pissed off and angry because I felt I could of done more to stop the molestation and protect my mom. Other times I would become angry with myself for allowing my thoughts and feelings to dictate my words, actions and how I treated others.

Situation / Problem – Nathan: As a child I embraced anger because it kept weakness at bay. When hurtful or painful things happened to me; anger covered them up. If I felt fear or shame because of something that took place, anger got rid of it. When I saw my mom getting red and begin to shake, or my dad get really quiet and breathe deeply, I would become internally scared and jump to anger feeling the need to protect myself. As I thought about my life and all the unfair things that happened and how helpless I felt all the time, a rage would build within me.

Internal: We began to develop thinking errors and create false beliefs such as: every man that drinks becomes a drunk and abuse their wife and children. We began to feel like everything that was done to us was done on purpose and intentional. We were frustrated, angry, irritated, mad, pissed off, resentful, forgetful, agitated, impulsive thoughts and we jump to conclusions.

External: Sometimes we would sweat a lot and grind our teeth. We were unable to sleep at night. Certain people, places and things would trigger us. Our demeanor and posture would change. Causing us to act aggressively and ready to defend ourselves. We walked around with a cold glare on our face.

Consequences: We lost respect for ourselves, other people and their property and misdirecting our anger at people for no reason. We ruined close relationships with the people we loved. Our anger taught people not to trust us. We were left out, not being invited places because our anger scared people.

Solutions / Coping Skills: Today, we are no longer broken, angry, immature or impulsive boys unable to control our thoughts and feelings. We have chosen to empower ourselves by taking charge of our lives. We are able to put things into perspective when triggered. We understand that a traumatic emotional experience can no longer transport us back to live in the hurt and pain of our past. We have addressed our causative factors, defects of character, triggers, and warning signs. We now know our strengths and weaknesses. We create new memories by honoring our accomplishments and engaging in a lifestyle that supports our calling in life to help others.

<u>Questions for the Class:</u>

1. What feelings trigger you into anger?

2. What thinking errors and warp beliefs do you struggle with?

3. How do you stop bad thoughts and unhealthy feelings without suppressing and ignoring them?

4. What coping skills have failed you in conquering your anger?

5. How has your anger allowed you to avoid accepting the consequences of your actions?

The Cycle of Anger

3. Actions & Behaviors = Immediate & Long Term Consequences:

Situation / Problem – Ray: I developed a one track mind to fix my problems when I was hurt, lied to, forgotten, abandoned, not appreciated, scared, belittled, ignored, or blamed for something I did not do. I acted on impulse. When I became angry; I was biased, aggressive, violent, and without compassion or empathy. There were times as a kid when I got upset because I could not change the TV channel; even though my stepdad would not be watching anything. (He was knocked out on heroin.) Or when my sisters would be playing with their dolls or jacks, and I still couldn't change the channel. My anger would make me call my stepdad a "junkie or drug addict." (I would get beat for saying that.) I felt my sisters were favored, so I would pick fights with them and play rough to make them cry. I would get hit with the broom or extension cord. As I got older, my anger would turn to rage and violent acts. I understood that the more aggressive I became, the more power and respect I seemed to gain.

Situation / Problem – Nathan: When I was young and faced with any situation that brought up negative emotions within me, impulsive anger was my go to. I felt the only way to solve my problems was to lash out with verbal or physical aggression. Whether it was my parents always on my back, some kid making fun of me, an adult giving me a hard time or if I could not figure something out. I would fly off the handle into a rage over the littlest thing. I felt both in and out of control when I was angry. I did not care what the outcome of my outburst were. In that state I had no compassion, consideration, or empathy for what someone else was going through. My anger ultimately led to violent acts and into the cycle of violence. Aggression and violence commanded attention and respect, but it was a warped respect. The long term consequences of this led to a murder and life sentence in prison.

Internal: As children we felt guilty, shameful, drained, and confused. As teenagers we felt like it was our place to act out however we wanted because we felt like everybody was wrong. As adults we felt justified acting out in anger because we had no regret, empathy, or compassion for others. We felt superior to others and believed we knew it all.

External: We cut people out of our lives for trivial reasons. We tried to embarrass others, talk down to them and provoke them to fight by revealing personal things we knew about them. We also acted like tough guys.

Consequences: We ended up hurting our loved ones and hurting people we did not know. We got locked up, lost jobs, our family and friends became scared of us. We ruined our community and created countless victims. We could not control our anger, especially when it to turn into rage.

<u>Solutions / Coping Skills:</u> Today, we understand the purpose of emotions. They are to help us identify and process what we are feeling. When we open up and become vulnerable, it allows us to embrace who we are and function in healthy ways. No matter the situation or who we are around. Emotions can be understood as our own personal GPS tracking system given to us by God for our safety and well-being.

<u>Questions for the Class:</u>

1. What has anger destroyed in your life that you can never get back?

2. What external evidence can people see in your life that's connected to your anger?

3. What beliefs were formed in your life due to your anger?

4. Why do you think a person misdirects their anger? What are the consequences of misdirected anger?

5. How hard is it to control your anger?

6. What tools have you acquired to help you deal with your anger?

Summary: Understanding the cycle of anger is pivotal, critical, and necessary for living a balanced life mentally, emotionally, physically and spiritually. Anger is not always a dangerous thing, it can become helpful when properly acknowledged. For instance, it can inform you when to leave a toxic and dangerous situation. It can remind you of the consequences. It can get you fired up so that you are able to overcome obstacles and achieve goals. When you find healthy ways to vent your anger, it allows you to live in the solution not the problem. Failing to deal with your anger continues to give your causative factors the power to influence your behavior. Having no self-awareness can ignite your internal triggers, causing them to be manipulated by what you think and feel. Your past then takes control of your current reality. Without control of your anger; you give yourself permission to justify every reason to act out in aggression and violence without regards for the consequences.

Quote

"A wise man was asked, what is anger?

He gave a beautiful answer.

It is a punishment we give ourselves,

For somebody else's mistake."

Criminality

A criminal is a person who has chosen to live an illegal lifestyle. They have no regard or consideration for the rules and laws of society. Nor do they respect the freedom and rights of people or society as a whole. They are driven by their thoughts (imagination), their emotions (what they feel), and what they accumulate materially because it brings (self-gratification). A criminal has no empathy or compassion; making the consequences of their actions lethal because they have learned to adapt to any circumstances during the course of their crimes, they are willing to do anything and hurt anyone to get away with their criminal activities.

1. Cultural Influences:

Situation / Problem – Ray: Growing up there was a lot of criminal activity in my home. There was drug sales/use, overdoses as well as stolen property and guns. Outside of my home was no different. Most kids I went to school with grew up the same way. Their parents, siblings, and cousins also engaged in criminal activity. Watching my stepdad, uncles and cousins count money and hearing how they got it by committing crimes had a powerful impact on the way I thought and behaved. Criminal activity was normalized in my neighborhood, nor was it frowned upon. I began to steal food stamps from my mom's purse. I then escalated to stealing ten cent bottles from behind Vons grocery store. Next, I began stealing skateboards and bikes from the rich side of town with my teenage cousins. My mom would ask "where did you get these bikes?" I would tell her "I stole them from across town!" She told me not to get caught.

Situation / Problem – Nathan: Growing up there was no criminal activity in my home. My small town community was mostly crime free. In my early childhood; I was not exposed to drugs or gangs. I learned about criminal activity through TV, watching movies and listening to music. After the molestation (10 years old) I committed my first crime; vandalism and petty theft. I felt a rush of adrenaline and a sense of power and control. I began looking up to criminal role models in movies, music and older peers who were already involved in crime and drugs. The criminal activity escalated as outside influences put ideas into my head. My criminal peer group would always challenge each other to "be down" (be ready) to commit crimes.

Internal: We felt justified by our actions because it helped block out our pain. My (Ray's) family taught us to steal. We felt scared at first, but when we realized how easy it was; we felt smart, brave, and more confident in ourselves. We wanted to fit in and be like the others in our household and neighborhood. At first we felt some guilt and shame but that feeling soon left us over time.

External: Our criminal activity escalated. We became bolder and acted crazier when we were with our criminal peers and others. We became greedy and started to rob and sell drugs by ourselves so that we did not have to share the profits.

Consequences: Our lives began to spiral out of control as we continued to seek acceptance. Our criminal thinking patterns led us to believe we were unstoppable! We had no moral values which we lived by. We became greedy, selfish, and irresponsible and lived in denial from the harm we caused other people. We destroyed relationships by influencing others to commit crime. We did not care about our safety or the safety of others. Our actions led to incarceration; both ours and others.

Solutions / Coping Skills: Today, we live with integrity because we have taken the necessary steps needed to correct our thought process. We now have morals, values, principles and ethics we live by. We understand that there is no such thing as a victimless crime. We have taken several victim awareness classes and we are able to place ourselves in our victims shoes. We have empathy and compassion for people's feelings, their property and for animals. We respect the life and liberty of all mankind. We have taken responsibility and accountability for our actions and now know the importance of making amends.

Questions for the Class:

1. What crimes committed against you, made you feel; hurt, angry, scared fearful and or unsafe?

2. In what ways do you still think like a criminal?

3. Have your children or any other family or friends followed in your criminal footsteps because of your influence? How does that make you feel?

4. What consequences of your criminal behavior do you regret the most?

5. Was there a defining moment (major event) in your life that caused you to rethink /stop your criminal lifestyle? If so what was it?

Criminality

2. Criminal Behavior:

<u>Situation / Problem – Ray</u>: The more I was exposed to criminal activity, the more I realize that every crime had to be approached differently. When conning people; I had to act innocent, friendly and civilized. It was all about manipulation. Other times I had to become aggressive in order to get what I wanted, but being sneaky was the easiest way to take things. Especially when a lot of people were around, because they did not know who to blame. Some crimes took planning; while others were spur-of-the-moment acts. (If the opportunity presented itself.)

<u>Situation / Problem – Nathan</u>: The more crimes I committed with my peers; the more entrenched my criminal thinking and behaviors became. I began to see myself as a criminal and started looking for opportunities in my daily life to commit crimes. I gained a sense of power and control over my life by using trust as a cover to commit crimes. Keeping my crimes secret allowed me to get revenge on those who I felt had harmed me in some way. Spur-of-the-moment crimes were rare; they usually took place when I was under the influence of substances or my criminal peers.

<u>Internal</u>: We were nervous, scared, tense, stressed, afraid and full of panic. When committing certain crimes, we got a rush when we got away with a crime or took something from someone we did not like.

<u>External</u>: There were times we committed senseless crimes out of boredom and anger. Overtime the crimes we committed became more sophisticated. Our demeanor, clothing, words and overall behavior changed to match our vision of what a criminal should be.

<u>Consequences</u>: We became lost in the criminal lifestyle and could not stop ourselves from cutting corners seeking to make some kind of profit. It did not matter if it was cheating at school, sneaking into the movies, doing beer, food, clothing or taxi runs. Selling drugs or robbing someone, we had become addicted to the lifestyle. Our compulsive behavior only focused on short-term benefits, ignoring the long-term destruction.

<u>Solutions / Coping Skills</u>: Today, we are able to control our compulsive desires, wants, and cravings. We are comfortable living within our means and have set healthy boundaries in our lives. We no longer entertain criminal thoughts or put ourselves in situations that trigger us. We understand that certain people, places and things are dangerous for us and should always be avoided. We have disciplined ourselves and established healthy routines, found new friends and hobbies to occupy our time. Like, reading, working out, going to church, self-help groups, listening to music or playing sports. We also have our own accountability partners.

Questions for the Class:

1. When did you become confident in your criminal Behavior?

2. What was your crime of choice and why?

3. What was the hardest crime to stop committing?

4. When a crime did not go your way, what did you do?

5. Why do you think some of your crimes failed?

Summary: Sometimes a person has to experience the consequences of their criminality in order to learn their lesson. Other times a person can see and realize where their actions are leading them, and correct themselves. It could take someone you love like your parent(s) siblings, spouse or children to be victimized by criminals before you can put yourself in your victim shoes. This may be the people you have harmed. It's possible this could spark a conscious decision to live a more responsible, honest respectful life rooted in integrity. When you learn to live within your means, and work for what you have you will find a new appreciation for the healthy life you can build by simply living a crime free life.

Gangs

When it comes to gangs, one must understand they function totally different then of a criminal. Although all gang members are criminals, they become more dangerous and brutally callus in the heart because they are inspired, driven and motivated by their pride and loyalty to their barrio neighborhood, set, turf or block. Everything they do is for this cause. Gang foundations are built upon the traditions, beliefs, manners and habits that have been passed down from one generation to the next. A gang member's character and identity are rooted in their status, rank and position with the gang they represent.

1. Beliefs & Traditions:

Situation / Problem – Ray: Growing up in a gang-infested household and neighborhood made it easy to adopt gang culture. My earliest memories were visiting my stepdad in the early 1970's in San Quentin prison. I remember taking pictures; my stepdad would fold his red rag and wrap it around my head, pick me up and tell me to throw up four fingers. I did not understand what that represented. However, I did not think it was something bad because his friends would smile and laugh saying "that's right little homie." Hearing those words gave me a sense of belonging and acknowledgement. In my household there was a code to stick by one another, remain loyal at all cost and to have respect for the Gang Lifestyle. My stepdad would call home and my mom would make us thank him for buying us clothes and paying the rent. I never thought about where the money was coming from until one day, I heard them arguing at a family visit. My mom did not bring him heroin like she was told to. My uncles were also gang members and in prison. I asked my cousins if their moms brought drugs to their dad's in prison, and they said "yes." My neighborhood was known for selling PCP. I grew up and joined the gang, I became a part of the drug trade and sold PCP too.

Situation / Problem – Nathan: I did not grow up with gangs in my household. I first saw gang activity watching movies on TV. I became aware of the gang in my small town during Junior High School. When my peers began forming different groups; some of them became involved in the gang. By that time I viewed myself as a criminal and began to look for a group to be a part of. I gravitated towards the older kids and was accepted by them for my willingness to use substances and commit crimes. While we were not gang members, we function like a gang pledging our loyalty, being down for each other and selling drugs. We built traditions around going on missions committing crimes, mixing gang style music and substances to influence each other and throwing or going out to parties together.

Internal: I (Ray) felt since my family were gang members and sold drugs, it was my duty to follow in their footsteps. Once we embraced the lifestyle we felt acceptance and no longer alone. Feeling the impact others had on us and also the impact we made on them, was a sign of respect. We felt scared and nervous at times but our homies calmed us down. There were other times when we were scared, but we hid it and remained loyal to the cause.

External: We passed down our gang's traditions and beliefs to others. We became delinquents and mislead others through deception and manipulation. Our actions demonstrated that we were prejudiced towards the law and others who were not loyal to our gang.

Consequences: I (Ray) exchanged every freedom I had for the gang. I was consumed in advancing my gang and making my name "known" at all cost. My beliefs became warped as I created new traditions. I pushed a harder line and became deeply involved with the politics in CYA, County Jail and Prison. I also began to chase after money at all costs.

Solutions / Coping Skills: Today, we no longer try to entice people through the lure of the Gang Lifestyle. We choose each day to be a productive member of our community by celebrating our recovery and helping those who are still lost in their own addictions. We believe in meeting people wherever they are at in their lives and showing them that change is possible if they truly desire it. Today we understand that gangs weaken us by providing a false sense of security and taking away the essence of who we really are.

Questions for the Class:

1. Have you ever made a woman carry your weapon or bring you drugs?

2. What beliefs and traditions have you followed as a gang member?

3. Who have you influenced by teaching them gang culture?

4. How powerful is your need for acceptance, explain your feelings and thoughts on acceptance?

5. What consequences have you yet to experience do to your gang involvement?

Gangs

2. Loyalty & Respect:

Situation / Problem – Ray: I understood that loyalty earned respect at a very early age, because my family demonstrated that to me. I remember my mom going to jail because she would not snitch on my stepdad and uncle. They would do robberies and bring the stolen property to our house and divide it, my mom always got her cut. One day the cops came to our house and confiscated the items that were stolen from one of the robberies. They repeatedly asked my mom where she got the stolen items from. She would tell them "a yard sale." The cops knew she was lying, they hand cuffed my mom and charged her with receiving stolen property. She was bailed out by my stepdad the next day and praised for keeping her mouth shut. (I never forgot that.)

Situation / Problem-Nathan: My loyalty earned me a place among my criminal peers. Without that; I would not have received the respect that I was looking for. Many times I was confronted by my parents or other adults who were suspicious of what my friends and I had done or were planning. I always denied or lied to protect us, especially when the cops showed up to my parents' house. I would deny knowing the reason why they were there. I was rewarded for lying and not snitching. That increased my status and respect amongst my friends. They would let it be known that I was with them and nobody should mess with me. As we committed more crimes and became more violent, our loyalty to each other deepened. My reputation was based on my willingness to be blindly loyal. Other people knew this and gave me respect.

Internal: We were scared because we knew on some level that being loyal would eventually get us into trouble. The praise we received for being down and loyal gave us a sense of belonging in a way we had never experienced before. To have respect was to feel loved, wanted and appreciated. Our confidence and self-worth as criminals and gang members strengthened our commitment to the lifestyle.

External: When we were out with our friends we began to act more bold, disrespectful and proud because we knew we had back-up! If you messed with one of us you messed with all of us! I (Ray) would dress in all red, wearing red rags and Bulldog clothing. I would throw up gang signs and start trouble in public.

Consequences: Our loyalty and respect to the lifestyle allowed us to despise those who really loved us; like our parents, siblings, aunts, uncles, cousins and friends. We lost our humanity, becoming numb to compassion and empathy. The results of this lifestyle was; two innocent people being murdered.

Solutions / Coping Skills: Today, we are no longer gang members. We chose to drop out several years ago. We are loyal to our family and friends who have stuck by our side even when we were at our worst. We now have positive self-worth and a respectable reputation in our community. We understand that true loyalty can only be found in doing what is right. Today, we respect the rights of all mankind. Our loyalty can be seen in our commitment to helping those in need. Our commitment involves us rebuilding the people, places and things we once destroyed.

Questions for the Class:

1. Did your loyalty always lead to respect?

2. Have you ever abused your respect?

3. Do you struggle with loyalties to family and old friends who are still stuck in the gang lifestyle?

4. How did you deal with those individuals who lost respect for you?

5. What habits, mannerisms and beliefs do you still carry from the gang life?

Summary: Youth often display certain character traits such as having; low self-esteem, depression, always angry and hate for any type of authority. These character traits lead them to seek acceptance among their peers. When they actually join a gang (especially teenagers) they will have a specific dress code they honor, own things they can't afford, brag about their new friends who can only be identified by a nickname. Use hateful or racist language, get certain tattoos and they may begin to use drugs and alcohol. When you first become a gang member you are tested to ensure you will fulfill the need that your gang expects from you. The gang will become your new family because of the social support and validation it brings you. It helps you form a new identity that you believe is the real you. People also join gangs for protection from bullies and other gang members. You can avoid joining a gang by thinking for yourself. Maintaining healthy relationships with those who raised you, and by being willing to communicate how you feel about certain things going on in your life. Getting involved with sports, education and other positive things can bring you a sense of satisfaction and motivate you to seek out positive peers and recognition.

Substance Abuse

When people engage in substance abuse; it is rooted in being hurt, broken, lost, confused, and unable to cope with life, and peer pressure. The effects of substance abuse comes in two forms: (Internal and External) bringing to life the addiction process. They are compulsive behaviors that seek short-term gratification and satisfaction, and gives no thought to the long-term consequences of ones actions.

1. Internal Effects:

Situation / Problem – Ray: As a child, I remember my step dad and uncles telling me to get them beer whenever they needed another one. They would say "I left you a sip, don't tell your mom!" I would run to the kitchen and drink it, before I knew it I would have a little buzz and fall asleep. I was 11 years old the first time my sister got me high on weed. I was paranoid, scared, and wanted the high to go away. She would laugh at me and say "if you tell Mom I'm going to beat your ass!" My family sold PCP and so did the neighborhood I was from. As a teenager I began to use PCP due to peer pressure. I would hallucinate and have a sense of strength, or be stuck and not able to move for hours. I did not like the high, but felt that I could not escape it because I was surrounded by it in my neighborhood. My grandma was a pill addict and would make me go pick up codeine pills for her. She would always give me one pill for the errand. It mellowed me out, but I did not like the feeling the pill gave me. I have lost three uncles, two aunts and my sister to alcohol and drug abuse. All dying from cirrhosis of the liver.

Situation / Problem – Nathan: Growing up there was always beer in the refrigerator at home. I remember at family get-togethers the adults would always be drinking something us kids could not have. At my parents work parties beer kegs were everywhere and many adults would be drunk. At a very young age I remember going around and drinking the leftover alcohol in bottles and cans. I stumbled around and then got tired. Afterwards I felt sick and frightened. At 13 years old I began sneaking my parents' beer and drinking them with friends until we got light buzzes. Not long after I smoked marijuana for the first time with some older friends. I began drinking and smoking weed with friends, it made me feel good. Going to high school; substance use was a rite of passage and brought acceptance which is something I craved. I often drank and smoked too much lowering my inhibitions to do risky things like; try acid, meth and magic mushrooms. While drunk or high I could escape my life for a little while be free of any responsibilities and have more confidence.

Internal: We felt scared the first time we tried drugs and alcohol. Over time we use them to feel accepted and to also drown out our hurt and pain.

External: We acted like we enjoyed getting high or drunk, when in reality it scared us. We also started to hang out with drunks and addicts which led to more substance abuse. We understood that if we had drugs and alcohol people would flock to us.

Consequences: When we were intoxicated our choices became careless and impulsive, we thought we knew it all. We were more prone to act out in violence, mistreating our parents and other authority figures by disobeying and talking back to them.

Solutions / Coping Skills: Today, we no longer put ourselves in situations that would willingly trigger us. We choose to live with integrity and act responsible in all of our affairs. We live with a constant awareness of the Serenity Prayer and understand that we have a choice in our actions and behaviors. We have sponsors and accountability partners we can talk to. We also trust the process of living in recovery by using the tools we have gained in our self-help classes.

Questions for the Class:

1. What was your worst experience getting drunk or high?

2. What have you done under the influence that you would not do sober?

3. What role did alcohol or drugs play in your upbringing?

4. Have you ever took advantage of someone that was under the influence?

5. Why did you drink or use drugs if you did not like them?

6. Have you lost someone you love due to substance abuse? Did you continue down the same path?

Substance Abuse

2. External Effects:

Situation / Problem – Ray: Growing up I witnessed the external effects of what substance abuse does. I did not like people who drank nor did I ever want to drink because my eldest sister's dad would always abuse my mother, sisters and myself when he was drunk. My younger sister's dad was a heroin addict and would beg, cry and manipulate my mom for money and steal from us in order to get his next fix. When he or my uncle were sick (kicking heroin) I would think they were dying because they would be moaning, sweating and rocking back and forth in pain. When it came to my older sister, the guys in the neighborhood would take advantage of her because they knew she loved smoking PCP. I never understood why people got drunk or high if they could not handle it.

Situation / Problem – Nathan: My parents drank alcohol and smoked cigarettes in the backyard during my childhood. I rarely saw the fall down drunk, or acts of violence while intoxicated. I did not see a problem with drinking. When I got drunk, I was more outwardly happy and willing to engage in risky behaviors. My friends and I would use substances out of boredom and then go out and commit crimes. When I was 15 years old, I began drinking one night and did not stop, I felt nothing! I passed out and woke up in the hospital. I had almost died from alcohol poisoning. My parents grounded me for a few days and then acted like nothing had happened. I went right back to my friends and our culture of substance use. In high school, some of my friends were in car accidents due to alcohol, a few of them died. My dad came home drunk one night and picked a fight with me. After the fight, I left the house and smoked some weed to cope with the fight and the feeling of how my life was spiraling out of control.

Internal: We felt scared, paranoid, lost and not in control of our emotions. At other times drugs and alcohol numbed the pain, on other occasions the use of substances brought energy, courage and excitement into our lives.

External: I (Ray) was known as a lightweight when it came to being under the influence. We could not handle our high nor did we know our limits. Under the Influence, we stole, vandalized and acted out in violence. We would mistreat the people we loved. I (Nathan) ended up being hospitalized for drinking too much.

Consequences: Under peer pressure, we used substances to hide our pain and seek acceptance. Eventually we no longer needed an excuse to partake in substances. Our hearts turned cold, our feelings stayed numb and we became a danger to ourselves and others. My co- defendants (Ray's) were all intoxicated the night of my life crime.

Solutions / Coping Skills: Today, we understand that being under the influence has contributed to us creating victims in our lives. We abstain from drugs and alcohol and are no longer in denial about our causative factors. They will not be excuses to contaminate our minds, spirits, emotions or our bodies. Nathan and I are happy with the men we have worked so hard to become. As mentors and sponsors we choose to live in sobriety and be an example of what change looks like.

Questions for the Class:

1. What external effects still haunt you, which are connected to substance abuse?

2. What were your excuses to get intoxicated?

3. Is your life crime a result of substance abuse?

4. What is the worst external affect you face due to substance abuse?

5. Have you or someone you know, developed a disease due to substance abuse?

Summary: Seeking a lifestyle that brings balance is where sobriety and living in recovery begins. The relapse process is having an imbalanced lifestyle. Understanding your external and internal causative factors puts you in the position to respond to triggering events, instead of reacting to them. Developing self-awareness allows you to identify warning signs and put into practice your coping skills. Knowing you ALWAYS have a choice is where your power lies in conquering any temptations, cravings or desires you might have to use mind altering substances.

Seeking Acceptance

Seeking acceptance is a very dangerous and dark road to travel. There is no certainty you will come back alive, or return the same person. Often times the need for affection, recognition, friendship, belonging, acknowledgement and acceptance stems from being rejected and abandoned by those we love. When we act upon loneliness to fit in we become the person people want us to be. The lure of being accepted is so strong it will allow you to live a lie with no sense of reality. You will go to extreme measures in order to fill the Brokenness in your life. Once in this state of mind, you're unable to be concerned with how your actions affect or harm others.

1. Pre-Life Crime:

Situation / Problem – Ray: The constant lack of attention, abandonment and rejection I received as an adolescent and teenager became the fuel and driving force in me chasing after acceptance. It began in small and simple stages like throwing out the trash, washing the car, raking the yard or putting away the groceries to be recognized. In elementary school it came in the form of peer pressure. My cousins would dare me to steal marbles and gum while we were playing video games at the Safeway grocery store in my neighborhood. I didn't want to steal and I told him "no!" They started calling me names like "sissy" or "coward" and they said they were going to tell their brother on me. He was my friend and I did not want him to think less of me. I eventually caved in and started on the road of crime. I got away with the deed and was immediately rewarded with a sense of belonging. It was an overwhelming feeling. In my teenage years I became bolder and my crimes were more dangerous. When I knew my stepdad, uncle and sister we're going to commit crimes, I would now volunteer to be their lookout. I was willing to hold my uncles and cousins drugs in the car. When I was out with my friends; I would be quick to fight or steal anything just to fit in and be recognized and trusted.

Situation / Problem – Nathan: Growing up feeling disconnected from my parents and other adults in my life, I struggled with issues of abandonment, rejection and low self-esteem. I sought acceptance through acting out in order to make my peers laugh and like me. When I was young I used to do chores around the house in an attempt to connect, but it would be treated as a transactional thing and I would receive a small allowance instead of meaningful praise. When kids would dare me; I had no problem with going to the extreme chasing their acceptance. I lit a fire which burned a field, on a dare. After my friend molested me, I lost all trust and felt disconnected from my peers. Moving forward I saw and understood acceptance to be solely based on materialistic, transactional things and actions. When I began committing crimes, my views on acceptance centered on a person's willingness; I became willing to do whatever was needed to be accepted. This meant almost dying from alcohol poisoning. I got kicked off the basketball team for getting into trouble at school. My criminal behavior escalated. All of it in excess, seeking acceptance.

Internal: We felt the need to do whatever was necessary to be loved, acknowledged, recognized, heard and accepted even when we knew it was going to harm us. When we were praised by our peers, the pain, hurt and loneliness in our lives seem to vanish. However, when we were by ourselves, all the ugliness and brokenness we tried to escape, returned much stronger, leaving us in a worse state.

External: We wore a different mask for each adventure and occasion we encountered. We became a puppet for others and lost respect for ourselves, friends, family and society as a whole. We abused innocent people. Some we knew, and some we did not know, in order to make ourselves appear more than what we actually were.

Consequences: We lost sense of ourselves. We were unable to live in reality. We lacked compassion and empathy. We scared our loved ones, and shut down mentally and emotionally from our problems. We no longer trusted ourselves, and eventually stop caring about anything in our lives.

Solutions / Coping Skills: Today, through much introspection, self-help and counseling, we have developed a healthy sense of who we are as individuals. We have established healthy boundaries. We live within our means and have gratitude for what we do have. We have become productive members of our communities, and we have earned trust and respect. (We) Ray & Nathan are an example of what change looks like. We are comfortable living in the present; focusing on what is important to ourselves and others.

Questions for the Class:

1. When you were younger, what were your reasons for seeking acceptance?

2. When you received recognition or acknowledgement from your peers, how long did the feeling of acceptance last?

3. Do you still seek acceptance today?

4. What is the worst part of seeking acceptance?

5. What are your warning signs for feeling an unhealthy need for acceptance?

Seeking Acceptance

2. Life Crime:

Situation / Problem – Ray: At this point in my life, I had many unresolved issues that plagued my daily living. I never dealt with my molestation, the domestic violence I grew up with, my mother's rape or her accepting my sister's dad back. To add to that I was in a relationship with someone I did not love. Our relationship was falling apart and we were about to have our first child. I tried to change my life the best I could by getting a job, an apartment, a car and ending my partying but somehow I still managed to fail. So I did what I knew and ran out on my relationship. I left home angry and drove to my sister's house. Where I ran into an old friend who asked me to do a lick with him. I said no at first, but he was persistent by saying things like, "Come on dog I ain't never did a lick with you!" I eventually gave in and said yes. So, he left and came back to get me with one of his friends who had brought someone else. I was then introduced to them. I told my homie I was cool on these dudes I did not know. That's when one of the dudes said, "Come on dog my primo said he was in CYA with you." I felt the peer pressure once again and the need to be accepted. So I agreed to do the robbery; which ended up turning into a murder.

Situation / Problem – Nathan: My life was spiraling out of control. None of the issues in my life had been spoken about or dealt with. I held all of my emotions inside; in a toxic brew of anger and self-hate. I held a job but stole from my employer. One night I got into a fight with my dad. I was sent out of the house. My mom had to separate us with a knife in her hand. I then retreated to my group of older criminal friends where I could do no wrong. My parents stopped keeping a curfew on me. I felt lonely and desperate because most of my older friends were about to leave town. One of them brought up the idea of murdering our friend. Another friend of ours hated the victim and blamed him for getting kicked out of school. My co-defendant said we needed to, "Be down" and "do it!" I felt the pull of not wanting to disappoint him. I began to de- value the victim's life. I felt powerful and in control. I made the decision to murder him. My co-defendant and I murdered our friend.

Internal: We were lost, scared, broken, hopeless, frustrated, confused, hurt, and we wanted to be loved and accepted. We lacked the strength to walk away from the situation because inside we did not have the coping skills we needed.

External: We adapted to the situation and participated in our life crimes without turning back or half step'n. We used weapons in our life crimes to get the task done.

Consequences: We created new internal and external problems for ourselves. Creating primary victims and secondary victims (as it extended to the victim's family) as well as victimizing our communities. We lost our freedom and were sentenced to (35 years to life) and (life without parole) (LWOP). Costing taxpayers hundreds of thousands of dollars to incarcerate us.

<u>Solutions / Coping Skills:</u> Today, we understand the power of having a voice. We have learned in recovery that it is okay to say "No!" We no longer live our lives seeking approval or validation from people living criminal lifestyles. Today we listen to our conscience and choose to live at peace within ourselves. We now have the self-awareness we need to avoid certain people, places and things that bring us mental, emotional, physical, spiritual and financial harm.

Questions for the Class:

1. In what ways were you seeking acceptance during your life crime?

2. Do you know why you lacked the strength to say no in your life crime?

3. How did your life crime change you as a person?

4. When did you stop seeking acceptance from people living criminal lifestyles? What caused this change in you?

5. Why did you feel the need to be accepted?

Seeking Acceptance

3. Post life Crime-Prison:

Situation/Problem-Ray: As a youth offender, being sent to a level 4 yard at Pelican Bay State Prison was an eye-opener. I was entering a world I had no control over. At the time I believed my only option was to survive by any means necessary and that's exactly what I did. I chose to adapt to the culture of violence and breaking laws. I was taught it earned me respect. I made a vow to make a name for myself and never to become someone's victim. Not long after I kicked off my first riot in Pelican Bay. From that point on, I committed to raising my hand when anyone needed to be beaten up, jumped, or stabbed. In that process, I discovered an outlet to release all the hurt, pain and anger I had built up in my life.

Situation/problem- Nathan: At the age of 17 years old, I was just sentenced to life without parole and sent to High Desert State Prison. I was full of fear in my new surroundings. A few days after being released to the yard, two prisoners attacked my cellie and cut his throat. In that moment I realized in order to survive I must become violent. I sought out older prisoners for advice. They told me in order to survive you could not show any weakness and must always be prepared to do violence. I fell in with their teachings and was accepted by them. In no time, I embraced prison politics and continued with my criminal thinking and behavior. To prove myself, I beat and stabbed my fellow prisoners, get into riots, assault officers, and broke any rules I did not like. The more violent and destructive I became, the more praises and acceptance I received.

Internal: We felt fear, peer pressure, anger and the need to fit into our new world. Our thoughts and imagination focused on seeking ways to survive prison life.

External: The violence we acted out was a direct manifestation of the chaos that was going on inside of us. We learned to live within the rules of our gang, to respect prison politics, and to adapt to the everyday culture of prison life. Our attitudes, habits, mannerisms and conduct changed dramatically. The laughs and smiles we displayed were fake and usually came when someone else was being harmed.

Consequences: We became who we hung out with; people who were callous in their hearts, cruel, disrespectful, hateful, demanding, unreasonable and violent when we felt we were being disrespected. We lost the support of some family and friends. We felt it was not necessary to ask for help.

Solution/Coping Skills: Today, we have embraced our true identities as special and unique people in this world. Developing character traits such as; self-awareness, self-worth, and self-care. These things have put our lives into perspective, freeing us from seeking approval and acceptance from others. Today we enjoy our solitude. We no longer desire to be accepted by the wrong people. Our journey of self-discovery has been worth all of the hard work and sacrifices we have made along the way to rebuilding our lives and reinventing our character.

<u>Questions for class:</u>

1. Why did you keep chasing after acceptance once you got locked up?

2. Why did you stop trying to make a name for yourself?

3. What is the hardest part about seeking acceptance while you were locked up?

4. Today, are you able to withstand peer pressure by yourself?

5. What new problems has seeking acceptance caused you while incarcerated?

Summary: When a person comes to terms with their past, and realizes that seeking acceptance has come at a painful and fatal price, they gain the confidence to take back control of their lives. You can then position yourself to take the appropriate and necessary steps towards closure, healing and forgiveness in your life. This leads towards self-acceptance and the beginning of the rebuilding process by establishing true identity, character development, and spiritual principles that give meaning and purpose to one's life.

Hope/Early Change

Hope is a powerful motivator for change. When hope is alive within ourselves, we begin to think that things can improve in our lives because we desire something more than the hurt and pain of our past. Hope often finds us at our lowest point, when our lives have become unmanageable. Hope sets in motion the process of change. Hope and change manifest themselves in different ways through our thoughts, and our actions. Many times defining moments in our lives plant the seed of hope, in which that seed grows into our change.

1. Opening Our Hearts and Minds to the Possibility of A New Direction:

Situation / Problem – Ray: Receiving my 3rd SHU term (special housing unit), and being placed in Ad/Seg (the hole) multiple times began to break my pride. I was tired of the drama, prison politics and having to fight other people's battles. In 2004 while I was in the hole I had a defining moment in my life. I became overwhelmed both mentally and emotionally. I was full of fear, panic and paranoia. I believed I was going to die somehow that day. For the first time in years I tried to pray and cry out to God, I felt nothing. In order to feel something, I began to relive all of my negative childhood experiences, especially the molestation and the rape of my mom. Hours later, tears began to roll down my face in a sense of release. My life began to change from that day on.

Situation / Problem – Nathan: Being sent to the hole again in 2008 left me with a lot of time to think. Many hardships in my life were beginning to quickly pile up. I was in the hole for my involvement in violence on the yard. As I laid on my bunk thinking about all the negative experiences I suffered in life. All of the violent and destructive things I had done, and my responsibility to it all. I realized I was exactly where I belong. Nothing I thought about brought me relief. My mind only raced as I fell into a fitful sleep. I woke up the next day and felt like everything had changed.

Internal: We felt fearful, anxious, overwhelmed, lonely, confused, paranoid, anger, shame, self- hate and we suffered depression.

External: We were unsure of what to do and retreated into ourselves to think. We became withdrawn and spoke less. We felt trapped in the lives we had chosen for ourselves.

Consequences: Our actions brought us to the SHU/hole yet again. We faced the harsh reality that our lives were spiraling out of control. We thought change wasn't an option for us.

Solutions / Coping Skills: Today, we know that change begins with the ability to embrace hope. We understand that change happens when we decide to break the cycle of negative thinking and actions. By taking back control of our lives, we begin to steer ourselves away from the people, places and things that triggered us to act out violently and destructively. In order for us to change our lives, we dared to do something different. We asked the prison officials for help in leaving the gang and violent prison environment behind us.

Questions for the Class:

1. Is there something negative impact in your life that you feel is out of control? If so, what is it?

2. What role has hope played in your life so far?

3. What do you feel when hope comes alive within you?

4. Do you think change is an option for you? Why or why not?

5. Can you see a way out of feeling hopeless? If so, what does it look like?

Hope/Early Change

2. Voicing/Expressing the New Direction We Seek:

Situation / Problem – Ray: In 2005, I finally had the courage to seek help for the first time in my life. I asked prison officials what the process was for dropping out of my gang. Once I said it, I knew there was no going back. I did not know what to do, how to feel, or how to act standing on my own. All I knew was that I was doing the right thing. The next thing I did was ask to talk to the psychologist so I could start to address this new change in my life. I finally worked up the courage to write home and tell my family, who were still active gang members and criminals, what I had just done. (Dropped out of the gang.) This was by far the hardest thing I had done in my life. I did not want my family to abandon me because I believed they were all I had left.

Situation / Problem – Nathan: I asked prison staff for help in moving me to a yard with less violence and prison politics. I struggled finding my way in this new environment which was unfamiliar to me. I still naturally gravitated towards people, places and things I was used to. Although I wasn't involved in the violent and destructive things I had just left behind, I was hanging around the fringes of it. By me not addressing or talking about the problem, I allowed myself to be triggered by something connected to my past sexual abuse. At this stage of my life; I suffered a setback by getting into a fight. I was sent to the hole, received a SHU term, and was transferred back into a more violent environment.

Internal: We felt lost, unsure, emotionally raw, sad, lonely, vulnerable, anxious, insecure, overwhelmed, angry and indecisive.

External: We had difficulties finding places where we felt safe to work on our change. We fell back into familiar patterns of interacting with people, places and things that would trigger us to act in negative ways. At times we became aggressive and prejudice towards others.

Consequences: Our old habits resurfaced and we suffered setbacks in our change. We questioned ourselves and lost confidence in the positive progress we had made. We did not always feel comfortable expressing ourselves, and our setbacks had real consequences.

Solutions / Coping Skills: Today, we know one of the most powerful tools for change is when we use our voice to express the exact change we desire. When change is new, avoiding the people, places and things that trigger us is important. We need to surround ourselves with positive people to protect our progress in change. Asking for help with positive solutions to our problems is one way we take control of our lives, being kind with ourselves when setbacks occur will help keep our self-esteem high and our determination for change firmly in place.

Questions for the Class:

1. What does hope and using our voice for change feel like?

2. Does having a voice for change increase your sense of responsibility?

3. What are you currently voicing to others about hope/change?

4. Who can you ask for help with changing your life?

5. What do you do when your old negative habits resurface?

Hope/Early Change

3. Building Momentum for Continuing Change:

Situation / Problem – Ray: Even in my new surroundings, I continue to find myself around familiar negative influences. I thought when I dropped out of the gang all my problems would be solved. I was mistaken and unprepared for what was in store for me. I thought about celling up with a friend of mine who I knew before we were gang members; thinking that would be the best situation to protect the change I was seeking. I told him I no longer wanted to be around alcohol because that is how my sister Laurie had passed. He said he would respect that and not drink. So I moved in, but what I did not know was that he was hustling drugs for people. He said since he had nobody on the streets taking care of him, and he could sell drugs in every building being a barber, he made a living doing that. I made the decision to continue living with him. I got comfortable, and within a few months got high and overdosed. I woke up in the hospital. I was placed in Ad-Seg and was asked to take a urine test. I refused it and received a 115. I understood right then and there that I could not do this alone. I vowed to myself not to give up.

Situation / Problem – Nathan: Due to the length of my sentence, many opportunities for rehabilitation were off-limits to me. I read books and sought out ways to continue my education. I was doing my best to build momentum in my change. Constant lockdowns and being told "No" by prison officials left me struggling to get on track. I would make some progress for a time and then be told "it's over." I was left wondering if real change was an option for me. A riot took place on the yard, and even though I did the right thing by not getting involved, I was still sent to the hole. The progress I did make was brought to a halt. I told myself; "this setback is only temporary." I did not give up hope.

Internal: We felt frustrated, disappointed, irritated, worried, incomplete, confused, discouraged and angry.

External: At times we became stagnant in our change. We often gave half-hearted efforts when things did not happen the way we wanted it to. We were not always honest with those around us. We acted petty and negative when setbacks happened. We made poor choices even when it was clear danger was nearby.

Consequences: We missed out on opportunities to build momentum in our change. Other people were not so quick to help us. We were still putting ourselves in positions to fail. We got into trouble and suffered setbacks in our rehabilitation efforts.

Solutions / Coping Skills: Today, we know that building positive momentum begins with putting ourselves in a position to succeed. We stopped making excuses and sought out ways to become involved in self-help and educational programs. We began to structure our lives around positive and our social people and endeavors. We accepted responsibility for our change by opening up and being honest about our past, our emotions, and our desires for real change. We decided that half step'n with the process of rehabilitation was no longer an option.

<u>Questions for the Class:</u>

1. What are you currently doing to build momentum in your change?

2. Do you find yourself experiencing more positive emotions now? If yes, what are they?

3. What do you do when a setback take place?

4. What excuses did you make for not changing? Do you still use those same excuses? How can you change that?

5. What does responsibility mean to you? Give an example of how it applies to your change?

Summary: When we truly embrace hope and change, we slowly begin to shed the masks we wore throughout our lives; covering up the hurt and pain we endured. Today, we reject violence and destruction and all of its terms. We now take control of our lives and make responsible choices to put ourselves in positions to succeed by becoming involved with positive people, places and things. We continue to practice self-kindness in order to build our self-esteem and protect our progress in hope and change.

Education/Self-Help

Education and self-help are important foundational building blocks for us to continue growing into responsible, positive and productive people. Education gives us the knowledge we need to participate in our society. Self-help is an educational tool used to help us understand our emotions, where they come from, and what to do with them. For many people school was a place of embarrassment, frustration, anxiety and rejection. For others; self-help is still an unknown source of emotional education. When we are actively participating in education and self-help we are positively investing in the potential for our future success.

1. The Importance of Education:

Situation / Problem – Ray: In the 7th grade I was placed in opportunity classes because my grades were so low. Not long after, I ended up dropping out of school altogether. I did not think school was important because no one in my family had ever graduated. Plus, my mom did not care if I went to school at all. When I was placed in juvenile hall and then CYA, I flat-out refuse to do school work. I still did not care about school, especially when I was an active gang member in prison. It wasn't until 14 years into my sentence that I began to pursue my GED. My son was a teenager at the time and I tried to tell him why it was important he graduated and how it would open up doors for his future. He asked me "did you graduate?" I told him "no" I could sense him challenging me so I told him "if I get my GED would you be willing to finish school and graduate?" He said "yes" I then went back to school in 2010 and earned my GED. My son was proud of me. Our accomplishments brought us closer together.

Situation / Problem – Nathan: I was locked up shortly after completing the 10th grade. I had no love of education. When I was younger, it was a place of confusion and rejection. It became a place of anger as I got older. I went to school because in my small town, all my friends were there. Coming into prison with a life sentence, I saw no place for education in my life. In my mid-twenties, my dad was diagnosed with cancer. One of his wishes was for me to finish High School. I contacted the education department and was refused entry into the high school program. I appeal their decision and was eventually accepted into the program where I graduated with my diploma in 2009.

Internal: We felt frustrated and disappointed, determined, curious, confident, interested and challenged.

External: We decided to persevere in seeking to achieve our goal of continuing our education. We did not become discouraged during the process. We put in the hard work.

Consequences: We were allowed to participate in the education department. After fulfilling the requirements and completing all the work, we achieved our goal earning our GED and High School Diploma. Having felt a sense of pride and accomplishments, we realized that our self-esteem was beginning to improve. We continued our education by entering college and earning multiple degrees. Our loved ones were proud of us, and our relationship with them improved.

Solutions / Coping Skills: Today, we see the value in our education. It has brought stability to our lives. Establishing a daily routine for class and study time taught us time management skills. As we learned we felt intelligent, satisfied and overall happier. Our progress was a source of encouragement for our fellow prisoners. We became role models, which was something new to us. We became members of a new community in prison.

Questions for the Class

1. What is your opinion on the importance of Education?

2. What kind of student are you? Do you give up easily?

3. Do the adults in your life encourage your education, how so?

4. What emotions are connected to your school experience?

5. What are your future educational goals?

Education/Self-Help

2. The Importance of Self-Help:

Situation / Problem – Ray: In 2009, the first self-help class I ever took was Stress and Anger Management. I did not understand or know the power I actually had over my life. Although I changed who I hung out with, how I talked, dressed and how I began to see life, I realized I had never faced my past. I still got angry and would be stressed out; I was unable to pinpoint why. I continue to pursue self-help classes. In 2019 Parenting and Victim Awareness was the next class I took. Moving forward I took Emotional Processing Psychotherapy, Insight into overcoming criminal behavior therapy, and Impulse Control. My life began to change drastically as I learn to understand and identify my triggers and warning signs, along with learning coping skills. I slipped up a few times but never gave up. I used my coping skills to avoid a full-blown relapse. I learned the difference between lapses and relapses, as well as defects of character and short comings. A lapse and short coming is recognizing that you have a flat tire. A defect of character and relapse is driving on the flat tire.

Situation / Problem – Nathan: Even though I had changed my thinking and behaviors away from violence, and started to open up about my past and emotions, I still did not have an understanding of the bigger picture - why I still reacted negatively in situations and made poor decisions. I was holding on to a need to protect myself, in part due to my past, but also in avoidance of taking responsibility for the pain and destruction I caused to other people. I had not fully examined my deep emotional scars. Often I was triggered by things people said and did. I would lash out with angry and hurtful words to express the pain I felt. My first experience in self- help was with the Alternatives to Violence Project (AVP). AVP open my eyes to the idea that a positive community could be built with honesty, respect and caring.

Internal: We felt shame, fear, hurt, pain, sadness, anger, uncertainty, resentment, suspicion and we ruminated in these toxic emotions.

External: We were physically drained. We slept more than normal. We stayed tense and wound up. We became physically overwhelmed.

Consequences: We avoided and resisted fully opening up about our past. We stayed guarded in our relationship. Others saw this and felt uncomfortable around us. We still made poor decisions due to our negative mindset.

<u>Solutions / Coping Skills</u>: Today, by fully embracing self-help and opening up honestly about our past, the emotions attached to it, and how they caused us to think and act. We now understand our (**Causative Factors**.) Once this connection was discovered, we were able to begin working on breaking the negative cycles we were stuck in. We began signing up for specific self-help groups that addressed our issues. Whether it be anger, criminality, substance abuse, domestic violence, gang involvement or any other type of mask we wore. All of these issues stemmed from our childhood violence and the neglect we suffered. Exposing these roots released us from the secrets we held deep inside. We gained emotional literacy, and we learned coping skills and other tools from these self-help groups. We then began to practice these new skills and tools to help us respond rather than react negatively to any situation in our lives.

<u>Questions for the Class:</u>

1. What was the first thing you learned in self-help that made an impact in changing your life?

2. What has self-help done for your self-esteem and self-worth?

3. What do you still struggle with in self-help?

4. Do you open up and take responsibility for your life in self-help?

5. Why do you believe that so many people do not believe in self-help?

Education/Self-Help

3. New Values, New Beliefs, New Man:

Situation / Problem – Ray: In my adolescent years I never felt nurtured, loved, protected or cared for. So in response, I sought acceptance, validation, acknowledgement, and belonging. I felt I needed to be loved by dangerous people. Having been abandoned, neglected and rejected left me confused and full of insecurities, fear, and panic. This paved the way for me to create my defects of character. These defects allowed me to function and get by each day being angry, disrespectful, dishonest, selfish, violent and manipulative. The end result was me establishing a warped belief system to live by. The way I treated myself and others was based on my warped and negative belief system which changed every hour every day.

Situation / Problem – Nathan: At age 10, I started to build my values and beliefs around very toxic themes, born out of a need for self-protection and to avoid feeling powerless. I believed that I could only count on myself because the source of negative feelings in my life where from the people I knew. To avoid living in a miserable state, I lived by the belief that if it makes me feel good; then it was all right. Due to this belief I committed criminal acts and hurt people. Coming to prison at 17 years old and being exposed to violence, I saw the value in being willing to "get them before they get you." Whenever I felt in danger, these values and beliefs kept me safe. I used extreme violence and broke the rules as I saw fit, even though it was often not called for.

Internal: We felt hurt, fear, shame, unloved, rejected, humiliated, insecure, hateful, worthless, confusion, betrayal, abandoned and angry.

External: We stopped trusting people. We became secretive, aggressive and resisted authority. We put on masks that reflected our warped belief systems, feeling the need for self-protection.

Consequences: We became anti-social towards society. We had no respect for people or their personal property. We committed crimes and hurt people. We fed off our anger, and used the pain from our past to justify our actions.

Solutions / Coping Skills: Today, we have constructed new values and beliefs centered on responsibility and accountability for the damage we have inflicted upon others. We understand the warped values and beliefs we built were based on our lack of emotional literacy and not having any coping skills or tools. We now use our education and what we have learned from self-help, our improved self-esteem and our ability to forgive and establish healthy relationships. Learning as well to speak out assertively about things that bother us. We now have a support network; we never feel like we are alone. We now realize that people are not out to get us. We act with integrity and treat people how we want to be treated.

Questions for the Class:

1. What values and beliefs did you live by, that seemed to be healthy but they were not?

2. What is your new belief system? What do you value today?

3. How do you deal with dangerous, rude, aggressive and dishonest people without going back to the old you?

4. What warped believes do you still struggle with?

5. Why did it take you so long to change and become a new person?

Summary: When we educate ourselves, open up and make peace with our past, we gain emotional literacy. In our daily lives; when we practice using coping skills and tools, we begin to establish positive, healthy values and beliefs. We become new men and women who act with responsibility and are accountable for our actions and the welfare of others. Education and self help boost our self-esteem and growth in maturity.

Remorse

Remorse is more than just feeling bad for the violent and destructive things we have done. When you are remorseful you have to accepted responsibility and take ownership of the harm you have caused. You no longer make excuses for your actions. Remorse also entails taking accountability for what you have done by being answerable for your actions. True remorse is understood by putting yourself in the shoes of those you have harmed. This includes what their loved ones feel too. You must be able to apologize by articulating the exact harm you have caused.

1. Responsibility:

Situation / Problem – Ray: Before the child abuse, emotional neglect, molestation and witnessing the rape of my mother, I had empathy and compassion. I would cry watching a movie. However once I experienced a consistency of the above-mentioned damage, I no longer felt a sense of innocence. I adopted a belief that it was (my duty to protect myself at all cost.) If someone was harmed by me defending myself I felt no need to apologize. Overtime when my life began to change I began to experience remorse in different ways. When my sister Laurie died from cirrhosis of the liver (drinking alcohol), I felt so much guilt and shame for never being able to apologize for mistreating her. I knew I never wanted to hurt any of my sister's or drink ever again. When I was diagnosed out of nowhere and for no reason with valley fever, I experienced remorse towards my victim, Daniel Cox, in new and profound ways. This was the same way my victim died, out of nowhere and for no reason. I became broken and vulnerable, reliving what took place the night of my crime. I vowed to never commit an act of violence ever again.

Situation / Problem – Nathan: I live my life in denial. I refuse to take responsibility for anything I did. Nothing was my fault because I believe the harm done to me in my life absolved me from any blame. Growing up I never apologized or felt bad for the harm I had caused others. I murdered a human being. I did not take responsibility for the terrible thing I did. I avoided taking that responsibility by lying about what I had done. I came into prison, broke the rules, and continued to be violent. I felt I had the right to do what I wanted because it was not my fault for being in prison.

Internal: We felt anger, resentment, betrayal, confusion, rejected, violated, indifferent to others suffering, and that an injustice had been done. Later we felt shame.

External: We felt tense all the time, blamed others and acted like they were crazy. We could not make eye contact. We became judgmental and took a victim stance. We apologized without really meaning it.

Consequences: Our family and friends stop trusting us, we became those people that others avoided. We use substances to avoid thinking about the bad things we did. Eventually our lives fell apart as the law and others held us responsible for what we had done.

<u>Solutions / Coping Skills:</u> Today, we take full responsibility for our actions and the consequences of them. We no longer minimize or blame others for the things we did. We admit when we are wrong and apologize right away and correct the behavior. We seek out and accept help from others. We worked to refute our irrational beliefs and overcome our fears. We let go of our anger, fear, blame, mistrust and insecurities. We recognize that we are the sole determinants of the choices we make.

<u>Questions for the Class:</u>

1. Why is remorse hard to feel?

2. Why is remorse so hard to accept?

3. Does remorse free a person from inner pain?

4. What does remorse mean to you?

5. What is false remorse?

Remorse

2. Accountability:

Situation / Problem – Ray: I now understood that accepting responsibility for my own actions meant to acknowledge and own up to my part in a wrongdoing. However, accountability was something new to me. I soon found out that accountability was me having to give an answer for my wrongdoings, which was something I was taught from childhood to never do if I got into trouble. I struggled with being able to give an answer for my actions because I did not know the root cause of why I hurt people or participated in my life crime. I did not want to be blamed in any way for the murder of Daniel Cox because I was not the one who shot him. Therefore I minimized my part in the crime by living in denial which was easier to accept. What I learned about remorse, responsibility and accountability was that you are unable to live in that emotional state for very long, because deep down you know you have a responsibility to be accountable and make things right.

Situation / Problem – Nathan: I saw the negative impact of my actions but refused to change my ways. In no way did I want to be held accountable for murdering my friend. I committed crimes and blamed others because my values were centered on self-protection. I avoided accountability in my life crime by refusing to give a truthful account of what happened. In prison, whenever I received a write-up for a violent or destructive act, I would say I wasn't guilty. Since I had no blame in anything I did, I saw no reason to change my ways. Once something happened or was over and done with, I saw no reason to revisit it because it could not be undone. After I committed murder, I simply forgot about it. I thought no good would come out of me revisiting it or by being accountable for it.

Internal: We felt fear, worthless, violated and humiliation, betrayal, embarrassed, anger, self-hatred, inferior, and had internal negative self-talk. Which led to low self-esteem, later we felt the shame.

External: We tried to run away and avoid people we had wronged. We felt run down and often were still at ease in our own skin. We were terrified of suffering the consequences of our actions. We played the victim at all times. We refused to apologize or offered fake apologies, blaming others for our actions.

Consequences: Our lives became stagnant. The only people who associated with us were criminals and substance users. All of our meaningful relationships became strained. We were constantly under suspicion because people lost trust in us, and others who followed the rules and laws of society distanced themselves from us.

Solutions / Coping Skills: Today, we are accountable for our actions because we correct our behavior after making a mistake. We communicate honestly and take blame when we are responsible for harm. We protect and nurture our emotional health and well-being. We act with compassion and integrity towards ourselves and others. We ask for help when we need it. We no longer avoid holding ourselves accountable in any aspects of our lives. We seek understanding and not blame, by listening to what others have to stay. We are sincere when apologizing.

<u>Questions for the Class:</u>

1. Who have you answered to for your crimes?

2. Why is being accountable for your actions important?

3. When did you begin holding yourself accountable?

4. What have you not taking accountability for?

5. For you, what is the hardest part of being accountable?

Remorse

3. Empathy:

Situation / Problem – Ray: My unresolved hurt, pain, anger and resentment would not allow me to feel empathy. I believed putting myself in someone else's shoes served no purpose because it couldn't undo or reverse any of the damage I had caused. Going to juvenile hall, CYA and prison also factored into my lack of empathy. I believe nobody cared about me growing up, so why should I care about anyone else? Especially if there was no benefit in it for me. When I began to partake in self-help programs, I became aware of the consequences of my actions. Attending victim awareness classes and hearing the victim's stories open my mind to their sufferings. At that time, I began to have a better understanding for what they went through, and I began to feel empathy for them. Coming into prison as a youth offender I now realize I lacked empathy because when I saw someone getting stabbed or jump I just laughed. When I knew I had empathy, I began to hurt for all the people I had harmed in my life.

Situation / Problem – Nathan: The last thing I cared about was what someone else was going through or feeling. I went through life doing what I wanted in order to make myself feel better. I took from people without any concern for how it would affect them. I hurt people without a care for what it would do to their long-term health. I murdered a human being without a care or thought for the pain and suffering he would feel. I never worried about how it would affect his family, friends, the community, or, how anyone who heard about it would feel. Coming to prison, I continued with this behavior. Justifying it as a need for self-protection.

Internal: We felt insignificant, small, alienated and needy. Fearful, abandoned, lost, vulnerable, angry, victimized, hatred, humiliated and rejected by society.

External: We lashed out at others to release the hurt and pain we felt. Our lives were miserable, we had no inner peace and low self-esteem. Deep down we felt like cowards, acting selfishly at all times.

Consequences: We became scared to death; thinking about others doing to us, what we did to them. We betrayed those closest to us. Our relationships were surface-level and not many people wanted to be around us. We were constantly on the run from the people we hurt, and law enforcement for the crimes we committed. We could not look in the mirror without seeing a hollow shell.

Solutions / Coping Skills: Today, we think before we act. Often putting ourselves in the shoes of others to get different perspectives on the impact of our actions. We are compassionate with ourselves and others. We listen to what other people have to say, what their needs are, and express our own needs in order to reach a compromise. We think about the victims we have made in life, and see through their eyes, in order to understand what we put them through. We feel a deep sorrow and regret for the fear, pain and violence we brought into their lives. We now act with humility and integrity in our daily lives. We also deal with our shame in healthy ways through self-forgiveness and forgiving those who have harmed us. We now carry healthy guilt as motivation to never be the source of pain for others in this world. We will never create another victim in our lives. Empathy connects humanity as one.

Questions for the Class:

1. In your opinion, what is the difference between sympathy and empathy?

2. How does one develop empathy?

3. Whom can't you have empathy for?

4. Why is empathy important for your growth?

5. Lacking empathy harms you in what ways?

Summary: When we feel true remorse for the harm we have done to people, and society as a whole we begin to change the way we think and act. This has allowed us to become honest and responsible people who freely admit when we have wronged others. We immediately take the appropriate steps to right our wrongs without being forced to do so We are constantly aware of how people feel by putting ourselves in their shoes. Embracing empathy within our hearts has allowed us to feel included, rather than excluded, from humanity. Our remorse motivates us to always take full responsibility and hold ourselves accountable for the consequences of our actions.

Amends

Once you take responsibility for your crimes and become accountable (answerable) for them, and feel remorseful for the harm you caused, then you can take the steps to begin making amends. When you make amends, you take action to express your remorse through some form of restitution. Direct Amends is; any form of amends directly related to the victim. It includes apologizing directly to the victim and their family, writing an apology letter or paying monetary restitution to the victims. Indirect Amends is giving your time, or money to people who are the closest to the victim as possible. This could include helping or assisting at churches, youth centers, schools or the community in which you harmed. Living Amends is the way you live your life by making it your mission to show kindness, gratitude and give assistance. Even in the smallest encounters you have with others. Living amends is a vow one makes to never create victims again.

1. Direct Amends:

Situation / Problem – Ray: I did not know how to make direct amends because my victim was deceased. I went through the stages of remorse and decided to write a remorse letter. I found that I lacked the words to properly express my sorrow and the regret I felt. I would start letters, and then rip them up. My remorse weighed so heavy upon me, too strong to allow me to avoid making amends. With a heavy heart and tears in my eyes, I wrote my victim Daniel Cox a letter. It took weeks to write the letter because the guilt and shame was too painful and strong, but I was able to finish it. Once I did, I felt a heavy burden lifted within me. I first read the letter to God, then I read it to Daniel as if he were standing right in front of me.

Situation / Problem – Nathan: For years I avoided making any kind of amends because I had not taken responsibility or expressed remorse for murdering a human being. I was in prison away from all those who I had harmed so I thought there was no point. When I found out that my victim's sister had written me a letter 17 years earlier, (which I never received) it deeply affected me. All the years that had gone by with no response from me only deepened her anger and hate for me. It seemed like there was now no avenue for me to make direct amends to her or the family.

Internal: Thinking about making amends we felt scared, anxious, inferior, dismayed, overwhelmed and then apathetic. At the time we were unsure, but began to think about making amends.

External: We felt comfortable in prison and continued in our criminality not worrying about making amends. Over the years we began to feel a heavy burden and the weight of responsibility; we needed to make amends to the many victims we created in our lives.

Consequences: For many years, we did not make any true direct amends. Leaving the families we harmed in a state of despair not having any closure. We continued in our violent and destructive ways creating new victims.

Solutions / Coping Skills: Today, we take direct amends seriously. We have an obligation to those we have harmed. Even though they are not living, we have written letters of remorse and apologized to our victims *Daniel Edward Cox and Erik Ingebretsen* and their families. We pay our victims restitution fines. While knowing that no amount of money will give the victim's family their loved ones back. Today, when any of our actions cause harm to another, we make direct amends and offer an apology. We live by a moral code; nobody has the right to harm another person for any reason. We treat all people with compassion and kindness.

Questions for the Class:

1. Who does an amends letter help?

2. Have you made direct amends?

3. If so, what took you so long?

4. If you have not made direct amends, what is stopping you from doing so?

5. Why is direct amends necessary?

Amends

2. Indirect Amends:

Situation / Problem – Ray: Making indirect amends was no easier than direct amends. Many of my victims and their loved ones used their voices to belittle me, protest against me and wish me dead. Later on, the memory of all the people I had indirectly hurt kept popping up in my mind. I remembered their faces as they spoke, one by one, with tremendous pain and suffering. When I understood that making indirect amendment meant educating myself and correcting my behaviors, I began participating in domestic violence, victim awareness and other abuse related classes. I dedicated my life to staying involved with these groups. I vowed to share my life story to help others. This led me to starting two self-help groups: The Road to Redemption Project and (BIO) Building Individual Ownership.

Situation / Problem – Nathan: After many years into my incarceration, when I learned about indirect amends, I was at a loss. I never thought I owed anything to people I had not directly hurt. I had no plans to make any indirect amends to the community I harmed. I was at a loss to understand how I could make indirect amends to my small community, who clearly wanted nothing to do with me.

Internal: We felt inadequate, unworthy, scared, embarrassed, hesitant and worried that we could never make any meaningful amends.

External: We physically felt overwhelmed and confused on how to begin making amends. The fear of causing further harm left us feeling sad and depressed.

Consequences: We avoided thinking about taking responsibility for our actions. We left innocent people with many unresolved questions and feelings. We could not bring ourselves to be fully responsible for the harm we caused to our communities. We struggled with our self- esteem, questioning whether or not we had any redeeming qualities. We began to ask others for help with understanding the impact of our crimes.

Solutions / Coping Skills: Today, we fully understand that the crimes we committed have a ripple effect of pain, hurt and fear that can last generations. We have learned that we harm society when we victimize one of its members. As criminals, we owe a debt of obligation to find ways to make restitution for the harm we have caused. By growing to understand the responsibility we have to any community we are a part of, we have learned how to give back to that community in order to right our wrongs.

<u>Questions for the Class:</u>

1. In what ways have you made indirect amends?

2. What self-help classes do you need to be a part of that addresses indirect amends for your specific crimes?

3. What is the benefit of making indirect amends?

4. Is indirect amends a lifelong process for you? Why or why not?

5. How do you feel about making indirect amends for your crimes?

Amends

3. Living Amends:

<u>Situation / Problem – Ray</u>: Working to understand my causative factors, defects of character and being able to identify my triggers and warning signs, put me in a position to find answers and develop coping skills for my past, present and future. It has not been easy trudging the path of recovery out of the insanity of my life, but it needed to be done to become human again. It was my only option because I never wanted to go back to the person I was. Changing my thoughts, speech, conduct and actions has freed me from my past. By reinventing myself in new ways, I allow my real identity, personality and character to shine through and be a blessing. I am then able to enjoy and share my gifts and talents with others.

<u>Situation / Problem – Nathan</u>: The baggage of my life caused me to question whether I could ever truly impact the world in any kind of positive way. Many times in my life I crossed a line doing criminal and violent acts that no person should ever be able to come back from. I sit here in prison convicted of murdering my friend, how can I make my life matter or hope to replace a fraction of the vast amount of happiness, safety and love I have taken from the world? I have heard people say that you can give back to the world by living your amends daily and never again being a source of harm and pain in the world. I was open to the possibility of change.

<u>Internal:</u> We felt shame, dismayed, sorrow, and regret. Worthless and uncertain that real change could happen for us.

<u>External:</u> We felt down and depressed under the weight of how much pain and suffering we caused. We felt exhausted and overwhelmed at putting into practice our daily change.

<u>Consequences:</u> Whenever we thought about the impact of our crimes, we became overwhelmed and withdrawn to ourselves. Our family and friends noticed we were acting differently and they became concerned. We continue living in denial for many years with low self-esteem. Eventually we educated ourselves on how we could make a difference in our community. With the help of others we made the necessary change.

<u>Solutions / Coping Skills:</u> Today, we have come to realize that our lives do matter and that we can make a difference in someone's life in a positive way. When we live our amends we live a life of service by helping others heal from their past. We help them feel safe enough to begin their journey in taking responsibility and making amends. We live our amends daily by acting with honesty and integrity. We have become mentors and role models in building a positive community.

<u>**Questions for the Class:**</u>

1. When did your living amends begin?

2. What part of living amends do you still need to address?

3. Why is living amends necessary for your recovery?

4. By living amends, what do you think will change in your life?

5. How do other people know your living amends is genuine?

Summary: Amends is the culmination of introspective emotional healing we express outwardly through actions that help others heal. The insight we gain during our healing process compels us to share our compassion, love, empathy, peace, hope, humility, kindness and truth with both those we have harmed and others in the world. In that respect we articulate our deep sorrow and regret for exactly how we victimized and changed the lives of others. We take full responsibility and accountability, express our remorse and apologize for our intrusions into people's lives. We vowed to live our lives as law-abiding citizens and be of service to those in need of our help.

PHASE TWO

Upon completion of Phase One:

The founding members will assist the BIO program graduates in developing a personal biography to utilize in Phase Three.

To The Department of Corrections and its Employees

Progress Report Summary

A Defense on behalf of Current and Future Rehabilitation Programs at High Desert State Prison

Written by: Inmates at H.D.S.P.
December, 2019

To the Governor of California and the Department of Corrections

(Secretary, Warden, Facility A Administration, and Community Resource Managers Office).

Second
Progress Report
90 day follow up
September-December
2019

What was accomplished, what is yet to be done with future plans and Proposals?

*"If hindsight is 20/20, then, let us learn
From 2019 and do better in 2020!"*

"Don't complain about the problem unless you're a part of the solution."

Greetings and special regards to all of you for reading this Report and all that you do on behalf of Inmates welfare and human progress!

Back Story

In September, 2019, a group of inmates put together and submitted a Progress Report to the California Department of Corrections and its personnel. The above Report was submitted to the following CDCR Employees:

- Ralph Diaz, Secretary of CDCR
- Joleen Speers, Community Resource Manager
- M.E. Spearman, former Warden of H.D.S.P
- M. Carrillo, former Captain of Facility A

Various Inmate Advocacy Groups also received it including, Place 4 Grace, Path 2 Restoration, and Alternative to Violence (AVP), just to name a few.

Surprisingly, Ralph Diaz contacted former Warden Spearman about the Progress Report and wanted to speak to some of us who were responsible for organizing it. On the same day a conference call was held with the Secretary, the former Warden, Captain Carrillo and the inmates.

The secretary wanted to thank us for contacting him with the report, and he also wanted to hear some suggestions on how we could further progress here at High Desert State Prison.

A summary of those requests are as follows:

1. Work on changing the culture from the employee level, for those correction officers who are skeptical of rehabilitation, and therefore resist its legitimacy, to some degree.

2. Encourage more corrections officers to accept the challenge and sign on to be sponsors of Self-Help Groups and grant them additional incentives for doing so.

3. Recruit more outside Sponsors on the above premise (a culture of rehabilitative acceptance from the top down).

4. Permit the Chairman of Self-Help Groups, their Executive Body and group Facilitator's an opportunity to meet regularly to communicate, train, and make the existing groups more effective.

Currently on Facility-A, there is building access authorization for Education Clerks, Tutors, Special Purchase Clerk and Inmate Advisory Council (I.A.C.); however, the men responsible for Rehabilitation programs are restricted from access to buildings to:

1. Meet with Members of their Executive Body.

2. Confer with building or RAC approved group Facilitators.

3. Assist Self-Help Group Members with curriculum or other rehabilitation matter.

4. Circulate Self-Help materials.

We felt, and expressed that, the (R) in C.D.C.R. was not being genuinely respected. The Secretary asked us to get with our Facility Captain about this matter, who was present and now gone. Actually, in response to this issue the former Captain ordered a memo to be drafted for him to sign permitting such Chairman movement, but, sadly this effort was defeated by others in Facility-A Administration. So, to date, no progress has been made concerning this matter.

Some Progress

The Secretary also recommended that we forward the progress to Governor Gavin Newsome, which we fulfilled in November 2019. At this point in time we haven't heard back from the Governor's Office. However, the Secretary informed us that the Governor was diligently working to make rehabilitation a reality throughout the Department and actually sent him to Denmark to study their prison model and the outstanding success that occurred in Connecticut where a Corrections Officer took interest in an inmate involved in a Self-Help Group and ultimately assisted him with getting into college upon release. This former inmate is now playing basketball for a college team (The book, "The Meaning of Life" reads in Books Without Bounds provides insight into the progressive Denmark Prison Model). The Secretary said, "The Governor is working to improve the culture to that extent which requires change in policy, especially as it relates to staff/inmate relationships that lies at the heart of what occurred in Connecticut." That can happen anywhere.

Further, out of this discussion a proposal was drawn up by a few inmates requesting a meeting place for Chairmen, Executive Body Members of ILTAG programs, and Facilitators. This Group was titled: Inmate Rehabilitation Committee (I.R.C.) and could possibly be in effect in early 2020.

Summary of Former Report

The September, 2019 progress report was somewhat massive, containing 123 pages. Below is a summary of its content:

1. An overview, Evidence of inmate's interest in rehabilitation programs.

2. A request for addition Sponsors and Self-Help Groups.

3. A list of all the Self-Help Groups founded or brought to HDSP (Facilities A&B), since 2016, confirming inmate's interest in, and qualification for Self-Help Group Leadership and participation. Here's is a list of those groups:

- GOGI
- Life Choices
- TRY
- Fatherless Fathers
- KID CAT
- NEW H.E.A.R.T.S
- The Self-Improvement Class (Chapel)
- Books Without Bounds
- Reaching Out From Within (in-cell)
- CGA
- Academic Chess and R.E.V.E.L
- R.A.M.P.
- Victims Impact
- Initiate Justice
- Veterans Support Group

4. A list of proposed groups was included:

- The freedom Committee (For Lifers and long term offenders)
- G.A.M.E (A Sports Activity Group which was recently approved)
- Write Our Wrongs (Victims Impact Group)
- The Phoenix Rose
- American Legion (Vets Group), and
- Road to Redemption

5. A section for events and proposals for future events:

- Juneteenth/Interfaith Community Celebration
- Stop the Violence Talent Show
- Proposal for Staff/Inmate Homerun Derby Challenge and
- Various other past events from Facility B

6. Brief representation of curriculum material for current and past Self-Help Groups.

7. Bio-sketches of organizers of the Progress Report

8. A section for future plans; they included:

- The Strongman/Ironman Challenge
- The Pledge of Peace event and
- A Multi-Cultural Holiday Event (for Christmas, Hanukah, Kwanza, and the Chinese New Year's)

Thanks largely to the support we've received from the Warden, the CRM's Office, and the Facility Administration. We are proud to report that the Ironman Challenge and the Pledge of Peace celebration were achieved (November 2019). The Holiday Event has been rescheduled and we're confident that it will happen in the month of December or shortly thereafter.

Moreover, adding to our two-day Leadership conference followed by the Ironman and Pledge of Peace raising the frequency of consciousness and activity which proves rehabilitation works; and if given the opportunity, with the support from CDCR personnel, true change and progress is the probable result.

<u>Summary Progress Achieved</u>
<u>Since Last Report</u>

- Inmate Rehabilitation Committee (IRC) preliminary approved
- Ironman Challenge
- Pledge of Peace
- Initiate Justice (approved on Facility B)
- Leadership Conference
- G.A.M.E approved

<u>Looking Towards 2020</u>
<u>Future Plans and Proposals for CRM's Office, and</u>
<u>High Desert State Corrections and Administration</u>

We are currently making efforts to reach out to San Quentin Newspaper and Ear Hustle podcast for some publicity. We are waiting for pictures from the Coach for the Ironman Challenge and the CRM's Office for the Pledge and Leadership Conference to be sent with our letter.

- <u>Inmate Donation</u> drive for Lassen Family Services (Dec. 2019)
- <u>The Leaders of the Future Workshop</u> (Jan. 2020)
- <u>The Veterans Event and Walk</u> (Feb. 2020)
- <u>Donation Drive to Assist</u> Elderly indigent inmates with receiving appliances, clothing, etc. (undated)
- <u>Initiate Justice Conference</u> for frequently asked questions (FAQ's) regarding the law, recently passed and proposed legislation (undated)
- <u>An 1170(d) Conference</u> to inform inmates about this process (undated) actually Nate Williams wanted to coordinate this conference with the Pledge of Peace event but had to reschedule.
- <u>GOGI (Power-UP!) Yard Event</u> (near spring 2020)
- <u>LWOP Conference</u> (spring 2020)
- <u>Leadership Conference</u> (spring 2020)
- <u>Inter-faith Community Event and Talent Show</u> (summer 2020?)
- <u>Ironman Challenge</u> (fall 2020)

- <u>Pledge of Peace Event</u> (fall 2020)
- <u>Multi-cultural Holiday Event</u> (winter 2020)
- <u>Path 2 Restoration</u> with Nate Williams and Karen McDaniel is scheduled for their second round of "Choices for Freedom" in January/February. We believe a graduation for these classes will occur in the spring of 2020 as well; possibly in March.

<u>Needs for Continued Progress</u>

1. Groups in need of Sponsors:
   - NEW H.E.A.R.T.s
   - Reaching Out From Within
   - Beginning Drawing
   - Victims Impact
   - Positive Parenting Program
   - Freedom Committee

2. Building access for Chairmen of Self-Help Groups

3. Regular monthly meetings between the CRM's Office and inmate leaders in the rehabilitation community

4. Continued support for the community event that provide unique opportunities for inmates to meet, learn and forge positive relationships

Thank you to all of all readers for your time, support and consideration. Together everyone accomplishes more!

<u>Authors Note</u>

The following inmates have contributed to the work mentioned in this Progress Report.

<u>Data Collectors and Authors</u>

J. Wilson AU5200...Author of Report
D. Poston AT2512...Co-Author of Report

<u>Contributing Authors</u>

R. Bracamonte K85547
S. Allee BA8058
D. Wilkerson AE1573
M. Adams BE6337
N. Ramazinni P04587
A. Woodard K03234

Special thanks to these men and their service!!!

Date:April 11,2016

From:Founding five members of (T.R.Y.),signatures on page 3.

To: V. Zumpano,Facility B Captain

Subject:Proposal for inmate self-help group,ie;Truly Redefine Yourself
        (T.R.Y.)

BACKGROUND

The idea for T.R.Y. came about during a discussion between five
inmates in the recreation dayroom at High Desert State Prison(H.D.S.P.).
The initiator behind this idea was our youngest member,Renwick Drake,
who encouraged us to continue gathering weekly during our dayroom
time,to discuss issues related to our past mistakes,our desire for
change and the possibility of creating an environment conductive for
peace,growth and progress for both inmates and staff.

VISION STATEMENT

T.R.Y. stands for "Truly Redefine Yourself", T.R.Y.'s vision
statement encourages it's members to:

1. Confornt and redefine any negitive self images we have imposed
   on ourselves.

2. While this process is underway to continue to reinforce one's
   new self image with positive and productive education and
   activities.

   Basically, we accept accountability for how our lives have turned
out and therefore we are required to avail of our self initiative and
free time to confront our once negitive past and continue to change ourselves into better people regardless of our circumstances.We humbly
and willingly accept this work.

PROGRAM

To accomplish our goals we:

1. Meet Monday,Wednesday, and Friday of each week at our own dayroom time for service of T.R.Y. and days between for further
   educational pursuits.

2. Discuss past behaviors and ways to change them.

3. Participate in writing about our lives and sharing the content
   of our transformation with others.

4. Being daily accessible to other inmates for mentorship in
   progress and positive life skills.

5. Promoting conflict resolution concepts and methods.

6. Continuously building positive relationships with individuals and other self-help leisure activity groups, including members of diverse religious denominations.

OUTREACH EFFORTS

Aside from building positive relationships and mentoring willing inmates we have collected our personal writings about our lives and have assembled them into a booklet we call "The STEP". "STEP" stands for "Solutions To Every Problem" and every month we'd like to gather other inmate stories of change and circulate them amongst the General Population to inspire hope and possibly a willingness to transform individual lives. Everything T.R.Y. does is produced from the efforts and initiative of willing members and other participants.

BY-LAWS

1. We accept members of all races and ethnicities.

2. Members of all religious beliefs can participate in T.R.Y.

3. We are politically neutral.

4. We believe in practicing what we preach and putting our best foot forward.

5. We believe in pursuing academic, spiritual, and self-help education.

6. We believe in brotherhood and that all Human Beings are members of one universal family.

7. Our purpose is to create an environment conductive for peace, growth, and progress for both inmates and staff members.

REQUEST

1. That we be allowed to use dayroom tables and benches to continue meeting at our dayroom time.

2. That other interested inmates on the opposite tier be permitted to attend our group meetings provided they participate for it's duration (one hour) and then return to their cell at staff's discretion.

3. That we be permitted to make a "reasonable" amount of copies of our STEP booklets to circulate to other interested inmates.

SUMMARY

In conclusion we welcome staff observation and scrutiny to promote a better understanding of our proposed program. We believe that our current relationships with other inmates, and our building staff suggests that our proposal is worth consideration.

FOUNDING MEMBERS

Renwick Drake Jr.,AL-9471

Marty LeMaster,G-00937

James Wilson,AU-5200

Orlindo Myles,AF-1849

Charles Smith,AA-7523

    If needed any or all of the above founders would be happy to meet and further discuss any issues you may have in consideration of approving our leisure time activity group.Thank You!

V.Zumpano,Facility B Captain   Approved   Disapproved

Date: February 25, 2019

To: Warden ME. Spearman, CRM's Office, Fac-A Administration (Capt., Lt., etc.)
    and any prospective sponsor

From: Jakier Roseman BC-9919, A1-202; Donel Poston AT-2512, A2-107; James Wilson
        AU5200, A1-249; Demetrius Wilkerson AE-1573, A1-202

RE: Approval of New Program (Reaching out From Within)

Greetings,

Attached to this proposal is a curriculum created by a 24 year old prisoner at
H.D.S.P (Jakier Roseman). Mr. Roseman, seeking to improve his own life, sought
out several older gentlemen on Fac-A to make his vision become a reality on
paper. Hence, the attached curriculum.

Proposal

The request is to have this program, Reaching out From Within, implemented on
Fac-A through the following possible means:

1. <u>In-Cell Program</u>: For C-status inmantes, and other inmates in the prison
   population, including new arrivals and

2. <u>Il-Tag Program</u>: with a sponsor once one becomes available

3. <u>Future Dayroom</u>: Facilitated program

The first goal is for this program to be received and accessed for operation
regardless to the program function (In cell, Il-Tag, etc.)

Back Story

Jakier Roseman is a 24 year old first termer serving a seven year sentence. Mr.
Roseman is a "survivor" of several forms of abuse, including sexual abuse as a
child. Through reaching out to older mentors in the prison population, he has
put his life on a new trajectory and serves as a model for what other inmates,
young and old, are capable of. Mr. Roseman wants to be a voice and example of
positive programming.

<u>Time and Place of Program</u>

Reaching out From Within could run during:

1. Inmates personal cell time

2. During the available time schedule of any sponsor and/or

3. During inmates dayroom time (any time program is running).

<u>By Laws</u>

Reaching out From Within is a program that:

1. Admits for participation people of all races, religions, and sexual orientations,

2. Seeks to forward inmates interest in the area of self-improvement via rehabilitative programs,

3. Promotes academic and vocation accomplishments,

4. Encourages its participants to positively program and avoid violent conflicts

5. Teaches its members to strive toward better citizens outside of prisons.

<u>Goals of Program</u>

1. To assist inmates with using their life-story for positive motivation.

2. To encourage inmates to transform their pain into self-empowerment.

3. To promote a positive self-image by encourages inmates to search out their hearts for their true core values and purpose.

4. To reward inmates with laudatory chrono's for their efforts to positively program.

Thank you for your time and consideration. We really appreciate your cooperation.

<u>Members of Reaching out From Within</u>

Jakier Roseman
Donel Poston
James Wilson
Demetrus Wilkerson

Memorandum

Date: Thursday August 8, 2019

To: Warden M.E. Spearman, Facility A Captain M. Carrillo, and Coach Boyer

From: James Wilson AU5200 (A1-249), Donel Poston AT2512 (A5-137), and David Johnson AR2179 (A4-237)

Subject: **SPORTS ACTIVITY ACADEMIC WORKSHOPS (G.A.M.E.-GAINING A MEANINGFUL EDUCATION) PROPOSAL**

Members of the sports community would like to expand our weekly athletic programs to include an academic and rehabilitative component. We believe that health is a balance between the body and the mind. What we would like to do thirty minutes prior to every game is:
1. Implement a ten minute meditation session.
2. A five minute study course and,
3. End each day game with a team-work pledge (Pledge Attached).

Brief Overview of G.A.M.E
G.A.M.E is an acronym for <u>G</u>aining <u>A</u> <u>M</u>eaningful <u>E</u>ducation. Our goal is to make both mental and physical education an aspect of our daily life, including our sports activities. Sports have meaning beyond "winning", which includes:
- Knowledge
- Roles and positions
- Team work
- Support
- Rules
- Time-management
- Leadership
- Training and skills
- Respect
- Purpose

We believe the basic elements of any game are:
1. Knowledge--To play any game requires knowing the fundamentals.
2. Skill--In order to advance at any game a certain skill-set is required.
3. Rules—Rules are necessary for structure and fairness.
4. Time—No game (nor life) lasts forever; therefore there must be an end-game (goal) in sight.
5. Purpose--The purpose of most game players are to win. Wining has different meanings for people. Another word for winning is success or completion. Even in sports, if you lose a game it must play out to the end.

Educational Material
For weekly lessons we will rely on:
- Men's Health Magazines
- San Quentin News (Sports Section)
- Books written about and by sports figures and,

- Our own knowledge and experience of the game of sports, life challenges, and where the two intersect.

Facilitators

We have a few inmates who will mediate and lead us in this ten (10) minute activity.

Location and Time

We are requesting the gym area or the Facility A yard basketball court for this program forty five (15) minutes before 0900 yard release at 0845 Saturday and Sunday one day for each tier.

Participants

The class will consist of 10 to 15 inmates for whatever tournament sport(s) scheduled to play that weekend. A list will be generated every 30 days (a 4 week course twice a week). Fifteen inmates per tier, one group Saturday, one group Sunday, and only during their assigned yard schedule.

Benefits

Not only would inmates gain a more informed perspective of sports, they will also enrich their minds and experience. We would like to provide the following:
1. A 5 minute group warm up course (push-ups, jumping jacks, stretches, relay's, etc.)
2. Laudatory chromos for organized sports with a learning component

We anticipate an increase in recreational and health related activities as a result of these incentives. Note: Please review attached articles from San Quentin News about sports and rehabilitation.

Thank you for your time and consideration concerning this matter.

J.HARTGROVE   RECOMMEND/ NOT RECOMMENDED

Facility A Sergeant

M. HUDSON   RECOMMEND/NOT RECOMMENDED
Facility A Lieutenant

M. CARRILLO   APPROVED/DISAPPROVED
Facility A Captain

High Desert State Prison
INMATE ACTIVITY GROUP BY-LAWS
Review Year 2019
The GAME Plan

Name
The name of the group shall be The Games, Athletics, Maintenance, and Exercise (GAME) Plan.

Purpose
The purpose of The GAME Plan is to thoroughly inform its members about health and best practices for staying in shape. The mission is to help its members live a healthy lifestyle while incarcerated and to continue upon release.

Operation
- Participants will follow the Curriculum created by the inmate population.
- The group should complete the course work and activities in 8 weeks
- After each 8-week session, new members will be added to the group, and the old members will be cycled out.

Membership
Membership is open to all interested inmates regardless of race, creed, color, or sexual orientation. A maximum of 50 participants will be added to the group at the beginning of each cycle.

Members will be assigned to the group from the Strategic Offender Management System (SOMS) waiting lists. The Community Resources Office will maintain the waiting list for each facility. Interested inmates must submit a California Department of Corrections and Rehabilitation Form 2016, Inmate Activity Group Program Request, to the Community Resource Office requesting to be added to the SOMS waitlist.

Removal from the Group
Any member of the group can be removed from the group by the staff Supervisor for disruptive or disrespectful behavior, lack of participation, or excessive absences. Two consecutive unexcused absences are grounds for removal due to excessive absences. Participants who are placed on C/C status or rehoused in Short Term Restricted Housing will be unassigned from the group.

Activities and Meeting Content
The group will meet weekly for approximately one hour. Scheduling of the meeting day and time will be determined by the staff Supervisor and availability of the Gymnasium. Attendance will be documented by the staff Supervisor, by way of sign-in sheets and counts. Meetings will follow the curriculum and guidelines of The GAME Plan Curriculum.

Deviations from the curriculum or any special activity/program will be determined by the facilitators and staff Supervisor during a regularly scheduled meeting.

Laws and Regulations
The operation The GAME Plan is subject to regulations in California Code of Regulations Title 15, the DOM, and related DOM supplements and prison procedures.

By-laws

The by-laws shall be reviewed by the group annually. Proposed changes of by-laws require the consent of two-thirds of the members present at a regularly scheduled group meeting. By-laws must be submitted to the Warden for approval via the Community Resource Manager annually.

APPROVED / DISAPPROVED

J. PICKETT	Date

Warden (A)
High Desert State Prison

<u>TEAMWORK PLEDGE</u>

TEAMWORK MAKES THE DREAM WORK, AND TOGETHER EVERYONE ACCOMPLISHES MORE.

"HOW TO"
WRITE PROPOSALS
AND BY-LAWS

Memorandum

Date: June 24,2016

To: Housing Units 1 & 2
Facility B, HDSP

From: T. Thompson,
Captain, Facility B
HDSP

Subject: ILTAG, HOUSING UNIT ACCESS

The following three ILTAG members of T.R.Y. (Truly Redefine Yourself) shall be allowed access to Housing Units 1 & 2 during programming hours for the express purpose of establishing core members within said Unit's with a view toward creating T.R.Y. groups in their communities; passing out T.R.Y. curriculum; and mentoring those willing to change their lives for the better through self-knowledge. These three men are:

- WILSON   AU-5200   5-118
- LEMASTER   G-00937   5-119
- RENO   G-61303   5-243

NOTE: If the above inmates are found to be doing any business other than the above-mentioned, or otherwise authorized matters by Unit Staff, a CDCR 128 shall be issued to my office for the appropriate disciplinary action; and the above-authorized access shall be immediately retracted.

T. Thompson, Captain
Facility B, HDSP

STATE OF CALIFORNIA

DEPARTMENT OF CORRECTIONS AND REHABILITATION
High Desert State Prison

Memorandum

Date: July 1, 2016

To: **B-5 Control Booth and Floor Officers**

From: T. Thompson, Captain
            Facility B, HDSP

Subject: **APPROVAL FOR I.T.A.G. : T.R.Y. (HOUSING UNIT SUPPORT GROUP)**

The following "Career Coaches" for T.R.Y (Truly Redefine Yourself) are approved to hold meetings in the Dayroom every **Tuesday** from **1400 hours to 1515 hours**:

Wilson	AU5200	5-118
Lemaster	G00937	5-119
Smith	AA7523	5-112
Reno	G61303	5-243
Penaloza	AF2264	5-127
Mahan	G01493	5-230

T. Thompson, Captain
Facility B, HDSP

Orig.   T. Thompson, Captain
CC.   B-5 Control Booth & Floor Officers
        Program Office
        MAC Files

CDC 1617 (3/89)

State of California   Department of Corrections and Rehabilitation

Memorandum

Date   :   August 28, 2019

To   :   Facility A Staff
           High Desert State Prison

Subject: **FACILITY A TALENT SHOW**

On Tuesday, September 3, 2019, the self-improvement class participants, in sponsorship with Chaplain T. Suleyman and Chaplain H. Mukdani, are hosting a Talent Show in the Facility A Gymnasium. This event will provide inmates with an opportunity to showcase their talent in a peaceful and productive manner. Inmate participants (list attached) will be eligible for Excused Time Off.

Facility A Gym Officer will be assigned to .count, out-count, and provide security as needed.

This talent show will showcase the following categories:

- Music of all genres (positive, motivational, and uplifting lyrics only)
- Dance acts (individual or groups)
- Poetry
- Motivational speaking presentations

If you have any questions please contact Community Resources Manager Jolene Speers at extension 5526.

M. E. SPEARMAN
Warden
High Desert State Prison

Attachment

State of California

Department of Corrections and Rehabilitation

Memorandum

Date :   October 15, 2019

To   :   All Staff
           High Desert State Prison

Subject: **FACILITY A PLEDGE OF PEACE EVENT**

The Inmate population on Facility A are sponsoring the Pledge of Peace event on November 18, 2019, from 0900-1300 hours in the Facility A Gymnasium (Gym). Each participating inmate will donate a minimum of $10.00 and all donations will go to the Susanville American Legion. The annual Pledge for Peace event, alongside the Veterans Support Group on Facility A, is to promote non-violence and rehabilitative incentive. The participants are pledging to remain disciplinary free for six months.

The Pledge of Peace event will include:

- Walk-a-thon (eight lap walk around the track)
- Speeches from staff and veterans group members
- A mini concert led by inmate musicians and singers
- Group trivia contest
- Last man standing burpee contest
- Dodge ball
- Pledge of Allegiance
- Pledge of Peace ceremony/signing of the Pledge

The only portion of the event that will take place outside of the Gym will be the Walk-a-thon. The Walk-a-thon will begin at approximately 0900 hours.

The coach will issue prizes for first and second place and Walkenhorst will supply participation grab bags (if available). Additionally, inmates will be given the opportunity to purchase ducats from Canteen and the inmate photographer shall take photographs to be purchased during the event.

The Community Resources Office will proved a microphone and speaker to be utilized during the event.

Six months from the date of the event, inmate participants will receive a Chrono stating they made a donation to the Susanville American Legion and succeeded in their pledge.

Thank you for your assistance in preparing for this important event. If you have any questions please contact Community Resources Manager J. Speers at extension 5526.

M. E. SPEARMAN
Warden
High Desert State Prison

State of California   Department of Corrections and Rehabilitation

Memorandum

Date :   August 29, 2019

To   :   J. Speers CRM (Community Resource Manager)

Subject: **PROPOSAL FOR NEW H.E.A.R.T.S./INTER-FAITH SPONSORED TALENT SHOW ON SEPTEMBER 3, 2019**

On August 27, 2019 the self-help and religious community would like to host a "stop the violence" talent show to provide inmates with an opportunity to showcase their gifts, skills, and talents in a peaceful and productive manner.

This talent show will showcase the following categories:
- Music of all genres (positive, motivational, and uplifting lyrics only)
- Dance acts (individual or groups)
- Poetry reading (including spoken word)
- Motivational speaking presentations

Also included in the day's events will be:
- Speeches from chaplains
- Prepared speeches from members of the Freedom Committee on the Write Our Wrongs victim's initiative project
- Snacks and sodas will be provided for those in attendance
- Circulation of positive community information

Criteria:
- One performance per person
- The performances theme must be positive, not controversial
- *No curse words, references to gangs, or violence*
- **NO C-Status inmates or any Serious RVR in the last year.**

Each performer will be judged based upon a point system, overseen by a 3-panel judgeship, following the guide lines listed below:
1. Quality of content
2. Theme of the performances
3. Overall performance (flawless, mistakes, re-starts)
4. Adherence to the criteria set above

Talent Show
Page 2

If at all possible the event organizers would like assistance from the CRMs office by providing a microphone and speaker (karaoke machine) to make this event successful.

Attached is a list of all those who will be attending and participating in the "stop the violence" talent show event.

Thank you for your time and consideration concerning this matter.

RECOMMEND/NOT RECOMMENDED

J. HARTGROVE
Facility "A" SGT
High Desert State Prison

RECOMMEND/NOT RECOMMENDED

M. CARRILLO
Facility "A" Captain
High Desert State Prison

APPROVED/DISAPPROVED

J. SPEERS
CRM
High Desert State Prison

STATE OF CALIFORNIA   DEPARTMENT OF CORRECTIONS AND REHABILITATIONS

DATE: February 14, 2017
TO: ALL FACILITY B STAFF
          HDSP
FROM: Truly Redefine Yourself, (T.R.Y.)
          Self-Help Group,
          Sponsored by C/O Brewer

SUBJECT: PROPOSAL FOR T.R.Y.'S FIRST ANNIVERSARY CELEBRATION

The attached list of Career Coaches request temporary space in the Facility B Gym or Kitchen
In order to celebrate the one year anniversary of T.R.Y.'S founding in HDSP here on Facility B.

We request this celebratory meet for the following activities:

- Congratulatory speeches
- Fellowship, and
- Eating

The members of T.R.Y. will be furnishing our own food products for this event and have designated

Specific T.R.Y. members to cook our meals.

We further thank you in advance for your consideration and assistance.

T. R. Y. CORE GROUP

_________________________   _________________________
T. THOMPSON, CAPTAIN   J. GINDER, LIEUTENANT

FACILITY B, HDSP   FACILITY B, HDSP

* EVENT WILL TAKE PLACE 2-15-17

MEMORANDUM

DATE   : April 7, 2017

TO   : ALL FACILITY B STAFF

FROM   : T. THOMPSON, CAPTAIN

        FACIITY B, HDSP

SUBJECT : T.R.Y. SPONSORED TOURNAMENT, BASKETBALL

During the early weeks of April, the sponsored ILTAG, T.R.Y. (Truly Redefine Yourself) will Conduct a basketball tournament "for the purpose of bringing more diverse people Together In our community for positive activities on a teamwork platform".

- Each building will be afforded an opportunity to assemble one team with an Integrated composition: one black, one Hispanic and one "other" or white inmate.
- There will be five teams with three men on each team.
- This event will include:
    1. A speech about community building, a teamwork effort, by a representative of T.R.Y.
    2. The actual basketball tournament
    3. A celebration with food and possibly other gifts (all food products will be provided by T.R.Y. members).

As the date approaches for this event, the designated REC CLERK will speak to all team prospects about the actual date of the event and further happenings.

_______________________   _______________________
T. Thompson, Captain   Date
Facility B, HDSP

To: Captain Thompson and Facility B Staff Members
RE: Proposal for Father's Day Weekend Event (on June 17th at
    1pm on the Yard)
From: T. R. Y. Group Members

During Father's Day weekend the T. R. Y. group would like to host a community event on Facility B for the purpose of:

1. Creating open dialogue with facilitators of all self-help groups about leadership and brotherhood
2. Breaking down barriers that may exist between the self-help leadership and inmate population on Facility B.
3. Broadening the concept of fatherhood to include the responsibility of community leadership and accountability for all men on Facility B.

This event will host the following:

1. Speeches from self-help leaders
2. Circulation of self-help information and
3. Feeding of all participants (T. R. Y. Group Members will provide all food items).

Thank you for your time and consideration.

T. R. Y. Core Group Members

To: Captain Thompson and Facility B Staff Members
RE: Proposal for Father's Day Weekend Event (on June 17th at
    1pm on the Yard)
From: T. R. Y. Group Members

During Father's Day weekend the T. R. Y. group would like
to host a community event on Facility B for the purpose of:

1. Creating open dialogue with facilitators of
all self-help groups about leadership and brotherhood
2. Breaking down barriers that may exist between
the self-help leadership and inmate population on Facility B.
3. Broadening the concept of fatherhood to include
the responsibility of community leadership and accountability
for all men on Facility B.

This event will host the following:

1. Speeches from self-help leaders
2. Circulation of self-help information and
3. Feeding of all participants (T. R. Y. Group
Members will provide all food items).

Thank you for your time and consideration.

T. R. Y. Core Group Members

State Of California   Department Of Corrections and Rehabilitation

Memorandum

Date: June 15, 2017

To: T. R. Thompson, Captain
          Facility 'B', HDSP

From: T. R. Y. Group Members

Subject: **PROPOSAL FOR FATHER'S DAY WEEKEND EVENT: JUNE 17TH @ 1300HRS**

During Father's Day weekend the T.R.Y. group would like to host a community event of Facility 'B' for the purpose of:

- Creating open dialogue with Facilitators of all self-help groups about leadership and brotherhood
- Broadening the concept of fatherhood to include the responsibility of community leadership and accountability for all men on Facility 'B'

This event will host the following:

- Speeches from self-help leaders
- Circulation of self-help information and
- Feeding of all participants (T.R.Y. Group Members will provide all food items)

Thank you for your time and consideration.

T. R. Thompson, Captain   M. Knedler, Lieutenant
Facility 'B', HDSP   Facility 'B', HDSP

M Pearson, Sergeant   J. Hawkins, Sergeant
Facility 'B', HDSP   Facility 'B', HDSP

Orig. T. Thompson, Captain
Cc.   ALL FACILITY 'B' HOUSING UNITS
       Program Office, Facility 'B'

State of California   Department of Corrections and Rehabilitation

Memorandum

Date   :   November 4, 2019

To   :   Coach Boyer

Subject: **IRON MAN CHALLENGE**

On November 16, 2019 inmates Stayer AX4000, Wilson AU5200, and Wilkerson AE1573 would like to host for the Facility A inmate population the Strong Man Challenge on the yard between the hours of 0900-1130 on the day indicated above. Attached is a list of all the inmates who will be participating in this event.

Thank you for your time and consideration concerning this matter.

J. HARTGROVE   RECOMMEND/NOT RECOMMENDED
Sergeant
HDSP Facility A

M. HUDSON   RECOMMEND/NOT RECOMMENDED
Lieutenant
HDSP Facility A

D. CLAIN   APPROVED/DISAPPROVED
Captain (A)
HDSP Facility A

State of California   Department of Corrections and Rehabilitation

Memorandum

Date   :   November 13, 2019

To   :   Facility A Administration, Community Resource Managers Office, Facility A Chaplains and
             Facility A Captain M. Williams.

Subject: **PROPOSAL FOR INTER FAITH HOLIDAY CELEBRATION**

The Inter Faith Community on Facility A, would like to host a holiday event. The
Purpose of the event is to express unity, peace, and goodwill amongst the religious
community.

The Event Contents

1. Selected speakers will discuss the meaning of holiday observations such as,
    Christmas, Hannukha, and Kwanza, all of which are celebrated in the month of
    December.
2. Uplifting and inspirational music will be provided by the Christian Choir and
    other inmate musicians.
3. Pastor Herry Mukdani will deliver a speech titled "Hope & Progress in Difficult
    times."
4. A resolution circle where all participants will be given an opportunity to state
    what changes they intend on making for the new year of 2020.
5. To conclude there will be fellowship and dialogue amongst the participants.

Date Time & Location

The Interfaith community would like to conduct the event December 5th 2019. The
community believes that this week will work best for the availability of the sponsors.
The community would like to host the event in the Facility A Gym during the hours of
0900 until 1300 hrs.

SPONSORS

Chaplains Herry Mukdani and Tahir Suleyman have already agreed to sponsor this
event and organize the choir and musicians for the event.

C. GALLYER
Correctional Officer
HDSP

Recommend/Not Recommended

J. HARTGROVE
Sergeant
Facility A
HDSP

Recommend/Not Recommended

M. HUDSON
Lieutenant
Facility A
HDSP

Recommended/Not Recommended

J. SPEERS
CRM
HDSP

Recommend/Not Recommended

M. WILLIAMS
Captain
Facility A
HDSP

Approved/Disapproved

Date   : October 4th, 2019
To   : Cpt. M. Carrillo
From   : I/M's Wilson (A1-249/AU5200) & Ainsworth (A1-126/AP0972
Subject: Inmate Rehabilitation Coalition (IRC)

Proposal

The Chairmen and Facilitators of Self-Help groups are requesting the following:

1. To have an opportunity to meet Bi-weekly for the purpose of:
   (a) Coordinating our rehabilitative aims (food sales, yard events, problem-solving, possible new groups & needs),
   (b) Distributing pertinent self-help material,
   (c) Organizing our educational activities and for,
   (d) Training purposes of current and future facilitators.
2. Building community and cohesion between all self-help groups.
3. Establishing a larger platform for cooperation with staff and other interested inmates.

Currently, there is a venue for the IAC to meet monthly with the Administration and Mac-reps but, no designated meetings have been allotted for those inmates responsible for overseeing the Rehabilitation community.

Name of Group

The Inmate Rehabilitation Coalition (IRC).

The Benefit

Relieving the IAC and program office clerks with having to advocate & provide any assistance with the needs of the rehabilitation community. Therefore, dividing the labor and making the program more efficient. Having a designated meeting time gives the administration access to speak with self-help representative all at one time.

Location and Time

We have various options:

1. The yard
2. The gym and if space is available
3. The Chapel

One hour on Saturday would suffice to accomplish our goals (1030-
1130 hours).

Thank you for your time and consideration.

M. Ainsworth
Group Facilitator
A1-126 / AP0972

J. Wilson
Group Facilitator
A1-249 / AU5200

M. Carrillo
Facility "A" CPT.
HDSP

Approved   /   Dis-Approved

Date   : October 4th, 2019

To   : Cpt. M. Carrillo

From   : I/M's Wilson (A1-249/AU5200) & Ainsworth (A1-126/AP0972

Subject: Inmate Rehabilitation Coalition (IRC)

Proposal

The Chairmen and Facilitators of Self-Help groups are requesting the following:

     1. To have an opportunity to meet Bi-weekly for the purpose of:

       (a) Coordinating our rehabilitative aims (food sales, yard events, problem-solving, possible new groups & needs),

       (b) Distributing pertinent self-help material,

       (c) Organizing our educational activities and for,

       (d) Training purposes of current and future facilitators.

     2. Building community and cohesion between all self-help groups.

     3. Establishing a larger platform for cooperation with staff and other interested inmates.

Currently, there is a venue for the IAC to meet monthly with the Administration and Mac-reps but, no designated meetings have been allotted for those inmates responsible for overseeing the Rehabilitation community.

Name of Group

The Inmate Rehabilitation Coalition (IRC).

The Benefit

Relieving the IAC and program office clerks with having to advocate & provide any assistance with the needs of the rehabilitation community. Therefore, dividing the labor and making the program more efficient. Having a designated meeting time gives the administration access to speak with self-help representative all at one time.

Location and Time

We have various options:

     1. The yard

     2. The gym and if space is available

     3. The Chapel

One hour on Saturday would suffice to accomplish our goals (1030-1130 hours).

Thank you for your time and consideration.

M. Ainsworth
Group Facilitator
A1-126 / AP0972

J. Wilson
Group Facilitator
A1-249 / AU5200

M. Carrillo
Facility "A" CPT.
HDSP

Approved   /   Dis-Approved

Date: September, 26, 2019
To: Facility-A Administration, Community Resource Managers Office,
and Chaplain Services
From:
RE: Inter Faith Holiday Celebration

Proposal

During the first week of December the Inter Faith community
on Facility-A would like to host a Holiday event which seeks
to express unity, peace and goodwill amongst the religious
community.

What the event will present

1. Select speakers on the meaning of Holiday observations, such
   as; Christmas, Hannukha, and Kwanza, all of which are to be
   celebrated in the month of December.
2. Uplifting and inspirational music from the Christian choir
   and other inmate musicians.
3. A message of hope and progress in difficult times Pastor
   Herry Mukdani.
4. A "resolution circle" where all participants will be given
   an opportunity to state what change they intend to make for
   2020.
5. Fellowship and dialogue.

Date, Time And Location

The first week of December is the best date for the availability
of the event sponsors.
We would like to host the event in the Facility-A Gym during
the hours of 9:00am through until 1:00pm.

Sponsors

Chaplains Herry Mukdani and Tahir Suleyman have agreed to
sponsor the event and organize the choir and musicians for
the event.

Captain   Carrillo

Sergeant Hartgrave   C/O   Gallyer

Chaplain Herry Mukdani   Imam Tahim   Suleyman

HIGH DESERT STATE PRISON
TRULY REDEFINE YOURSELF
(TRY)
INMATE LED GROUP BY-LAWS
REVISION DATE: DECEMBER 2016

ARTICLE I:
Plan of Operation for Truly Redefine Yourself (TRY)

Pursuant to Title 15 California Code of Regulations §3234, the following Plan of Operations is hereby submitted for approval for the establishment of the Truly Redefine Yourself (TRY) as an Inmate Led Group at High Desert State Prison.

ARTICLE II:
Name of Group

The name of this group shall be the "Truly Redefine Yourself (TRY)."

ARTICLE III:
Purpose of Group

The purpose of the TRY Group is to instill a new self-image of positive and cooperative citizenship centered upon traditional business and academic principals. The goal of TRY is to promote the basis for community and social development, which is self-development. The overall mission of TRY is to help inmates recognize their higher potential and to accept that reaching it requires a serious work ethic and violence is never a means to such an end. TRY members believe in adding by subtracting, by removing racial, religious, and political barriers that exist in order to take a brand new step toward a universal brotherhood and peaceful environment.

Meetings

Meetings will be held on a weekly basis on Facility B. The meetings will be conducted in a room/building/area designated by Custody Staff.

ARTICLE IV:
Membership Criteria

A. Qualification of Membership

Membership in the TRY Group is open to all interested inmates regardless of race, creed, color, or sexual orientation. Membership in TRY is voluntary and limited to a total of approximately 20 members per eight week session. The TRY Group will maintain a waiting list if membership requests exceeds 20.

B.   Conduct of Members

Members shall adhere to all rules, principles and purposes prescribed by the Constitution and Bylaws of this group.

1. No member shall subject the group to any event, action or influence of gang activity.
2. At NO TIME shall members display discourtesy towards any member, executive officer, speaker, sponsor, or guest of sponsor attending the group.
3. Member will not make fun of non-members concerning their lack of interest or participation in the business or activities of the group.
4. All members shall wear clean, state issued clothing. Tennis shoes are acceptable.
5. Refusal to comply with any of the established rules of conduct shall be justification for the individual to be turned away or asked to leave.

ARTICLE V:
Executive Body

The Executive Body shall consist of a Chairman, Vice Chairman, Secretary, Treasurer, and Sergeant-at-Arms. These positions shall be filled by majority vote of the group membership.

A.   Duties

1. Chairman:
   a. Conducts meetings.
   b. Introduces guest speakers.
   c. Serves as liaison between the group and staff.
2. Vice Chairman
   a. Serve as the chairman in his absence.
   b. Participate in meetings with TRY and institutional staff.
   c. Assist chairman with membership process
3. Secretary:
   a. Maintain records for the TRY Group.
   b. Maintains correspondence and takes minutes at all meetings.
   c. Maintains literature for the Try Group.
   d. Maintains the TRY Group membership roster.
4. Treasurer
   a. Work with Self Help Sponsors on fundraising activities.
5. Sergeant-at-arms:
   a. Maintain order
   b. Assist Chairman and Vice Chairman.
   c. Responsible for researching material.
   d. Handle any disputes that arise with members.

ARTICLE VI:
Elections

Regular elections for the offices of the Executive Body shall be held at the first meeting of the month in June. A nominating committee shall be comprised of three to five members, not nominated themselves and having the best interest of the group. The nominating committee will search for interested candidates that are most qualified for the position.

ARTICLE VII:
Outside Affiliations

The TRY Group welcomes and encourages cooperative participation with individuals and groups working to rehabilitate the prisoner population and develop communities.

ARTICLE VIII:
Structure of Governing Body

The Governing Body of the TRY Group shall consist of a Chairman, Vice Chairman, Secretary, Treasurer, and Sergeant of Arms. These members shall comprise the Executive Committee and will have been selected by a consensus process. The specific duties of the Executive committee members are as follows:

Chairman: The Chairman shall preside over all group business, functions and operations unless absent. In the same spirit, he shall function as spokesperson for the group and shall oversee all meetings, including announcing business items according to an agenda. The Chairman has the responsibility of setting goals for the group and planning, organizing, directing and controlling the group's day to day operations (within the confines of the group's by-laws). The Chairman is empowered to assign members of the group to various projects as needed. The Chairman shall ensure that written agendas are prepared prior to any meetings.

Vice Chairman: The Vice Chairman shall work closely with the Chairman in the execution of all duties, and shall temporarily act in the capacity of the Chairman in his absence or vacancy. He shall perform all tasks delegated to him by the Chairman and provide direct supervision over the Workshop Facilitator and all subgroups. He may appoint a member to the post of "Sergeant at Arms" and if so, shall set forth his duties.

Secretary: The Secretary shall assume all duties related to maintaining the files of all documentation generated and accumulated by the group. He shall take notes at and prepare minutes of all meetings. He shall assist the Chairman I preparing all written agendas and ensure the proper distribution of all necessary documents. The minutes of each meeting shall become a permanent part of the group's record. Calls roll.

Treasurer: The Treasurer shall maintain an accurate and current account of all property, supplies, and other materials maintained for the benefit and use of the group. He shall maintain proper levels of inventory items.

Sergeant of Arms: The Parliamentarian shall work closely with, consult and advise the Chairman and Vice Chairman on matters of parliamentary procedure, laws and administrative authorities. He shall have a thorough knowledge of Constitutional Law (federal and state), state statues, and administrative regulations. He should be an expert on "Robert's Rules of Order." He ensures that the group operates within the by-laws.

ARTICLE IX:
Executive Committee Facility Access

In an effort to facilitate their duties, the Executive Committee shall have access to all facility buildings and yards as determined by the Facility Captain. Any misuse of this access will result in immediate termination from the executive committee and possible CDCR 115 Rules Violation Report.

ARTICLE X:
Terms of Office

The term in office for Executive Committee members shall be two years with the term expiring in June. Officers shall serve a term of two years and may only serve one consecutive term.

ARTICLE XI:
Executive Committee Elections

The Executive Committee shall be elected by a majority of the group's total membership. In the event of a tie, a re-vote shall be held. The Executive Committee shall have the power to appoint a member to an Executive Committee position "pro tem" to ensure the continuous effective functioning of the group in the interim between a vacancy and an official election of an Executive Committee member. A prospective Executive Committee member must be nominated, by self or other, before running for a position. Official business requires three members.

ARTICLE XII:
Recall of an Executive Committee Member

An Executive Committee member may be recalled for the following:

- Non-participation and lack of interest in the Executive Committee and/or the group's general functions, meetings, projects, etc.
- Negligence and failure to complete individual / group assignments and duties.
- Repeated confrontation with Executive Committee members, the group, the Group Sponsor, Administration or guests.

Recall proceedings shall be initiated only after the member accusing the Executive Committee member of the above violations has attempted to resolve the matter with the accused at the informal level. If this fails to remedy the issue, formal recall proceedings shall be initiated. The Parliamentarian will be provided with detailed written account of the rules violations. The Parliamentarian shall ensure that everything is in order and shall submit the recall petition to the Chairman. The Chairman will then convene a meeting of the entire group and hold a recall election. If the Chairman is the subject of recall, the Vice Chairman shall assume his duties for this purpose. The members of the Executive Committee are only to be removed from their position by recall by a majority vote of the entire membership. During the recall proceedings, the accusing member shall formally read his charge(s) to the group and request a recall vote. The Chairman will then call for a vote.

ARTICLE XIII:
Termination from the Group

Any member of the group (including Executive Committee members) may be terminated from the group based on the following:

- Voluntary termination
- Failure to demonstrate, in words and actions, an interest in the group's objectives. This includes full participation in all activities
- Failure to place the objectives of the group before those of personal gain and recognition.
- Failure to continually strive for the advancement of the group.

- Failure to work in harmony with fellow members, Group Sponsor, and guests – disregarding differences in personality and beliefs.
- Physical violence or the threat thereof against anyone in the group.
- Failure to maintain the confidentiality of group discussions.
- A serious CDCR 115 within a one year period.
- Using membership to attract people who will cause embarrassment to the group, Group Sponsor, Administration and guests.

Any member in violation of any of the above will be brought before the group by any other member to initiate termination proceedings. These proceedings shall follow the same format as recall proceedings. The Group Sponsor shall make the final decision on termination. Any member involuntarily terminated shall not be allowed to reapply for membership for at least on full year. Voluntary termination carries no penalty and the former member may reapply immediately upon resolution of the issue causing the voluntary termination. Any member may take a "leave of absence" for 30, 60, and 90 days based on maters that prevent their full participation in the group's activities. These matters include family emergencies, legal matters, participation in academic/vocational programs, etc. Any member needing more time to resolve these issues may be required to voluntarily terminate himself from the group.

ARTICLE XIV:
Annual Update Provision

This Plan of Operation may be amended (updated) annually based on a majority vote of the entire membership and upon approval of the High Desert State Prison Warden.

(APPROVED) / DISAPPROVED

M. E. SPEARMAN
Warden
High Desert State Prison

1-10-17
Date

CHRONO FORMATS

Basic Class
Chrono 1

The purpose of this chrono is to recognize and congradulate this inmate for his participation in the workshops for T. R. Y.'s (Truly Redefine Yourself) weekly self-improvement classes from ________ 20__ through ________ 20__.

Through participating in T. R. Y. this inmate has learned concepts and practical insight into matters related to: Accountability and responsibility for past criminal behavior; goal-setting skills for planning organizing and managing one's daily life and intrinsic values; redefining self-concept and self-worth; mentor training and community building metho and; self-motivation teachings to reinforce everyday learning for positive and progressive social behavior, even beyond prison. This positive activity and programming is an asset to the institution, the inmate population and society once paroled. This inmate should be commended for his participation in T. R. Y. and continued positive programming.

A. Beck (CRM)

Advanced Class
Chrono 2

The purpose of this chrono is to recognize the continuous rehabilitative and positive accomplishments of this inmate by his participation in the (Truly Redefine Yourself) T. R. Y. Program's Advanced classes. By completing and continuing to apply T. R. Y.'s Advanced Curriculum this inmate has the ability and knowledge of: Teaching T. R. Y.'s Basic Curriculum by mastery of the material and by example; mentoring others continuously and training others to convey T. R. Y.'s lessons and positive information in general to everyday people.

This inmate is a pillar within the T. R. Y. community and continues to exemplify T. R. Y.'s goals of continuously redefining and improving oneself. As such this inmate would be a positive asset to the societal community upon parole.

A. Beck (CRM)

STATE OF CALIFORNIA

DEPARTMENT OF CORRECTIONS AND REHABILITATION
CDCR 128-B (REV 8/77)

NAME AND NUMBER: POSTON AT2512 HOUSING: A5-102

On behalf of High Desert State Prison (HDSP) Community Resources Office, we would like to thank you for your participation in making the hard times a little less lonely. Facility A created a drive for "The Elderly in Need of Love and Support," during the pandemic we face together. During the COVID-19 Pandemic, the elderly are at high risk of getting the virus, which means they have been quarantined and without visitors/loved ones for sometime now. The effort and love you put into your submission will not go unrecognized and will remind them they are not alone. Donations were given to Senior Citizens residing in our surrounding community.

Org.: Central File
Cc: Inmate

D. MORRISON, CRM Office Technician
High Desert State Prison

DATE: 8/4/2020   **PARTICIPATION CHRONO**   HDSP

CDC-128-B (Rev.4/74)

Name: Poston   CDCR#: AT2512   Housing: A5-102

Mr. Poston was appointed as Facility "A" Muslim Amir (Islaamic leader) December 17, 2017. During my time working with Inmate Poston, he has always been polite, courteous, and professional to staff and inmates when executing his duties. He is highly intelligent, articulate, and successfully in working across all racial and ethnic lines, in an effort to project a professional image and in fostering positive and assisting in coordinating effective religious services/programming. He is an exceptional asset, reliable worker, problem solver, and dedicated himself to participating in a cross-section of activities. He was instrumental in facilitating a variety of Self-Help and Religious Groups. He is more than willing to assist inmates in appropriately addressing their needs. I have never witnessed Mr. Poston demonstrate any form of aggression, violent, or, derogatory behavior while in my presence towards staff or other inmates. I have observed Mr. Poston facilitating effective communication between custody staff and recently arrived inmates, and, especially younger inmate population in order to maintain successful programming. This recognition is highly warranted and I commend Mr. Poston on his accomplishments and rehabilitative efforts.

C
Original: C-File
Cc: Inmate

Tahir A. Suleyman, Imaam
High Desert State Prison, Facility "A"

Date: 1/27/2021   **(LAUDATORY CHRONO)**   **GENERAL CHRONO**
Chapel

WORK SUPERVISOR'S REPORT

INMATE NAME	CDC#	FACILITY
POSTON, DONEL	AT2512	HDSP-Facility A

SECTION NUMBER	SECTION LOCATION
001	FAC A Peer Literacy Mentor

POSITION #	POSITION TITLE
LMP.001.007	Peer Literacy Mentor

ASSIGNED DATE	CURRENT PAY RATE
02/11/2020	$1.00 per hour

Evaluation Date: 09/01/2020   Period Covered: 07/07/2020 to: 09/01/2020

Hours Assigned: 30   Hours Worked: 238

GRADE		GRADE	
2	A. DEMONSTRATED SKILL AND KNOWLEDGE	1	F. TEAMWORK AND PARTICIPATION
1	B. ATTITUDE TOWARD FELLOW INMATES AND WORKERS	1	G. LEARNING ABILITY
2	C. ATTITUDE TOWARD SUPERVISORS AND STAFF	2	H. USE OF TOOLS AND EQUIPMENT
1	D. INTEREST IN ASSIGNED WORK	2	I. QUALITY OF WORK
2	E. EFFORT DISPLAYED IN ASSIGNED WORK	1	J. QUANTITY OF WORK

Pay Changes		
Effective Date	Pay Scale	Status
02/11/2020	1.00 per hour	Applied

Recommended for: ⦿ Retain ◯ Reassignment

☐ Pay Increase   ☐ Pay Decrease   New Pay Rate: $ Effective Date:

Code of Safe Practices Reviewed	Supv. Initials __________	Inmate Initials __________

Supervisor Comments

Mr. Poston has made satisfactory progress for the learning period.

He has completed over 720 hours of the internship, tutoring, teaching and collaborating with other tutors. He has a strong work ethic, he can read complex materials, understand them, and apply them to his teaching craft. He is passionate about helping his students and his passion for helping doesn't waiver. He collaborates well with other tutors. He is the kind of tutor that this program was designed to support and recognize with the certification and EMC.

Inmate Comments

J. Giles

SUPERVISOR

LENGTH OF SUPERVISION:

J. Giles

CDCR-128-B (Rev. 4/74)

NAME: POSTON   **CDCR NUMBER: AT2512**   **BUILDING/CELL: A2 - 125**

The above listed inmate has completed the Fatherhood Focus parenting study program. Focus areas include parenting education; employment skills; high school completion; substance abuse treatment (if applicable); anger management; child support; positive relationships; increased employability, and pre-release planning.

Linda Hedgpeth
Family Liaison Services Specialist / Friends Outside
High Desert State Prison

Original: Central File
CC: CC II
              Writer
              Inmate
              11/18/2017   Fatherhood Focus Program   **GENERAL CHRONO**

CDCR-128-B (Rev. 4/74)

NAME: POSTON   **CDCR NUMBER: AT2512**   **BUILDING/CELL: A2 - 125**

The above listed inmate has successfully completed the 30 Hour Positive Parenting Program under the sponsorship of Friends Outside. This program meets all CA court mandates. It meets the requirements for court-ordered parents and the methodology is designed specifically for the special needs and interests of incarcerated parents.

Linda Hedgpeth, Family Liaison Services Specialist
Friends Outside, High Desert State Prison

Original: Central File
CC: CC II
        Writer
        Inmate
11/25/2017   POSITIVE PARENTING PARTICIPATION   GENERAL CHRONO

Mountain View Adult School

This certifies that

Donel Poston Jr.

**HAS COMPLETED THE PEER LITERACY MENTOR TRAINING PROGRAM
AND IS NOW A CERTIFIED TUTOR AND MENTOR**

Monday, August 17, 2020

The year of training involved rigorous assignments on the topics of brain based learning strategies, adult learning theories, personalized learning plans, motivational interviewing, emotional intelligence, as well as a 700 hour supervised internship. We at Mountain View Adult School found him to be hard working, dedicated and result oriented. His contribution to the team was invaluable We take this opportunity to thank him and wish him many years of helping others reach their educational goals.

J M Giles - MA - Literacy Teacher
Mountain View Adult School

J. Huber - MA - Assistant Principal
Mountain View Adult School

VA 2959

NAME and NUMBER: <u>POSTON</u>   <u>AT2512</u>   CDC 128-B (Rev4/74)

Inmate Poston AT2512, has participated in "CHOICES" A Juvenile Diversion Program (JDP) from June 2016 to April 2017. In fact, he has been instrumental in establishing this program on Facility A at High Desert State Prison. Without his ongoing commitment to help at-risk youth, this group would not have been possible.

The purpose of the JDP is to provide at-risk youth with an in-depth understanding of how devastating the effect their criminal behavior has upon themselves, the victim of the crime, as well as upon their own immediate family. The JDP offers the juvenile participants skills and knowledge in understanding the mental and emotional aspects that have motivated their anti-social behaviors, choices, and perceptions. As a mentor he hopes to convey to the youth that they have the opportunity to make a positive change in their lives.

Inmate Poston has successfully completed the mentorship training and has graduated to be a JDP Mentor. He has completed an extensive training manual that covered workshops on sharing his life story, improving active listening skills, identifying and understanding core subjects and core issues, identifying at-risk behavior, and learning open-ended questions. He has also completed a parenting workshop and is currently working on a victim impact workshop to better understand how dysfunctional family behaviors have had an effect on his own life as well as how these behaviors can affect the at-risk youth.

Inmate Poston has been meticulously screened and approved before becoming a member. He has proven to possess sound leadership skills, maturity, and seriousness for a positive purpose. He is highly dedicated and determined to utilize his knowledge and experience in reshaping the troubled youth of today. He has exhibited genuine compassion for his fellow mentors in the group and is supportive of their rehabilitative efforts. I believe he will exhibit this same compassion with the at-risk youth. He understands the devastating and far reaching effects his past behavior has caused and has expressed sincere remorse for the pain he has caused. He is willing to share this experience with the youth so that they can make the choice to make a positive change in their lives. He has been an integral member of this extraordinary program.

Orig: ERMS
  cc: Writer
    Inmate

R. Nez, Self Help Sponsor, JDP

DATE: 4/17/17   **Choices, Juvenile Diversion Program CHRONO**

Name: POSTON   CDCR# AT2512

(Rev.7/2005)

This chrono is to document Inmate POSTON, AT2512, participation in "Life Choices", a self-help program at HDSP. He was continually involved in this program; first as a participant, and then as a mentor upon finishing his mentorship training. Inmate POSTON should be commended for his hard work and dedication as this program has come to a completion.

I have witnessed Inmate POSTON allow himself to become vulnerable as he opened up about his life story. Although it was difficult for him at times, he persevered throughout the entire program, knowing that there was a greater purpose. He was supportive as a team member as well as taking on leadership roles. This helped in not only identifying the past issues of his peers, but him as well. Inmate POSTON has progressed and matured in his recovery and shows a strong commitment to helping others identify the issues of their past as he himself has done.

I believe Inmate POSTON is an asset. I have no doubt that the knowledge he has unlocked from his past and the skills he has developed through this program would complement a similar program.

X. Medvedeva, Self Help Sponsor

Orig: C-File
Writer
Inmate

Date 6/9/2020   General Chrono

Name: WILSON CDCR#: AU5200 Housing: A1-249

The above inmate organized a talent show which gave inmates an opportunity to express their gifts, skills and talents in a non-adversarial manner. This event was sponsored by staff and chaplains; the focuses of the talent show was 'Stop the Violence" so all participants had to adhere to a strict criteria to perform (i.e. no cursing, violence, gang, race, or gender references). The above inmate participated and maintained a high standard of conduct during the event and this event and this behavior and/or performance is worthy of note.

Original: C-File
Cc: Inmate

T. Suleyman, Chaplain
High Desert State Prison, Facility "A"

Date: 8/20/2019

(LAUDATORY CHRONO) **GENERAL CHRONO**

CDC-128-B (Rev.4/74)

Name: WILSON CDCR#: AU5200 Housing: A1-249

This above inmate participated in a talent show which gave inmates an opportunity to express their creative talents, gifts and skills in a non-adversarial and constructive manner. This event was sponsored by custody staff and chaplains. The focus and theme of the program was "Stop the Violence". All participants agreed to adhere to a strict criterion of performance (i.e. no profanity, violent, gang, race, ethnic, or gender references). The inmate participated in and maintained an exemplary standard of conduct during this program. The inmate's behavior and performance is to be commended. It is because of his prosocial behavior in this constructive outlet that he is recognized as a positive asset to the institution and the community. He is to be applauded for this achievement.

Original: C-File
Cc: Inmate

Suleyman, Tahir, Imaam
High Desert State Prison, Facility "A"

Date: 08/20/2019

(LAUDATORY CHRONO) **GENERAL CHRONO**

NAME and NUMBER   WILSON   AU5200

CDC-128 B- (Rev. 10-06)

The purpose of this chrono is to recognize the continuous rehabilitative and positive accomplishments by his participation in the Truly Redefine Yourself (TRY) Program advanced classes. This inmate has completed training in teaching TRY Basic curriculum, mentoring and training other members to convey TRY lessons and positive information. This inmate is commended for his participation in TRY and continued positive programming.

Original: Central File
    CC: Inmate

G. CROWE
Lieutenant

Inmate

HDSP

DATE: 7/22/2017

INFORMATIONAL CHRONO

STATE OF CALIFORNIA

DEPARTMENT OF CORRECTIONS
AND REHABILITATION

NAME and NUMBER   WILSON   AU5200

CDC-128 B- (Rev. 10-06)

The purpose of this chrono is to recognize this inmate for his participation in the workshops for Truly Redefine Yourself (TRY) weekly self-improvement classes from July 2016 to May 2017.

TRY teaches concepts and practical insight in accountability, responsibility for past criminal behavior, goal-setting skills, planning, organizing, managing daily life issues, intrinsic values, redefining self-concept and self-worth, mentor training, community building methods, and self-motivation teachings to reinforce everyday learning for positive and progressive social behavior, even beyond prison. This inmate is commended for his participation in TRY and continued positive programming.

Original: Central File
    CC: Inmate

G. CROWE
Lieutenant

Inmate

HDSP

DATE: 6/26/2017

INFORMATIONAL CHRONO

CDC-128-B (Rev.4/74)

Name: WILSON   CDCR#: AU5200   Housing: A4-244

Seeking to forward progress in his life and community, the above inmate has participated in the Day of Peace and Reconciliation conducted by staff religious representatives and inmate leadership.

Original: C-File
Cc: Inmate

Chaplain H. Mukdani
High Desert State Prison, Facility "A"

Date: 1/28/2020   **(LAUDATORY CHRONO)**   **GENERAL CHRONO**

CDC-128-B (Rev.4/74)

Staff Appreciation Day Speaker

Name: WILSON   **CDCR#: AU5200**   **Housing: A4-244**

On March 6, 2020, Inmates on Facility-A organized an Event to show appreciation for various Staff Members in the areas of Academics, Religious, and Rehabilitative Services. The above Inmate was present and gave a speech for recognizing Staff for their amazing contributions to progress at High Desert State Prison. His actions should be acknowledged.

Original: C-File
Cc: Inmate

Chaplain H. Mukdani
High Desert State Prison, Facility-A

Date: 3/12/2020   **(LAUDATORY CHRONO)**   **GENERAL CHRONO**

CDC-128-B (Rev.4/74)

Name: WILSON   CDCR#: AU5200   Housing: A4-244

The above inmate made a cash donation to the American Legion Veterans Group as a participant in the Pledge of Peace ceremony. For his effort to support a worthy cause to those who have served our country he should be commended.

Original: C-File
Cc: Inmate

T. Suleyman, Chaplain
High Desert State Prison, Facility "A"

Date: 11/18/2019   **(LAUDATORY CHRONO)**   **GENERAL CHRONO**

591

NAME AND NUMBER: WILSON   AU5200   **HOUSING: A4-244**

This Laudatory Chrono is being generated on behalf of Inmate **WILSON** for your effort to promote peaceful co-existence among the prison population with your participation in The Day of Peace and Reconciliation at High Desert State Prison on January 28, 2020.

Thank you for your willingness to participate in The Day of Peace and Reconciliation. You shared your thoughts and experiences with the inmate population, which were extremely motivational and useful. The event was a huge success thanks to you and the other guest speakers.

Additionally, Inmate **WILSON** played an essential role in organizing the event.

Org.: ERMS
Cc: Inmate

INMATE COPY

J. SPEERS, Community Resources Manager
High Desert State Prison

DATE: January 31, 2020   **LAUDATORY CHRONO**   HDSP

CDC-128-B (Rev.4/74)

Name: WILSON   CDCR#: AU5200   Housing: A4-244

The above inmate organized a Leadership Workshop and he actively participated in group discussions and writing exercises that focused on topics, such as: Leadership methodology, problem-solving and characteristics of a leader. He also worked on cultivating the qualities of leadership he aspires to develop as a future leader in his community. He also strived to develop the skill set needed to collaborate with individuals of diverse beliefs.

Original: C-File
Cc: Inmate

Suleyman, Tahir, Imaam
High Desert State Prison, Facility "A"

Date: 12/6/2019   **(LAUDATORY CHRONO)**   **GENERAL CHRONO**

NAME: JAMES WILSON   CDCR: AU5200   HOUSING: A-1-249

Mr. Wilson has been in prison since September of 2015. Despite some of his early challenges, he has accomplished some exceptional goals, especially after walking away from the gang life, which once dominated his existence. Beginning in February of 2016, Mr. Wilson has contributed to the goal of rehabilitation by Co-founding four Self-Help classes, two of which are RAC approved groups (T.R.Y., NEW H.E.A.R.T.S., Reaching out From Within, and the Self Improvement class. He has Co-Authored various other curriculums that are under proposal for additional self-help programs. Further, Mr. Wilson has received his G.E.D. and completed various rehabilitative classes, such as: AVP, GOGI, C.G.A., Purpose Driven Life, Suicide Prevention Work Shop, Cancer and Veterans Walks, Peer Health Education Program, Transitions Courses, Book Report Awards, various spiritual development classes, Alcoholics and Narcotics Anonymous, 12 Step Programs, Lifers Support Group. Mr. Wilson is currently the Facilitator / Co-Facilitator of six Self Help Groups: T.R.Y., NEW H.EA.R.T.S., Reaching Out From Within, Self-Improvement class, Alcohol and Narcotics Anonymous, 12 Step Programs. Regrettably, Mr. Wilson allowed his frustration to prevail and received an admin strative RVR October, 2019.

But, Mr. Wilson is an avid reader and a mentor of men in the prison community. Further, he has organized various pro-social events: Inter-faith Community Celebration, Stop the Violence Talent Show, Pledge of Peace, Sports Tournaments, Father's Day Celebration, Facilitator Symposiums, Leadership Classes, Motivational Speaking engagements. On September 27, 2019, the Secretary of CDCR, Ralph Diaz, called and spoke with Mr. Wilson in the presence of Warden Spearman at High Desert State Prison regarding his and other inmates progress there. Mr. Wilson should be acknowledged for his personal progress & contribution to others Growth & Development.

____
KAREN MCDANIEL PLACE 4 GRACE
November 18, 2019

____
NATE WILLIAMS PATH 2 RESTORATION
November 18, 2019

State of California   Department of Corrections and Rehabilitation
CDC-128B Rev 1/15

WILSON, JAMES - #AU5200 - YARD: B

The above individual successfully completed no less than 12 weekly meetings and daily writing assignments in a group and self-study format. The intense self-improvement course requires the development of insight through the learning of Cognitive and Behavioral Tools for positive Decision Making and encouraged pro-social peer interactions and support. The course they completed is the GOGI GROUP CERTIFICATE COURSE.

Original: Central File
     CC: CRM
        Inmate

DATE: September 25, 2016   GETTING OUT BY GOING IN

CRM or authorized institution
staff signature

GOGI Education Course Completion Certificate

The recipient of this award is acknowledged by Getting Out by Going In (GOGI) for the successful completion of the **GOGI GROUP CERTIFICATE PROGRAM** which required self-study as well as weekly group meetings for no less than 12 weeks.

JAMES WILSON, #AU5200

September 25, 2016
Date of Issue

GOGI Founder
Dr. ML "Coach" Taylor

CDC-128-B (Rev.4/74)

Name: WILSON   **CDCR#: AU5200**   **Housing: A4-244**

.This Laudatory Chrono is being generated for the recognition of Inmate's active participation in INDIVIDUAL SELF-IMPROVEMENT efforts while housed in HDSP. As a Chaplain, I've had the opportunity to continue to observe inmate, JAMES WILSON towards positive personal growth, positive reformed behavior and programing, and contribution to his immediate community. My professional observation leads me to believe that Mr. WILSON has invested countless hours, especially devoted an incredible amount of personal time, to develop his leadership skills in leading and participating in various Self- Help groups.

Mr. WILSON has demonstrated and provided evidence of his skills and growth by guiding, coordinating, collaborating, and supporting his peers in his community in discussions, studies, and/or rehearsals. He has shown his efforts in being a life--learner of both social and life skills while being incarcerated. He has also shown developmental efforts in time management, effective communication, positive reflection and expression of self and emotions, and last but not least, service to one's community and choosing not to be idle, but striving to be a productive member of society. This list does not include all the details and balancing efforts-more than likely to be an extensive and immense list-which the inmate should be allowed to describe and narrate on his own to convey his story and developmental growth. So Mr. WILSON should be commended for his tireless work on leadership with a high-spirited and humble attitude.

Original: C-File
Cc: Inmate

____
Chaplain H. Mukdani
High Desert State Prison, Facility A

Date: 2/26/2020   **(LAUDATORY CHRONO)**   **GENERAL CHRONO**

OCTOBER 2019 – FEBRUARY 2020

INDIVIDUAL WORK INITIATIVE

PLEDGE OF PEACE

JAMES WILSON AU5200

During the month of November 2019, the above inmate came together with several other inmates to organize a pledge of peace event, which brought together members of all races, creeds, and religious backgrounds to encourage positive social activities, breakdown barriers and inspire positive programming. As a result of his efforts dozens of inmates donated money to American Legion (Veterans Group) and Place 4 Grace Family restoration program. Further, many inmates took the Pledge of Peace and vowed to carry its message of peace, cooperation and progress in their daily lives and interactions with others, inside and outside of prison.

DATE: November 18, 2019

CHAPLAIN TAHIR SULEYMAN

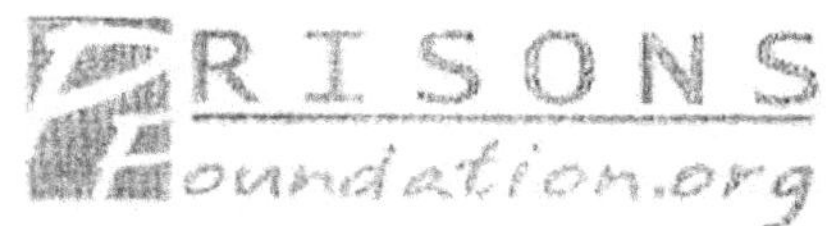

2512 Virginia Ave NW, # 58043, Washington, DC 20037
Staff@PrisonsFoundation.org

June 4, 2020

To: Adrian Woodard, Author
From: Dennis Sobin, Publisher

Thank you for sending us your book. I am pleased to inform you that it has been accepted for publication.

Anyone can read or download your book on our website at www.PrisonsFoundation.org where it has been posted. I am sure that they will find reading it a most worthwhile and interesting literary experience. We certainly enjoyed it when we read it.

You, Adrian Woodard, can rightly be proud of your achievement. The challenge of accomplishing anything worthwhile in prison is very difficult, and you have accomplished much. As your publisher, we applaud you on your new book. Excerpts of your books may be read during our podcasts *Podcast from Prison* (see prisonsfoundation.org)

If you find it necessary to communicate with us in the future, please do so by mail. Kindly include a SASE so that we will be sure to respond without undue delay. We intend to be very busy promoting your book and other fine books we have published.

Let me hasten to say that I would like you to know how we very much value you as an author and would be pleased to publish any future books you care to submit to us. Please refer to the enclosed submission guidelines.

You will also find enclosed a few promotional sheets about you and the publication of your new book. Please use them to distribute as you see fit, including to inside and outside contacts, newspapers and TV stations, and anyone else you care to contact and influence. You are free to copy them if you need more since we will not be able to supply you with additional copies.

Congratulations again, Adrian Woodard, on the publication of your book. As someone who spent many years in prison, I know first hand the tremendous challenges you face and the great value of your important work.

With sincere appreciation,

Dennis Sobin
Director
Dennis@PrisonsFoundation.org

Special Note; If you or your friends or family care to support our work with a donation, we will reward you by featuring your name and book on the front homepage of our website and a FREE link to your book. This gives you double the impact since your book will be viewable at two locations on our website. Whether you donate or not, your book will still be published and remain on our website indefinitely. But a donation gives you and your book prominent front-page publicity and a second link, which no other author receives. A $50 donation covers one year's publicity, $100 covers two years, etc. (Non-prisoners and businesses must donate twice that much for this special publicity and link.) Donations can be made online by using the donate button on our website or by sending a check or money order to the address at the top of this page. Thank you.

*The Foundation exhibits art by imprisoned artists, publishes books by prisoners, and presents prisoner-written works at the **Kennedy Center** and **Podcast from Prison**. Its director, Dennis Sobin, spent 10 years in prison after being falsely accused of a nonexistent crime. Upon his release, he wrote several books and received many awards for his fight against injustice and over-incarceration in America.*

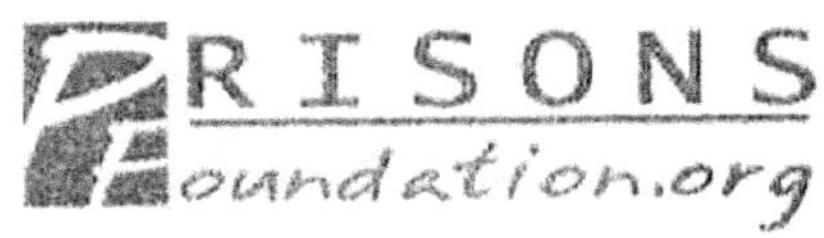

Prisons Foundation 603
2512 Virginia Ave NW, # 58043, Washington, DC 20037
Staff@PrisonsFoundation.org

April 12, 2019

To: Poston & Wilson, Author
From: Dennis Sobin, Publisher

Thank you for sending us your book. I am pleased to inform you that it has been accepted for publication.

Anyone can read or download your book on our website at www.PrisonsFoundation.org where it has been posted. I am sure that they will find reading it a most worthwhile and interesting literary experience. We certainly enjoyed it when we read it.

You, Poston & Wilson, can rightly be proud of your achievement. The challenge of accomplishing anything worthwhile in prison is very difficult, and you have accomplished much. As your publisher, we applaud you on your new book.

If you find it necessary to communicate with us in the future, please do so by mail. Kindly include a SASE so that we will be sure to respond without undue delay. We intend to be very busy promoting your book and other fine books we have published.

Let me hasten to say that I would like you to know how we very much value you as an author and would be pleased to publish any future books you care to submit to us. Please refer to the enclosed submission guidelines.

You will also find enclosed a few promotional sheets about you and the publication of your new book. Please use them to distribute as you see fit, including to inside and outside contacts, newspapers and TV stations, and anyone else you care to contact and influence. You are free to copy them if you need more since we will not be able to supply you with additional copies.

Congratulations again, Poston & Wilson, on the publication of your book. As someone who spent many years in prison, I know first hand the tremendous challenges you face and the great value of your important work.

With sincere appreciation,

Dennis Sobin
Director
Dennis@PrisonsFoundation.org

PS. Please note our new guidelines which now impose costs on authors who wish to publish more than one book within a 12-month period. Sorry but this is necessary for our survival and we will discard anything that comes from you within the next 12 months without payment.

*The Foundation exhibits art by imprisoned artists, publishes books by prisoners, and presents prisoner-written plays at the **Kennedy Center**. Its director, Dennis Sobin, spent 10 years in prison after being falsely accused of a nonexistent crime. Upon his release, he wrote several books and received many awards for his fight against injustice and over-incarceration in America.*

EPILOGUE AND HISTORY

A Brief History of T.R.Y. and its' Founding and Members

An Anniversary Celebration of Trials and Triumphs

T.R.Y. Founded: February 12, 2016

in High Desert State Prison

"Out of Darkness Can Emerge Light"

Chapter One

Building New Bridges

I woke up mid-Sunday morning, January 17, 2016, in a cold cell wrapped in one sheet and blanket. I had no personal property or belongings so I decided to reach out, through the vent, to my cell neighbor. He introduced himself at T.I. but whose real name turned out to be Marty Lemaster, a young brother from Chico, California. T.I., who is a dozen years younger than myself, became my first guide through the complicated maze of SNY, particularly on B-yard. He ran me down on the best course of actions for programming here. He also furnished me with hygiene, food, and stationery throughout the entire lockdown until I received my own personal property.

T.I. would become a great source of friendship and was the bridge between my meeting two other men, Wrenrick Drake (Rick) and Charles Smith (Chuck), who would become my other close friends on B-yard. We would all hang out and discuss ideas related to change and progress. Following T.I.'s advice and my own conscience I stayed away from certain crowds of people, many who still held firm to their old gang codes and allegiances, even on SNY. Further, aiding my progress was the fact that T.I. was enrolled in college and loved learning and having positive dialogue. So when I introduced him to the booklets I had written with the other men on the main line and my desire to continue this same work here, he encouraged me to speak with Rick, an amateur artist, for the drawing of book covers for the writing project. This conversation would take place, in February, Black History Month.

Chapter Two

T.R.Y. is Born

On February 12, 2016 I approached Rick about my idea for a mini book writer's project. I showed him all the booklets I had and the drawings for their covers which were solicited from prison artists on Calipatria's main line. Rick liked the idea but thought it could be expanded to something different. He proposed a study group organized for the purpose of producing a monthly magazine we eventually called The STEP, Solution To Every Problem.

During our discussion about the project another inmate came to the table and joined us. His name is Orlindo Myles (Neno) and although he was Rick and Chuck's neighbor we had never spoken to each other before. Neno seemed, not only interested in what we were discussing, but eager to join in on the effort. Neno also added that his mother had attempted to start a nonprofit organization before and maybe we should all T.R.Y. to start a nonprofit organization and promote the magazine even beyond the prison walls. In our effort to think of a name for our nonprofit idea, Rick offered the acronym T.R.Y. This stood for "Truly Redefine Yourself". T.R.Y. was born!!

Chapter Three

Meeting of the Minds

As was customary, T.I. joined us at the table, and we expressed to him what we were thinking about and he was immediately sold on the idea. Since me and T.I. would talk about the progressive ideas daily this was right up his alley, especially his love for business. T.I. suggested that we develop a schedule, a time to meet, on our day room time, which wouldn't be too difficult since we were all on the lower tier in building five. Rick and Chuck were cell mates and Neno was their neighbor as me and T.I. were neighbors. It seemed like a perfect arrangement of people, timing and ideas. We chose the business and work concept as our model for personal and social change.

As a senior brother amongst us, Chuck threw his support behind our efforts and joined in. We started meeting three times a week (Mondays, Wednesdays, and Fridays) to discuss ideas about the magazine and its message. This was relatively easy since we hung out together every day anyways. Then word and our persistent meetings began to spread throughout the building. Now other inmates would come around the table to see and hear about what we were T.R.Y.ing to accomplish.

Unsurprisingly there was also the usual crowd of naysayers and haters who would go around badmouthing our efforts. There were even gang members from my past affiliation upset that I had hung out with my first T.R.Y. brothers instead of rallying with them. Without the physical violence, the atmosphere of animosity, felt similar to my recent experiences on the main line for T.R.Y.ing to do positive things. Staff had even spread rumors about me, our members, and opposed us in many ways. But to accommodate the interest of other inmates we opened our meetings to the "public" on Wednesdays and Fridays, but kept Mondays a private meeting just for the purpose of discussing the magazine and business materials related to nonprofit organizations.

During our public meetings we'd have an open group discussions called "round table" and "food for thought" which came from individual writings we all wrote on our free time and shared with the group. At this time, we had no curriculum nor an interest in approaching the administration about approval for an inmate leisure time activity group (IL-TAG) or support group. We felt that studying on our own time was our best proven ground as a self-help group, with a businessman's model for success and progress. However as our group expanded and even some of the Christian brothers who held bible studies in the building would join us on Wednesdays and we'd go to their studies on Sundays, the idea was proposed that we should move toward approaching the administration about IL-TAG status.

Our brotherhood and idea had grown and we would need more endurance and larger facilitation. Fortunately, Rick was friends with the inmate self-help coordinator, Dale Case. So we presented to Dale the rough draft of our program titled "T.R.Y.'s Orientation Guide" and he typed it up and mass-copied it for us. This pamphlet was our first offering to the larger prison population outside of our building. But still we hadn't approached the administration and by this time, it was around the month of April, many of our efforts were stalled due to a series of lockdowns and a lack of motivation and effort from a few members in the group for various reasons, one being, the fear of our own successes!

During the month of May we were told we would need to apply for IL-TAG status, namely an eight or 12-week curriculum and official bylaws, not just the summarized ones we offered in our orientation guide. There was a lot to be done and very few informed and disciplined enough to do it all. So T.I. and I went to work writing T.R.Y.'s curriculum and Nazim, another inmate, helped with supplying us with information on how to write bylaws. Jay, the inmate who brought Gogi to High Desert State Prison, typed everything up for us. By this time Isaiah Montgomery (K.O.) had joined our group and begun mentioning us to the new captains of the facility, Captain Thompson, along with Dale Case and Melvin Reno (Supreme), another inmate who joined T.R.Y. in June. We had improvised, adapted, and overcome many problems and trials. But the work wasn't complete.

Chapter Four

A Measure of Success

By June of 2016, all of our material, including our proposal for authorization, our curriculum and orientation guide were submitted to Captain Thompson for evaluation and on June 24th Captain Thompson met with our group and authorized us to begin recruiting career coaches (teachers, facilitators) for our group beginning in buildings one and two, first. By July, we submitted our By-Laws to the Captain and our entire program to the Community Resource Manager, Andy Beck, via institutional mail.

By August, TRY was operating in all five buildings on Facility B! T.I., Supreme, Samuel Mahon (Capone) and myself began the process of taking the message of TRY's program to all the buildings throughout the month of July and August. Several times our entire "B-five" group would go out on the yard and talk to people about TRY and it's where we recruited some of our first career coaches, like Antoine Thompson (Twan) whom Chuck approached. Supreme recruited B.J. Ladelle and Melvin Cunningham (Mel.)

Other men joined the effort, listed but not limited to: Robert Villalobos, Angelus, Tovar, Pablo Upchurch, Christopher Tlatelpa, Leav (Da-Da), Brandin Orchard, Raymond Mercado, Kailon Matthews, Jesse Rivas, Phil Lozano, William Thompson, Ortiz, Ainsworth, Bounheseng and many other men, unmentioned, but not forgotten! You great men of all races, creeds, and colors have been amazing examples of what inmates are truly capable of. Thank you all, and those to come, both staff and inmates, for keeping this idea and community alive.

Written by:

James Wilson (AU-5200)
TRYs first Chairman and Co-Founder

<u>Afterthought</u>

No, I was not "lynched" at High Desert State Prison. Although I have experienced some forms of bias and even racially insensitive comments by corrections officers have met my ears.

However, it is never my intent to play the blame game or insinuate that any place in my life that I'm failing at is the sole responsibility of other people. No, there is much blame to go around. Even my own personal flaws, mistakes, and errors in judgement, like the "riot" in recent days I've been accused of participating in.

Obviously, no one is above reproach. We all fall short of even our own standards. Yes, it has been a mixed bag of experiences here at High Desert State Prison. Still, I try to remain optimistic that inmates and the administration will change their "hardened perceptions" about one another and allow the current messages of Rehabilitation, CDCR, and the Warden, Mr Spearman, and his assistants are calling for to take shape.

On my part, I will never stop until I T.R.Y.-umph!

Written by:

James Wilson (AU-5200)

January 4th, 2017

<u>T.R.Y.'s Original Founders</u>

James Wilson AU-5200
HDSP / A5-229
PO Box 3030
Susanville, CA 96127

8 September 2020

Warden J. Pickett
High Desert State Prison
PO Box 750
Susanville, CA 96127

Dear Warden Pickett:

I have documented a history of abuses at High Desert State Prison in almost five years of my imprisonment here. In knowing that this is a rehabilitation center, all of my appeals deal with obstructions to the noble cause of rehabilitation.

Since arriving in 2016, I have been privileged to meet and collaborate with several other inmates to expand rehabilitation opportunities at High Desert State Prison. We have successfully co-founded the five self-help groups listed below:

- T. R. Y. – Truly Redefine Yourself
- New H. E. A. R. T. S.
- Reaching Out from Within (in-cell program)
- Self-Improvement class (chapel)
- G. A. M. E. (sports & athletics group)

In addition to these groups, I have been a co-organizer of various pro-social events and activities, including but not limited to:

- Sports tournaments
- Pledge of Peace
- Stop the Violence talent shows
- Iron Man challenge
- Veterans walk
- Peace and Reconciliation event
- Staff Appreciation Day
- Leadership Conference
- Interfaith religious dialogs
- Facilitator Symposia

Further, I have co-authored a book *Writing Our Wrongs* set to be published soon. The proceeds of this will be donated to victims' impact groups. Despite my human failings, this has represented the preponderance of my service at High Desert State Prison. The reaction to my work can be seen through the lens of the following appeals, many withdrawn in good faith agreements that staff have rarely upheld. Despite these obstacles, I am undeterred.

<u>Appeal Log Numbers</u>

HDSP-B-17-03547 HDSP-A-19-04745 HDSP-A-18-04531 HDSP-B-1800871 HDSP-B-17-01534 HDSP-B-17-03280	HDSP-A-19-04395 This appeal granted me access to meet with group participants in other buildings, which is constantly being infringed upon, hampered and undermined.

These are just some of my appeals to seek redress for obstructions to rehabilitation efforts. I have also written to wardens M. Spearman and J. Pickett, The Office of the Inspector General, Internal Affairs, the Ombudsman and Prison Legal Office. I have asked several friends to file Citizen's Complaints on staff members who have participated in harassment and obstruction of self-help activities, including my ability to meet and mentor inmates in our programs.

<u>Currently, staff is seeking to terminate the in-cell program</u>. While COVID-10 has limited building-to-building access, I was permitted to continue the inmate led in-cell program, *Reaching Out from Within* until group activities resume. I was also given the alternative of meeting with inmates during their yard time to distribute curriculum, pick up completed packets, and to assist inmates with learning the material. This was going well until harassment and obstructions resumed.

I filed an appeal on 19 August 2020 and wrote a letter to the Facility-A Lieutenant Hudson, who is currently on leave. Instead, I met with Mr. Kingsley, who said he would try to resolve the matter on 24 August 2020.

Copies of this letter were handed to the staff in question; they expressed anger toward me and threats of retaliation (e.g. RVRs) for my legitimate actions. Some of these correctional officers falsely accused me of fabricating my appeals disposition, granting me access to do my job as an Inmate Leisure Time Activity Group Chairman, just to layer on suspicion and further the harassment from their colleagues.

Seeking to encourage better relationships, I copied and circulated an article written by the Secretary of California Department of Corrections, Ralph Diaz, titled, "Now is the Time Not to be Silent." The staff's reaction to this article was poor. In their words, they said it was, "a bunch of B. S!" This article, dated 12 June 2020, acknowledged racism, injustice, marginalization, and indifference in the system, but also exhorted CDCR employees to transform the agency into the greatest on earth, so that it wouldn't be another system to fail its human occupants.

Despite the resistance, I will continue doing the great work of leadership. I request your help in further these aims on Facility-A. When possible, I would like to meet with you to discuss future progress and plans for rehabilitative programs at High Desert State Prison.

I thank you for your time.

Sincerely,

James Wilson AU-5200

JW/at

cc: Ralph Diaz

Epilogue

Thank you for taking the challenge, and reading this material. We hope that you were able to benefit from it on some level - physically, emotionally, mentally, or spiritually. While it is obvious that a lot of time and effort went into coming up with these ideas, and constructing them into curriculums, less is made plain about the struggles attending the processes that brought these works to fruition.

The following insight is shared with no ill will: for it is also the nature of darkness to reveal the light more readily, and make it more productive. With courage, and wisdom, we can allow our struggles to illuminate our service rather than damper, or upend it. There is a quote I'd like to share to put these testimonies in perspective:

> "The truth goes through three processes:
> First, it is ridiculed.
> Second, it is opposed. And
> third, it is accepted as self-evident."

I will begin with ridicule.

Contrary to what people might believe, not all inmates have an interest in rehabilitation programs. While this group is relatively small (and ever decreasing), it most typically includes "short-timers", despairing lifers, inmates who still believe their way of thinking is more self-constructive or profitable, and those yet to be properly informed, and inspired, about the value of rehabilitation courses. This segment of the population are sometimes the antagonizers of those inmates who seek to participate in, and expand, both themselves and self-help programming, as well as the usefulness of the principles within them. As you will read in the "Brief History of T.R.Y.", we were constantly ridiculed by other inmates for holding study groups during our dayroom time.

Prior to T.R.Y. being approved as a facility-wide program, the only supportive entities were those few of us building it to begin with. While inmates can be effective at discouraging inmate participation, the worst effect of inmate ridicule is that it gives insulation, and credence, to many Correction Officers (C.O.'s) who are not sold on the idea of rehabilitation. Inmates who have special rapports with this segment of staff bolster the (easily foreseeable) next phase to hinder progress: administrative opposition.

I'm not being metaphoric here. I could literally write an entire book on
the opposition I, and others (be it inmate, or outside pro-rehabilitation
facilitators), have experienced when trying to create, establish, and operate
self-help programs at High Desert State Prison (HDSP). Even after the HDSP
Captain had approved T.R.Y. for building operations, the C.O.'s in my building
told me: "That is not gonna happen in my building."

They made us fight every inch of the way to get the program up and running.
When a core group of us that did not acquiesce to this opposition, and campaigned
in support of rehabilitation by writing the Warden, the Captain, and filing
appeals, our naysayers only became more emboldened. They sabotaged hard drives
that contained group lists, cancelled classes without explanations, targeted
us with fabricated Rules Violation Reports, searched our cells excessively,
engineered lock-downs, encouraged inmates to intimidate us, denied us access
to buildings and thus the ability to do our jobs, and labeled us all kinds
of things to isolate us, and discourage inmates from dealing with us.

Five-plus years into our campaign, the opposition was still not letting
up (as you'll see with a letter I wrote to the Warden's office in 2020). Remember,
I started this work in 2016, just one month after my arrival in HDSP. I had
hit the ground running, but ran right into the "green wall" (as the C.O. proclivity
to always back each other's moves has been called). Even after transferring
to another facility (from B- to A-yard), I was told straight-away (as I walked
through the security gate between them even): "Don't come over here with all
that self-help group stuff." I hadn't yet been on the yard a minute. I immediately
knew there was more resistance to come.

Luckily, for my first four years at HDSP we had a progressive Warden (M.E.
Spearman), and a great CRM (Community Resource Management) team. I also met
some inmates on A-yard inspired about rehabilitation, like Donel Poston. We
teamed up, and with our collective efforts began to roll out self-help groups,
and pro-social events on the yard. Donel had experience with doing this already
as co-founder of the self-help group 'Life Choices'. He was older, more established,
had leadership experience, and had already built good working relationships
with some of the sergeants, and other staff, that I didn't enjoy on my previous
yard (B).

As time went on, we recruited more inmates with our vision of expanding
"all things rehabilitation", and as night follows day, the opposition arose

once again. Soon after, we co-founded 'New H.E.A.R.T.S.'. The staff approached me, and said: "I thought I told you not to come over here doing this." I had learned from past experience by this point to not argue with staff though, and just go on about my business. In prison (as with most things in life you know is right), you can not let the naysayers psyche you out, as there are multitudes. 'Reaching Out From Within' became approved on A-yard, and with progress came more struggle. The predictable agenda of delay, obstruct, and deter was in full swing. This time they employed the Inmate Advisory Council (IAC) against us. If we wanted to hold any special events (e.g. 'Pledge of Peace') in the gym, or on the yard, we had to agree that no program (dayroom and yard, and also canteen) would be ran during the time of the event.

Quite naturally, this upset the other 800+ A-yard inmates, who had to sequester in their cells as the event participants (about 100+) enjoyed themselves. The gym's capacity was about 120, or less (and was never open during program anyway, so there was no reason both couldn't run simultaneously). The staff would send the IAC with the memo for the event, and say: "It was modified to adjust for staff availability." This created increasing animosity towards us, and since Donel and myself are African America, it spawned racial animus against us as well. Nothing in prison can equal it's racial divisions amongst certain inmates.

Fortunately, many of the men who have spent some time in prison were wise enough to see the game being played. Donel was soon able to sway the opinion of one sergeant, who admired what we were doing. He saw that using punitive measures against the entire population to provoke them against programs / events that would actually improve the facility was a failed policy. We were soon able to hold events at the same time that program ran.

Unfortunately, not long after, the sergeant was "out-bidded" (a process C.O.'s go through where they can "win" their facility placement), and relocated, which put an end to our hosting events in the gym at all. The sergeant who had replaced him (and the subject of most of my subsequent appeals from 2019-20) was altogether a different breed. He could care less about rehabilitation, or program. We weren't going to let this one set-back deter us though. After all, we had fought hard, and won, many times before.

Since Donel was the 'Amir' of the Islamic community, and I was the facilitator of the self-improvement class (both of which operated in the chapel), we found favor in the eyes of the yard's Imam, and Christian Chaplain. These two individuals

• Imaam Tahir Suleyman and Chaplain Herry Mukdani

had already sponsored a few of our events held in the gym, so were quick to get on board. Due to the smaller size of the chapel, our events had a much reduced capacity. But, at least we were once again being allowed to move forward.

Between 2018 and 2021, myself and Donel were able to:

- Co-found four self-help groups.
- Host over a half-dozen pro-social events.
- Co-author several books.
- Inspire hundreds of inmates to get involved with rehabilitation programming.

This is the third phase of the struggle. Eventually, people get it, and the goal becomes clear (self-evident). As Frederick Douglass once said: Where there is no struggle, there is no progress." There can be no bountiful harvest without some storms.

It must be said here that none of these revelations were intended to discourage you, or place a bad rap on reactionary staff, or inmates. It is a truism that, "all new ideas are deemed blasphemous", and as a result appear subversive to institutions, and established thinking. Change is often resisted, and the familiar always more comfortable.

As CDCR embraces this new, and growing, culture of rehabilitation (the 'R' in CDCR was only relatively recently added), it is expected that there will be growing pains. There have been many staff members willing to help "deliver" (support) many of our brain-children. Not everyone was against us.

History has well established that, "standing armies can not prevent an idea whose time has come". The time is now for this change. Get on board. Accept the challenge!

By: James Wilson
&
Donel Poston